D1169646

"Brian Wruk and Terry Ritchie have put together the most complete resource book covering all areas of relevance for both Canadians and Americans heading south over the 49th parallel. A must-read and resource document for any practitioner serious about dealing with clients relocating south."

— **Doug Macdonald**, MBA, RFP, Macdonald, Shymko & Company, Fee Only Financial Advisors

"This is the best book I've seen on the myriad of financial and legal issues involved in moving to the U.S."

— **Ian McGugan**, Editor, *MoneySense Magazine*

"**The Canadian in America** is an excellent one-stop resource for Canadians living in the U.S. I will certainly recommend it to our clients."

— **Geoffrey D. Leibl**, Immigration Attorney, Leibl & Kirkwood, San Diego

The Canadian in America

Real-Life Tax and Financial Insights
into Moving and Living In The U.S.

BRIAN D. WRUK with Terry F. Ritchie

ECW Press

Copyright © Transition Financial Advisors Group, Inc., 2007

Published by ECW PRESS
2120 Queen Street East, Suite 200, Toronto, Ontario, Canada M4E 1E2

All rights reserved. No part of this publication may be reproduced, stored in a retrieval system, or transmitted in any form by any process — electronic, mechanical, photocopying, recording, or otherwise — without the prior written permission of the copyright owners and ECW PRESS.

LIBRARY AND ARCHIVES CANADA CATALOGUING IN PUBLICATION

Wruk, Brian D
The Canadian in America : real-life tax and financial insights into moving and living in the U.S. / Brian D. Wruk ; with Terry F. Ritchie.

Includes bibliographical references.
ISBN 978-1-55022-757-4

1. Canadians — United States — Finance, Personal. 2. Canadians — Taxation — Law and legislation — United States. 3. Canadians — Legal status, laws, etc. — United States. I. Ritchie, Terry F. II. Title.
HG179.W78 2007   332.024008911073   C2006-906831-3

Cover and Text Design: Tania Craan
Cover Image: Boden/Ledingham Masterfile
Typesetting: Mary Bowness
Printing: Marquis

This book is set in Minion and Franklin Gothic

The publication of *The Canadian in America* has been generously supported by the Government of Canada through the Book Publishing Industry Development Program. Canadä

DISTRIBUTION
CANADA: Jaguar Book Group, 100 Armstrong Ave., Georgetown, ON L7G 5S4
UNITED STATES: Independent Publishers Group, 814 North Franklin Street, Chicago, Illinois, U.S.A. 60610

PRINTED AND BOUND IN CANADA

ECW PRESS
ecwpress.com

Table of Contents

IV.   Moving Your Stuff   61

VI.   Show Me the Money   113

I dedicate this book to my grandparents who have gone home to be with their Saviour in heaven. They pursued their own dreams and left Europe to homestead in Canada, creating the next generation of Canadians.

Wilhelm and Louisa Wruk

Edward and Ottilie Hiller

The Lord your God has blessed you in all the work of your hands. He has watched over your journey.

Deuteronomy 2:7

Acknowledgements

Given the vast complexities and issues surrounding any move to the U.S., we are unashamed to say we don't know everything! However, we view ourselves as the quarterback of a team of people to effectively coordinate your move. To that end, our firm relies on a large network of trusted, competent professionals to assist with the variety of issues our clients have. We view our knowledge as being a mile wide and a foot deep, but we have experts in all areas whose knowledge is a foot wide but a mile deep. We have drawn upon these experts to review various parts of this book, and want to thank them individually for their assistance in making this large undertaking possible.

Richard Brunton, a fabulous Canada-U.S. tax accountant in Boca Raton, FL, thank-you for your encouragement of this project and for imparting your wisdom and knowledge whenever needed.

Brent Gunderson, an excellent attorney in Mesa, Arizona,

offering the unique combination of estate planning and immigration to our Canadian-American clients. Thanks for your counsel in these highly technical areas.

Terry Ritchie, a leading authority on Canada-U.S. transition planning. I'm honored to have you as a friend and partner heading up our Calgary, Alberta, office; thanks for all your contributions to this manuscript and your support in making this dream possible. I appreciate the common heritage we share.

Eva Sunderlin — My Canada-U.S. paraplanner and a cherished associate of mine; thank you for all the work you did to make this book possible. Thanks for all you do for our clients (and me!).

Our clients, without whom our firm would not exist; we enjoy the relationships we have with you and appreciate your excitement about this project.

My friends, in Canada and the U.S., who have pushed me over the years and helped me overcome many obstacles; thanks to Isaacs for your edits and Canadian perspective.

My family, especially Dad and Mom; thanks for all you have done for me over the years and your support of whatever I did. I appreciate the home cooking, your prayers and the wisdom you imparted. And finally, to my wife Kathy and daughters Corrine and Emily . . . I love you and thank-you for your support in this endeavor. I apologize for underestimating the time I would be away from you during the writing of this book.

And our readers, thank you for buying this book. We trust you will find it a useful reference as you begin, undertake and complete your move to the U.S. Our hope is this book will save you more time, money and frustration than I experienced in my Canada-U.S. moves. If you have any questions, comments, edits or things you'd like to see in later editions, please email us at book@transitionfinancial.com and tell us what is on your mind. For tax and other updates or changes in the book, please visit our website at www.transitionfinancial.com/us

Introduction

The complexities associated with moving to the U.S. are astounding, yet according to researchers, approximately 25,000–30,000 people move from Canada to the U.S. annually with little or no idea of these complexities. Often the similarities in culture, currency, language, and goods consumed between Canada and the U.S. lead people to think their situation is "simple." In fact, the differences in taxation, investing, health care, wills, and estates are profound. It was mind-boggling the complexities I had when I moved down to the U.S. in 1990 as a single man (poor student), moved back up to Canada in 1992 with my wife, and then moved back to the U.S. permanently in 1996. We have written *The Canadian in America* to equip you with the information you need to consider when making the transition to life in the U.S. That is why I started Transition Financial Advisors — to provide you with an experienced helper to assist you in making this transition. Our goal is to ensure our clients have a smooth transition to the U.S. from Canada versus an abrupt "move" and all the connotations that come with it. The constantly changing rules and their application to your unique financial situation require the right professional help.

My own fascination with the U.S. started in high school when I took a bus trip to Portland to participate in a band competition. I became interested in U.S. culture, geography, and so on. Then I took another bus trip with Campus Life that went through Montana, Idaho, Utah, and Las Vegas to Los Angeles. There I experienced Disneyland, Knott's Berry Farm, Magic Mountain, and Universal Studios. These experiences combined with the oceans, beaches, and warm weather had me hooked. From that point on, I decided I would eventually live in the U.S. My goal was to get a green card and have the ability to move, live, and work anywhere in Canada and the U.S.

The first part of my dream was shattered in 1981 when I applied for all kinds of jobs in the U.S. after graduating from high school, getting nothing but polite "no thanks" letters in return. I decided to upgrade my skills and graduated from the business administration diploma program at the Northern Alberta Institute of Technology (NAIT) before obtaining a bachelor of commerce degree from the University of Alberta in 1987. In the summer of 1985, I moved to Dallas to stay with family friends for the summer. I loved my stay and actually enjoyed the heat and humidity, which only served to renew my determination to reside in the U.S. someday. I resumed my application process in the U.S. only to be dismayed once again. I then accepted a position as an assistant product manager at Alberta Government Telephones (AGT) and began my 10-year career in the Canadian telecommunications industry.

In 1990, I decided a master of business administration degree would help my telephone career, so with the support of my employer I began applying to business schools across the U.S. and Canada. I maintained that, if I was accepted at any of the

U.S. schools I applied to, I was going to the U.S. Fortunately, I was accepted by two programs and responded to the invitation from the MBA program at the University of Arizona. I thoroughly enjoyed the "snowbird" lifestyle: winters in Arizona and summers in Edmonton (for summer internships). I resumed my application process and was getting interest from prospective employers when I gained the affection of a young lady while in Tucson. After graduating, Kathy and I got married, and we decided to move to Calgary to resume my telephone career while she began training as a nurse. It wasn't until four years later that I realized I was waking up next to a "green card" every morning and could escape the cold winters and punishing taxes. I obtained a green card through the sponsorship of Kathy, and in April of 1996 I was finally able to realize my lifelong dream of residing in the U.S.

My migrations between Canada and the U.S. came with much frustration and complexity even though I thought my financial situation was simple. The following examples illustrate how the simple situation of a single, poor student can become incredibly complex when moving back and forth across the border.

- Applying for and receiving a student visa required a lot of paperwork and coordination with the University of Arizona.
- I received an assistantship from the university that caused no end of grief in figuring out the payroll and income tax implications in both Canada and the U.S. because there was so little information to be found on the subject.
- Getting married in the U.S. and moving to Canada created untold difficulties with the Canada Border Services Agency when we brought our car, personal effects, and wedding gifts across the border.
- Clearing Canadian immigration with my wife, despite months of paperwork and phone calls beforehand, we were told we had broken five immigration laws when our plane landed. Thankfully, immigration officials issued a minister's

permit to allow Kathy into the country until we figured out our mess.

- We had to file U.S. income tax returns for my U.S. citizen wife each year we lived in Canada.
- We had to go through the green card application process when we decided to move to the U.S. and had to make at least two trips to Vancouver and wait in unbelievably long lines to get fingerprinted, complete the medical (including X-rays), and be interviewed.
- We had to complete paperwork to expedite U.S. Customs and Border Protection processing with our automobile and combined personal effects.
- We had to figure out what income to declare on which tax return and when to file in the year we left Canada and took up residency in the U.S. (including the tax implications of our RRSPS).
- We had to collapse our RRSPS, endure the currency exchange, suffer the Canadian government's withholding tax, and move our money to the U.S.
- Finally, we had to apply for a Social Security card, write the test to get our Arizona driver's licenses, and coordinate our health-care coverage during our move.

Now, let me be clear I will always be Canadian, will always love Canada, and will always visit as long as God gives me the health and strength to do so. However, I have settled in the U.S., become a dual citizen, love this country and what it has to offer. In particular, the weather of Arizona is much better for my health than Canada's winters, and I find I can remain active year round in biking, swimming, and golfing.

And that's the starting point for any move to the U.S., the desired lifestyle you are trying to achieve. You should never consider a move for monetary or tax reasons alone. I have witnessed many times a couple with young kids move to the U.S. because one spouse has a great job opportunity and will make incredible money. It doesn't take long for the other spouse to become disenchanted when there is no family nearby, no friends, no support structure, and the working spouse is at the office or traveling all the time in the new career. Good planning should help you to document your desired lifestyle, see the pros and cons of your move, and consider more than just the financial rewards or lower taxes.

1

American Aspirations

A simple man believes anything,
but a prudent man gives thought to his steps.
— Proverbs 14:15

So, you've decided to move to the U.S. It may be because of a great job offer, a spouse, or returning to your roots, but you have decided to leave Canada and move to the U.S. How do you prepare for such a major transition?

You have entered our world . . . the world of Canada-U.S. transition planning. With the laws and regulations of two countries such as Canada and the U.S., such planning quickly becomes complex. This unique niche has been termed "cross-border" planning by some, but we prefer to call it Canada-U.S. transition planning. We caution you now that you shouldn't proceed with your move to the U.S. without allowing yourself enough time to understand all the nuances of your unique situation and then take the necessary actions before leaving Canada. If you are reading this book, you are off to a good start.

What Is Transition Planning?

You have your stuff packed and the moving company selected, but suddenly you think, "How do I move my financial affairs to the U.S.?" Financial planning is the core of transition planning, but we clearly define which border we are talking about and, in particular, how to smoothly transition your finances from Canada to the U.S. while saving you time, aggravation, professional fees, and every tax dollar you possibly can.

According to the College of Financial Planning, comprehensive financial planning is "the process in which coordinated, comprehensive strategies are developed and implemented for the achievement of the client's financial goals and objectives." According to the Financial Planners Standards Council (the licensing organization for the Certified Financial Planner™ designation in Canada), financial planning consists of the following six distinct steps.

1. Establish the client-planner relationship.
2. Gather client data and determine the client's goals and objectives.
3. Clarify the client's current financial situation and identify any problem areas or opportunities.
4. Develop and document the financial plan and present it to the client.
5. Assist the client with implementing the plan.
6. Monitor and update the financial plan.

You will notice that financial planning is a process, not a transaction or an end in itself. The same applies to transition planning. Since the financial planning industry is only about 25 years old, a brief history might help. The industry started as a transaction-based business with life insurance agents selling policies over the kitchen table or mutual fund salespeople coming to your door. It has since evolved to a technically based business where people manage an investment portfolio or provide tax advice. Today the industry has realized that you can't make decisions with a person's money and ignore the person — the two are integrated. As a result, the industry is rapidly moving toward a relationship-based model where "Money is a means to an end, not an end in itself."

Comprehensive financial planning begins by understanding what you are trying to achieve in terms of lifestyle now and in the future. This is driven by your values and beliefs about money and what you have observed during your lifetime. It is akin to taking off in an airplane with a flight plan in hand. Once our firm knows where you are trying to go (documented goals and objectives), we can develop a specific plan to test the feasibility of your goals and figure out how to get you to your destination. Other factors constantly affect your ability to achieve your goals, such as changes in the tax and estate laws, your income and expenses, death, disability, and investment performance. Therefore, our firm views transition planning as a lifelong process, not an event or a transaction. Without a flight plan, how do you know which direction to go?

There is a difference between a goal and an objective. A goal is a desired end state, such as "I want to simplify my life" or "I want a better understanding of my financial situation." Only you will know whether you are accomplishing that or not. An objective is clearly measurable, and everyone knows whether it has been achieved or not. For example, "I want to move to the U.S. by December 31st of this year." Once in place, your plan provides the overall context in which to place the individual, day-to-day decisions. When people struggle with individual financial decisions, it is usually because they do not have a plan. They are stuck in the individual decisions and have lost the overall perspective in which to place each decision. For example, a popular question we field is "Should we withdraw our RRSPs?" The answer is "What are you trying to achieve?" The tax implications are one small part of the answer. Why do you want to take them out? When do you need the funds? What will you do with the funds

Table 1.1

Living Desired Lifestyle			
Values, Beliefs, Goals, Objectives			
Client (Spouse, Children, Family, Relatives, Friends)			
Transition Financial Advisors Group			
Comprehensive Overview			
Cash Management Planning	**Income Tax Planning**	**Independence/ Education Planning**	**Risk Management**
• Mortgage broker	• U.S. Accountant (CPA)	• Pension plan admini-	• Insurance agents:
• Banker	• Cdn Accountant (CA)	strator	• Property/ Casualty
• Currency exchange	• Bookkeeper	• Actuary	• Disability
firm	• Tax Attorney (Cdn, U.S.)	• Custodian	• Long-term care
• Realtor	• Canada Revenue Agency	• RRSP/LIRA/ RRIF	• Health
• Auto Dealer	• Provincial taxing	custodian	• Life
	authority	• RESP custodian	• Social Security
	• Internal Revenue	• College savings plan	Administration
	Service/ U.S. Dept. of	administrator	(Medicare)
	Treasury	• Social Security	• Provincial Health-
	• State taxing authority	Administration	care provider
		• Human Resources	
		Development Canada	
		(Canada Pension Plan/	
		Old Age Security)	

when available? Will you move the funds to the U.S.? How? Do you understand the pros and cons of doing so? Will you invest them? If so, how? For what purpose or objective?

Table 1.1 depicts the elements of Canada-U.S. transition planning. Based on this table, our firm's transition planning includes the comprehensive analysis of eight specific areas in any Canada-U.S. move.

Living Desired Lifestyle			
Values, Beliefs, Goals, Objectives			
Client (Spouse, Children, Family, Relatives, Friends)			
Transition Financial Advisors Group			
Comprehensive Overview			
Estate/ Charitable Planning	**Investment Planning**	**Immigration Planning**	**Customs Planning**
• Estate planning attorney	• Stock broker	• Immigration attorney	• U.S. Customs
• Charities	• Mutual fund manager/ company	• Immigration & Naturalization Services	• Canada Customs
• Trust administrator	• Brokerage firm		• Moving Company
• Estate/gift/trust tax accountant	• Investment manager		
• Custodian			
• Trustee			

1. Customs planning addresses issues in relocating your physical assets to the U.S. The transportation of items such as pets, guns, cars, or a wine collection across the border has unique issues that need to be dealt with in advance.

2. Immigration planning looks at the legal ways of moving to, working in, and residing in the U.S. either temporarily or permanently. You need some legal means of entering the U.S. because, despite popular opinion, the U.S. is another country, not another province of Canada!

3. Cash management planning includes the development and review of your net worth statement and a review of your cash inflows/outflows during your move. From there, our firm can analyze the ownership of your assets between spouses and between Canada and the U.S., and we can calculate various financial ratios to determine if any opportunities or issues exist. The net worth statement serves as a benchmark to evaluate the effects of your move over time. We also address the movement of cash from Canada to the U.S. and how to simplify your life prior to your move.

4. Income tax planning is a comprehensive review of your current and projected tax situation with an eye for opportunities to reduce your current and future tax liability both before and after your U.S. move. It is important to note the difference between tax preparation and tax planning. Tax preparation is a completely historical perspective and merely takes what has happened (your tax slips) and records it on a tax form for the Canadian and U.S. governments. At that point, whatever tax liability or refund results is what you must adhere to. Tax planning, on the other hand, tries to reduce your tax liability by reviewing any tax avoidance techniques that may apply to your situation. There is nothing illegal about proper tax planning or tax avoidance, but it must be differentiated from tax evasion, which is the intentional defrauding of government authorities of the tax dollars they are due.

5. Independence/education planning develops detailed projections out to age 100 using current assets, income, and expenses to determine the feasibility of your financial independence and lifestyle objectives in the U.S. Alternative scenarios and sensitivity analysis are conducted to provide insights into which actions, if any, may be necessary to achieve your goals. For example, do you need to save more and be more aggressive with your portfolio, or can a more conservative approach be taken? Education planning determines how much is required, at what point in time, and what you need to do to fund these future education liabilities. It also provides a review of your education saving options in the U.S. and what to do with your education savings in Canada before moving.

6. Risk management examines your current situation for risk exposures and determines the best course of action in addressing them. For example, illness, fire, theft, accident, disability, death, lawsuit, et cetera are potential catastrophic events that could devastate what has taken a lifetime to build. There are many differences in managing risk between Canada and the U.S. that need to be addressed to ensure you are fully covered.

7. Estate planning helps you to arrange your affairs so you can (1) continue to control your property while alive, (2) provide for the needs of loved ones in the event of disability, and (3) give what you have to whom you want, when you want, the way you want, at the lowest overall cost. The focus is on control first and on tax dollars, professional fees, and court costs saved second.

8. Investment planning determines your investment objectives as derived from your financial plan and then designs an investment portfolio to achieve your required rate of return while managing your tax liability. Ongoing monitoring, reporting, and rebalancing of your portfolio are required over the long term to ensure it is achieving your goals and risk tolerance.

Before You Go!

The two items you *must* have in place before you even consider a transition to the U.S. are adequate health-care coverage and a legal means of residing in the U.S. (a valid visa).

1. Health-Care Coverage

You may not be aware, but your provincial coverage will be of little or no use to you when you move to the U.S. The rules are different for each province, but typically, if you reside out of your province for six months or more, you lose your provincial health coverage. And, once you have lost your coverage, you may not be able to get it back immediately because of your individual provincial rules (Alberta allows you to have it back immediately, while Ontario has a three-month waiting period). As a result, you must have some form of U.S. medical insurance to cover yourself in the event of illness or injury in the U.S. because there isn't universal government coverage like there is in Canada. This coverage is best secured just before you make the transition to the U.S. in the event you, or someone in your family, has a "preexisting" condition and is "uninsurable." There are several options to cover you and your family that are discussed in more detail, along with items such as life, auto, and homeowner insurance, in Chapter 2, "Cover Your Assets."

2. Residing in the U.S.

Despite popular opinion, you must have a legal means (i.e., valid immigrant or non-immigrant status or U.S. citizenship) of entering and remaining in the U.S. for any period of time. To work there, you require the appropriate authorization as well. No matter what, you have to fit into one of the immigrant or non-immigrant "boxes" as outlined by the U.S. Citizenship and Immigration Services. Unfortunately, many Canadians go to the U.S. on a "visitor's visa" (good for six months) and mistakenly believe they can work in the U.S. just like they can in any province. This misconception comes in part because a B-1 (visitor for business) or B-2 (visitor for pleasure) visa is not physically issued when you cross the border (you may get a stamp in your passport, but that is it). This leads some to believe they can stay or work as long as they want. In fact, if you are caught working in the U.S. without a valid work visa, you will be considered an illegal immigrant and could face deportation and lifetime banishment from the U.S. There are numerous legal options you can use to enter the U.S., and you can review your possible visa options in Chapter 3, "A Pledge of Allegiance."

Once you have these two essentials in place, the following must also be considered.

Customs

This is where most people spend the bulk of their time, to the jeopardy of most everything else. No doubt the movement of your physical assets to the U.S. is time consuming. You have to make travel plans for yourself, your spouse, and your children to get yourselves down there whether you are going to fly or drive. There is also coordinating the visa applications for spouses and children that can cause havoc if not done correctly at the border. Then there is the packing of your household goods, selecting a moving company, filling out all the requisite forms for U.S. Customs and Border Protection, and so on. When you get down to your final destination, you have to coordinate the arrival of your moving truck with the closing on your house. And then there is unpacking and putting everything away. We offer some considerations in Chapter 4, "Moving Your Stuff."

Income Taxes

U.S.

There is much work to be done in minimizing your taxes before taking up tax residency in the U.S. If you choose not to do it, you can face unnecessary taxes and compliance issues that can be punishing. The Canada-U.S. Tax Treaty and the relevant provisions in the U.S. Internal Revenue Code and Canadian Income Tax Act are your protection from double (and triple) taxation in both countries. Obviously, a thorough understanding of these rules and their application to your situation is the key.

An analogy may help. Imagine you are the owner of a dinner theatre, and the Internal Revenue Service (irs) is sitting in the audience. You have one chance to "set the stage" before the curtains open and the irs has full view of your "financial stage." As soon as you become a tax resident of the U.S., you open your entire "financial stage" for the irs to see. At that point, you can no longer set the "stage" to present your financial situation in the best light possible to minimize your tax liability. Interestingly enough, you can be a resident for tax purposes in the U.S. yet be considered an illegal alien for immigration purposes. Alternatively, you can become a tax resident of both Canada and the U.S. and have to look to the Canada-U.S. Tax Treaty to avoid double taxation and to determine in which country you belong. All of this is explored in greater detail in Chapter 5, "Double Taxes, Double Trouble." As a side note, U.S. citizens, derivative citizens, and green card holders living in Canada must file U.S. income tax returns annually!

Social Security number/individual taxpayer identification number: (ssn/itin)to work or live in the U.S., everyone in your family must have an ssn (for those working) or an itin. The ssn will be required by your employer and is needed to file a tax return or open a bank account. The itin is required for those who are not eligible to work in the U.S. but allows you to reduce your taxes by claiming your spouse and children as dependents. See Chapter 5 for further details on obtaining an ssn or an itin.

Canada

Based on popular opinion, many people just stop filing Canadian tax returns when they leave Canada for the U.S. The rationale is usually "I don't live there anymore, so I don't have to file taxes there anymore." In fact, there are final filing requirements with cra that could increase your tax bill significantly due to the "departure" tax when you leave Canada. In addition, if you don't sever your ties properly prior to and after your move, cra could come back and "deem" you a resident of Canada, causing you a lot of inconvenience and the potential of additional income tax. Alternatively, the rules state that, if you are considered a treaty resident of the U.S., you are automatically deemed a non-resident of Canada and forced into the departure tax. You need to ensure you do the requisite planning before your departure to understand your departure tax, how to correctly sever your ties with Canada, and how to mitigate the taxes in your unique financial situation.

The bottom line: if you haven't done the prerequisite planning prior to your departure, many planning opportunities may be lost forever, and you will find yourself in a situation where you have to pay many financial professionals on both sides of the border to get yourself back in compliance with both taxing authorities.

Currency Exchange

Along with moving yourself, your spouse, your family, and your physical goods, you have to move some, or all, of your financial assets to the U.S. Doing so can be confusing, and most folks are unsure about how to tackle it. There are many misconceptions about currency exchange, and often people will leave assets in Canada because they believe they will "lose" money in moving it to the U.S., but other risks can be incurred by leaving everything in Canada. These myths and facts are addressed in Chapter 6, "Show Me the Money."

Estate Planning

In our experience, the area most often neglected is wills and estates. Unfortunately, many Canadians go to their attorney to "update" their Canadian last will and testament before moving to the U.S. to make sure they have it in order. What they don't realize is it may be a complete waste of time and money because their Canadian estate planning attorney typically doesn't know the U.S. rules for non-citizens living in the U.S. Further, you can have a valid will in the U.S., but the provisions contained in the document may not be executable in the U.S. (i.e., domestic laws, disinheriting heirs, etc.). The complexities of estate planning for non-citizens residing in the U.S. are considered in Chapter 7, "Till Death Do Us Part."

Independence Planning

Our firm does not use the term "retirement" because it conjures up images of an unscheduled, unproductive life pursuing leisure activities. In our experience, this pursuit of leisure is short lived, and it doesn't take long before people look for more meaning in life, including returning back to work! As a result, our firm prefers the term "financial independence" because it prompts the question "Independent to do what?" Associated with becoming financially independent are the issues of saving for the future with company pensions, U.S. Social Security, Canada Pension Plan, Old Age Security, et cetera. Typically, a move to the U.S. may mean the start of a new phase in your life. But now that you live in the U.S., it may not make sense to invest in an RRSP, so you need to understand the other alternatives for saving in the U.S. These issues are dealt with in Chapter 8, "Financial Freedom."

Education Planning

Once people have left Canada for the U.S., many wonder how they will be able to save for their children's education and what happens to the savings they have accrued so far in Canada. Can these savings be used at a U.S. educational institution? If you save for education in the U.S., can the funds be used in a Canadian educational institution? There are some landmines to be aware of here, and these issues are addressed in Chapter 9, "Smarten Up!"

Investment Planning

Many people have established a nest egg for their financial independence, but how do you deal with this in the U.S.? How do you move your current investments and RRSPS there? Can you? How do you invest in the U.S.? Which financial institutions or mutual funds should you use? It is a whole new ballgame in the U.S., and there are several things of which to be aware. They are addressed in Chapter 10, "Money Doesn't Grow on Trees."

Business Entity Planning

If you have a small business in Canada, it can afford you some unique opportunities in your move to the U.S. Business entities can be used to get you a green card in the U.S., help you qualify for free U.S. Medicare, establish a Social Security retirement benefit, and allow you to get disability coverage. There are many planning opportunities available and potential landmines to contend with for small-business owners that are discussed in Chapter 11, "The Business of Business."

Selecting the Right Professionals

When it comes to planning your move, we don't recommend you do it yourself. Trust me, I tried with my simple situation, and it didn't go well. That is why I started this firm! To us, it's like giving yourself a haircut — you might do fine on your front bangs because you can see them in the mirror, but what about the sides and the back? The complexities associated with a Canada-U.S. transition are far too complex, and based on our experiences it is in your best interests to pay for the right assistance. When you look at your time, aggravation, lost opportunities, and costly mistakes, it should be an easy justification to hire someone to provide the information you need when you need it. The key benefit of doing so is that you get an outside, unbiased understanding of your entire financial situation and the obstacles and opportunities it presents when moving to the U.S. With that in mind, Chapter 12, "Mayday, Mayday," presents some of the things you should look for in any qualified Canada-U.S. transition planner.

Simplify Your Life

This is probably one of the most neglected areas in dealing with making the transition to the U.S. Before you move, take the opportunity to consolidate all of your investment accounts, RRSP/RRIF/LIRA accounts, with one brokerage firm. Also, maintain only one checking account and one savings account in Canada where possible. Once you are in the U.S., the management of your financial affairs in Canada will be greatly simplified (i.e., one call to manage all of your accounts, one checking account to deal with, etc.). If you are a small-business owner, it is typically best to sell or wind up your entity prior to moving to the U.S., but it depends on your individual circumstances and how your business entity might be used for immigration purposes, qualifying for U.S. Medicare, et cetera. Either way, you should try to set up your affairs so that you are not required to manage the day-to-day operations of the entity. There are also many cultural differences, and differences in the postal system, of which you should be aware. There is a brief overview of some of the major differences in Chapter 13, "Realizing the Dream."

2

Cover Your Assets

Therefore, a man cannot
discover anything about his future.
— Ecclesiastes 7:14

There are many risks in everyday life that can have devastating effects on what has taken you a lifetime to accumulate. Unfortunate events such as a sudden illness, the death of a working spouse, an auto accident, or the disability of the primary breadwinner can cause severe problems. These risk exposures must be reviewed in light of your transition to the U.S. to ensure your current risk management strategies remain appropriate and new strategies are selected as required. Consider the following questions.

- When making the transition to the U.S., what coverage will your provincial health-care insurance provide?
- Are you currently eligible for U.S. Medicare coverage? If not, how can you qualify?

- Which alternatives exist for health-care coverage in the U.S. if you have a "preexisting" condition?
- You may have sufficient life insurance coverage in Canada, but if your death benefits pay in Canadian dollars what effect will the exchange rates have on how much benefit you receive in the U.S.? Are your life insurance needs higher or lower in the U.S. than in Canada?
- Have you considered the same issues with your disability insurance as well? Will your policy still pay in the U.S.?
- Will your Canadian auto and homeowner insurance cover you in the U.S.? What differences in homeowner and auto insurance need to be considered if you get U.S. policies?
- The U.S. is a more litigious society than Canada. How can you protect yourself in the event of a lawsuit?
- What do you do in the U.S. if you can no longer perform some of the activities of daily living and require skilled nursing care around the clock?

As these questions illustrate, there is the potential of creating new risk exposures when making the transition to the U.S. that were previously covered. The following attempts to establish the facts and dispel some of the myths surrounding the major risk exposures when moving to the U.S.

Medical Coverage in the U.S.

There are a number of rumors and opinions about the health-care systems in both Canada and the U.S. In our opinion, both health-care systems offer some of the best care in the world, but there is a greater availability of services in the U.S. There is more flexibility in scheduling various tests and in getting elective, non-emergency procedures, and there are more professionals available in a particular specialty. The main reason is the medical system in the U.S. is primarily "for profit." This means there is competition for patients and group health insurance contracts that leads to a clearer "customer/patient" service orientation. We have personally experienced hospitalization and medical treatment on both sides of the border. In our experience, the hospitals and physicians in Canada take the view that you are there for them to practice medicine on, while in the U.S. the view is they are there to get you better to live your life again. The drawback of the U.S. system compared with Canada's health-care system is the lack of universal coverage. We have seen several people come into our practice for pro bono budget counseling whose finances have been depleted because of high medical costs, co-pays, and prescription costs. It is interesting to note that approximately 50% of all bankruptcies in the U.S. are due to medical expenses. In Canada, national coverage means everyone pays (through higher taxes), and as a result no individual's health-care problems can leave them penniless. Unfortunately, that is not the case in the U.S., and it is not uncommon to see a bucket at a local cash register asking for donations to help an employee who was in an accident or needs a heart transplant because they can't keep up with the out-of-pocket medical expenses.

Despite popular opinion, the medical system in the U.S. will not leave you dying in the gutter outside the hospital because you don't have a health insurance card in your wallet. This would be against the law, and the liability lawsuits would be flying if such an incident occurred. There are county hospitals available to the general public, and if you are a U.S. veteran va (Veteran Administration) hospitals are available that are funded by the state and federal governments. There is even medical insurance available through your local state for those who cannot obtain coverage on their own. For example, in Arizona, ahcccs (Arizona Health Care Cost Containment System, a scary name) is medical insurance for those who cannot afford it on their own. However, someone has to pay for those without insurance, and this cost, coupled with the rising medical costs, is causing insurance premiums to skyrocket and people in the U.S. to shoulder more of the expenses individually. In our opinion, a combination of the Canadian and U.S. medical systems is probably the ideal scenario. The U.S. seems to be moving toward universal coverage on a more formalized basis so that individuals and families are no longer devastated financially. Canada appears to be moving toward a private, "pay as you go" system so that those who can afford it can shoulder more of the costs. This approach is evident with the increase in private eye clinics and MRI machines popping up all over the place (particularly Alberta).

Provincial Coverage

Your provincial health-care coverage may be good for up to six months after you leave Canada, depending on your province of residence (some terminate it sooner). There are several problems in continuing your provincial coverage in the U.S. that make it of virtually no use to you. First, your provincial health-care will only pay "table" rates. For example, the table rate for a hernia operation in Canada may be c$4,000 . . . that is all that will be paid. If you need a hernia operation while resident in the U.S. and it currently costs US$4,990, your provincial health-care will pay only c$4,000, and you will be billed by the U.S. hospital for the balance. Second, there are limits on the daily rate paid for hospitalization; this rate covers a very small portion of what is required (Alberta pays c$100 per day) and includes the room, bandages, food, medicines, et cetera. In the U.S., however, there is one fee for the room, another for the physician, another for the nurse, and each bandage, pill, and syringe is tracked separately. Needless to say, this system leaves you with the balance to pay personally. Third, you will have to prove to the provincial health authorities that your intent was to remain in Canada and not move to the U.S. It stands to reason that, if you are taking advantage of the Canadian health-care system, you should continue to pay into it. As a result, this could be viewed as a tie to Canada, and you could face continued taxation from Canada as well as the U.S.

Travel insurance can assist you on a temporary basis (usually up to six months) for any balance owing, but if you have a "pre-existing" condition you may not be able to get insurance coverage for it. Likewise, the insurance company may attempt to attribute any illness to the preexisting condition so it doesn't have to pay benefits. Therefore, it is always prudent to do the requisite planning beforehand to solidify your health-care coverage. If you are getting an individual policy, you should apply for U.S. health insurance just before you leave the safety of Canada's health-care system in the event you are "uninsurable." This can be difficult at times because the health insurance company will want you resident in the U.S. and may require a Social Security Number.

We have worked with a couple of clients who qualify for U.S. medical benefits as part of their Canadian employer's retiree benefits. Also, some Canadian federal government retiree medical benefits provide coverage in the U.S. Each situation is unique and must be examined individually for the opportunities or risk exposures that exist. Typically, these benefits offer some coverage but should not be relied on to cover everything in the U.S. Obtaining U.S. health-care coverage is your best alternative in the U.S., and using your Canadian retiree medical benefits for coverage when you are "sunbirds" in Canada may be a viable solution to achieve your Canada-U.S. lifestyle.

U.S. Employers

For those making the transition to the U.S. for employment purposes, the best coverage usually available is the group health-care plan through your U.S. employer. Typically, the larger the employer, the better the health plan choices you have. However, as with almost any health-care plan in the U.S., be prepared to pay a "co-pay" by cash, check, or credit card for any doctor, lab, x-ray, et cetera. My family of four is on a group health insurance policy with my wife's employer (Kathy is an RN at a local hospital). Since she is a part-time employee, my family shares more of the cost each month. To obtain full health-care coverage, dental, and prescription benefits, we pay approximately US$550 per month, which comes off her paycheck pretax. As a comparison, Alberta health care costs C$1,056 annually in 2006 for a family of two or more.

For those hoping to retire before age 65, you must be cognizant of the fact you'll be without health insurance once you leave your U.S. employer unless you have been employed long enough to qualify for retiree medical benefits. Typically, this means you have some combined total of age and years of service that equals 75 to 85. The situation is not the same as in Canada, where you automatically qualify for provincial health-care coverage provided you make the monthly premium payments. There is a federal law (called COBRA or Consolidated Omnibus Budget Reconciliation Act) that allows you to take your employer health insurance benefits with you for up to 18 months after you leave as long as you take over the premium payments, but this coverage tends to be very expensive. If you are not eligible for retiree medical benefits, you'll have to obtain an individual health insurance policy or consider working part time at a place that offers medical benefits to part-time workers. For example, most hospitals and even Starbucks offer medical benefits to part-time workers.

Individual Policies

In the U.S., individual health insurance policies are available to those who do not qualify for any group or government benefits. These policies typically offer "catastrophic" coverage and have high deductibles of $2,500 or more but only cost about $200–$300 per month depending on your circumstances and which state you reside in. This plan means you pay the first $2,500 of your medical expenses until your policy kicks in (this typically excludes prescriptions, vision, and dental) and then generally provides lifetime coverage up to $2 million. Recent changes in the law permit the holder of a high-deductible health insurance policy to set up a health savings account for any out-of-pocket expenses. You can put money into the account pre-tax and distribute it tax free for qualified medical expenses. In the meantime, this money can be invested and grow to pay for future out-of-pocket expenses. In my view, this is where the health-care insurance industry is going in both countries. The large deductible for these catastrophic policies can be quite shocking for most Canadians; however, when you calculate the lower taxes, lower medical insurance premiums, and readily available services in the U.S., you may actually come out ahead.

The problem with individual policies is that, if you have a "preexisting" condition, you may have a "rider" on your policy excluding the condition, or you may not be able to get under-written at all. A pre-existing condition is generally defined as a condition that has been treated by a physician within the past year. As a part of your underwriting, the health insurance company will need your approval to get copies of your medical records for their review or they won't issue you a policy. Whatever you do, don't be deceptive when filling out your application form. If you are found to be untruthful in answering any questions on the application form, you could find your claim denied. If there is an exclusion, any illness that occurs may have the insurance company trying to blame it on your preexisting condition so it doesn't have to pay benefits. You have to understand that the health insurance companies are in business to make money (and they make millions!). They try to offer insurance to those they believe on average they can make money on (i.e., those who will incur the least amount of medical expenses and still pay their premiums). However, there are health insurance companies that offer individual health insurance policies at reasonable rates to those making the transition to the U.S., including those with some preexisting conditions. Of course, your individual circumstances and financial situation will determine the best company and policy for you and your family. For example, you may want your health insurance coverage to include the best care possible like the Mayo Clinic or the M.D. Anderson Cancer Center. To assist you, we recommend you use an insurance broker that offers plans from several companies to best meet your needs and provide more objectivity in the process. Consult our website at www.transitionfinancial.com for insurance brokers we recommend.

U.S. Medicare

Canadians living legally in the U.S. for at least five years become eligible to pay for U.S. Medicare at age 65. U.S. citizens (naturalized, derivative, or naturally born in the U.S.) and their spouses (non-citizens included) are generally automatically eligible when the qualifying spouse reaches 65 (newlyweds have to be married for one year). Medicare is currently made up of four parts: Part A, Part B, Part C, and Part D. Part A is hospital insurance and helps to pay the cost for care while in a hospital. Part B is medical insurance and helps to pay for the doctors, outpatient hospital care, and a variety of other medical services not covered by Part A. Part C is a Medicare Advantage plan that combines Parts A, B, and D and is offered by private insurers through a Health Maintenance Organization (HMO) or Preferred Provider Organization (PPO) plan. Part D is the new drug prescription plan introduced in January 2006.

In 2007, Part A costs $410 per month ($4,920 annually) per person. However, to qualify for free Medicare Part A at age 65, you must have "earned" income that you paid Social Security taxes on in excess of the required amount ($4,000 in 2007) for at least 10 years. Once you have established the required 40 quarters of Medicare eligible earnings, you qualify for free Medicare Part A coverage. Once 30 quarters have been established, the premium for Part A drops 45% to $226 per month ($2,712 annually). Canadian spouses who have not paid one nickel into the U.S. Social Security system automatically qualify for free Medicare Part A coverage under the qualifying spouse. At times, Medicare planning can make or break your finances and bring into question your pending transition to the U.S. There are many strategies to get you qualified for free Medicare Part A, but it depends on what stage of life you are in, your unique financial situation, and your individual goals and objectives.

Part B coverage for doctors and outpatient hospital care costs $93.50 per month in 2007 ($1,122 annually) per person, and everyone pays it no matter how many quarters of eligibility you have. The monthly premium you will pay for Part B is broken down in the following table.

Table 2.1

Medicare Part B Premiums, 2007

2007 You pay ($)	If your yearly income is		
	Single	Filing married	Filing separate
93.50	80,000 or less	160,000 or less	80,000 or less
105.80	80,001–100,000	160,001–200,000	
124.40	100,001–150,000	200,001–300,000	
142.90	150,001–200,000	300,001–400,000	80,001–120,000
161.40	200,001 +	400,001 +	120,001 +

Part C is offered by a variety of private health insurance companies in all different states. These plans tend to be less expensive than Medicare with a supplement but they tend to be more restrictive in which doctors, hospitals and other facilities you use (must be in network). These plans may fit your circumstances and are certainly worth investigating.

The Part D drug coverage can cost as little as six dollars per month in some states and goes up from there (depending on which state you reside in and which plan is selected). There is a $250 deductible, and then prescription expenses from $250.01 to $1,250 per month will be on an 80%/20% coinsurance plan. While Medicare provides good base coverage, it should not be relied on to cover all of your medical expenses. In addition to the premiums listed above for Part A, there is a deductible in

2007 of $992 that must be paid for a hospital stay of from 1 to 60 days, $248 per day for days 61-90, and $496 per day for days 91–150, while hospital stays greater than 150 days are not covered at all! For Part B, there is a deductible of $131 per year, plus you pay 20% of the Medicare approved amount after that. You'll need to purchase a Medicare Supplement policy to cover the expenses not covered by Medicare. These Supplements have 10 government-defined types of policies, ranging from basic (A) to comprehensive (J). They are all the same no matter who provides them, so it becomes a matter of shopping price. Your Medicare Supplement does require underwriting, but it is very lenient, and we have not heard of an instance of anyone being turned down. Medicare Supplements cost approximately $1,500 per year per person.

Another important aspect of U.S. Medicare is the disability benefits you can receive. Generally, if you have worked for 5 of the past 10 years in the U.S. (establish 20 credits), you are eligible for a disability benefit. There is usually a one-year waiting period before benefits are paid, and the benefit is based on your Social Security earnings record. These payments can continue up to age 65 until you qualify for Social Security payments. Like any government benefits, it is difficult to qualify because you must prove you are unable to perform any work at all.

Life Insurance in the U.S.

Another area often overlooked when making the transition to the U.S. is the appropriate amount of life insurance to cover the risk exposure if the primary breadwinner dies prematurely. All of your policies should be reviewed with an experienced eye to ensure you have the right type and amount of coverage while avoiding potential U.S. income/estate tax issues (see Chapter 7 for more details). For example, your life insurance coverage could drop significantly as soon as you take up residency in the U.S. How? If you need c$500,000 in Canada to cover your needs and you move to the U.S. and have a need for us$500,000, you could be underinsured because, at an 85¢ exchange rate, you have only us$425,000 in coverage! This amount will leave you underinsured by us$75,000 in covering your risk exposure in the U.S. Another important aspect is to reevaluate your life insurance needs in the U.S. to see if you need more, the same, or less insurance than you did in Canada based on the change in your financial circumstances. For example, if your lifestyle goes up and you now need us$650,000 in life insurance in the U.S., relying on your Canadian life insurance policy alone could leave you underinsured by us$125,000. If you decide to collapse your life insurance policies in Canada and take out the cash value, you'll be subject to tax in both Canada and the U.S. As you can see, the complexities surrounding a simple item such as life insurance are often overlooked.

Long-Term Care Insurance

One of the largest issues facing the federal governments in both Canada and the U.S. is providing long-term care to the aging boomers and baby boomers. Long-term care consists of home care, assisted living, or skilled nursing care in a qualified facility for those who are unable to maintain the activities of daily living (dressing, eating, continence, transferring, and bathing). With today's medical advances, people are living longer but generally sicker, and as a result these costs can quickly become very expensive. There are government facilities available, but there are usually long waiting lists, and the quality is not as good as in some of the private facilities. Despite popular opinion, health insurance does not cover these costs, and U.S. Medicare provides limited coverage ($119 per day in 2007 for days 21 through 100). There are state government benefits available, but you qualify for free state government long-term care only when you have virtually nothing left to pay for it. As a result, you have a risk exposure that needs to be addressed.

Other Insurance: Auto, Home, Liability

Auto Insurance

Private companies run all auto insurance in the U.S., while in Canada some provinces have government-run auto insurance. One difference you will notice is that auto insurance is quoted on a six-month basis versus a year in Canada, and it tends to be more expensive in the U.S. You will also see underinsured and uninsured motorists coverage in the U.S. along with towing and rental car coverage. Uninsured/underinsured motorist coverage is used if a driver who doesn't have insurance, or doesn't have enough insurance hits you. This coverage pays for medical costs, loss of income for you, family members and your passengers. California estimates over 10% of drivers in the state don't have car insurance, but many experts believe the actual number is much higher. In the event your car is no longer functioning, your insurance will pay for it to be towed and pay for a rental car to use while your vehicle is being fixed or replaced. Liability limits are typically $100,000–$300,000 versus $1 million in Canada, and your state of residence will dictate the minimum amount of coverage you are required to carry. As you can see, there are a number of new terms and limits with which you will have to become familiar.

Homeowner/Condominium Insurance

Just like in Canada, in the U.S. you are required to have homeowner insurance if you have a mortgage on your home (the bank wants to protect its investment!). This coverage is fairly standard, and it is best to consolidate your auto and homeowner policies with the same firm since you can usually save on premiums. Ensure you get coverage to protect yourself in the event someone slips on your driveway or falls into your pool, as outlined in the liability section below. But beware, if you are running a small business out of your home, your homeowner insurance typically won't provide the coverage you need!

Liability

The U.S. is a much more litigious society than Canada because the laws are more liberal in permitting lawsuits, and the case law has proven that big payouts are possible. As a result, there are countless attorneys in the phone book and on TV and radio advertising for those who may have been injured in a car accident or medical malpractice. Make sure you protect yourself with an excess liability policy. We never recommend you retain your Canadian property and casualty insurance policies when making the transition to the U.S. — they just don't provide the coverage you need as a resident there, and may suggest a tax residency tie back to Canada.

3

A Pledge of Allegiance

I pledge allegiance to the flag of the
United States of America. . . . — Francis Bellamy

For some Canadians, quoting those words in a U.S. citizenship ceremony someday is the ultimate dream, while for others this is the deciding factor in returning to Canada when their kids come home from school quoting it from heart. The issue of immigration to and citizenship in the U.S. can be confusing, and this chapter aims to provide you with a basic understanding of the options you have for living and working in the U.S. To live year round or work at any time in the U.S., you must have the appropriate non-immigrant or immigrant status or be a citizen of the U.S. If you are not a U.S. citizen, your long-term objectives should determine whether you pursue a non-immigrant visa with or without employment authorization, a green card, or citizenship, because there are tax implications, health care, cost of living, and lifestyle issues to consider. Again, a thorough analysis of your unique situation is required to determine the best immigration strategy for you and how to best achieve your goals. For example, if you hope to move to the U.S. and remain there for the balance of your life, you need to ask your immigration attorney for the road map to get you from where you are now (Canadian citizen) to where you want to be (dual Canadian-U.S. citizen). Likewise, if you want to move to the U.S. for a short-term job opportunity and then return to Canada, a different road map is required.

A lack of planning in this area can result in some negative consequences. One scenario we often see is one spouse gets a job offer and sponsorship for a temporary visa from a U.S. employer, while an immigration strategy for the dependent spouse is not addressed. Once in the U.S., one spouse is working, and the other is left at home in a strange city because the other spouse cannot work, and there is no family or support structure in place. This situation tends to raise tensions in the non-working spouse and create a longing to go back to Canada.

The Trade NAFTA (TN) visa has caused some U.S. immigrants unforeseen difficulties as well. People often forget that this is a temporary visa. As a result, staying in the U.S. is entirely dependent on whether your employer will sponsor the renewal of your visa. We have witnessed poorly conceived immigration strategies where people have moved to the U.S. with a TN visa intending to stay permanently. In one situation, we worked with a scientist who faced a return to Canada because the company he worked with fell on difficult financial times, and a layoff was imminent. The scientist had six months to find another company to hire him in his field of expertise to continue sponsorship of the TN visa. Needless to say, this was a very stressful situation that could have been avoided with a well-thought-out immigration strategy, better negotiations with his employer upfront, and a plan for contingencies.

Another situation we have witnessed is becoming a naturalized U.S. citizen or holding a green card for a long time when you plan on returning to Canada. In both situations, you typically have to continue filing U.S. tax returns even if you live in Canada because the IRS taxes its citizens and permanent resident green card holders on their worldwide income regardless of where they are living at the time (see Chapter 5). As examples in this chapter illustrate, a lack of sound planning in this area can lead to some unintended consequences.

U.S. Immigration Visas

Despite the close relationship between Canada and the U.S., anytime you cross the border you mustn't forget you are crossing into another country. Therefore, you must have the proper documentation to prove your origin and identity. Historically, a birth certificate or driver's licence has sufficed, but recently the U.S. Citizenship and Immigration Services (CIS) has tried to implement a Western Hemisphere Travel Initiative. Initially, all travelers were required to have a passport by December 31, 2005, to enter the U.S. from Canada. The biometric identifiers in a passport and the documentation supporting it allow the U.S. CIS to better track and confirm whom they are allowing into the country. However, once the U.S. Department of State realized it couldn't process enough passports or alternative secure identification documents in time, along with the hindrance to U.S. international commerce, the plans were delayed to January 23, 2007 for travel by air and as early as January 1, 2008 for land and sea travel ports of entry. The plans have changed a few times already, and it is expected that they will change again.

There are two ways of obtaining legal status in the U.S.: through a business/professional relationship, or through a primary family member sponsoring you. The age of maturity to be considered for a visa based on a parent's status is 21; over that age, you must apply independently under a sponsoring parent, other qualifying relative, or business/professional relationship. Despite thoughts to the contrary, if you don't fit into one of the immigration categories outlined below and have not secured the appropriate visa, don't even think of moving to and remaining in the U.S. Unfortunately, no "special circumstances" are permitted.

Temporary Business/Professional Visas

The decision about which visa to pursue depends on what you are trying to accomplish and on understanding the pros and cons of each alternative. The most common visas Canadians use for making the transition to the U.S. on a temporary or permanent basis are the B-1, B-2, E-1, E-2, F-1, H-1B, K-1, K-3, L-1, L-2, and TN visas (see Table 3.1).

Table 3.1

Non-Immigrant Visas

A-1 Diplomats: for traveling ambassadors, public ministers, career diplomats, or consular officers.

A-2 Accompanying support: for other foreign government officials or the staff of A-1 visa holders.

A-3 Accompanying party: for an attendant, servant, personal employee, or immediate family member of an A-1 visa holder.

B-1 Visitor for business: this visa is what you receive when you attend a conference or visit a branch office or subsidiary company in the U.S.
- No application is required.
- No visa is issued.
- You don't typically receive a passport stamp.
- It is good for six months only.
- You are not eligible to work (earn a wage) in the U.S.

B-2 Visitor for pleasure: this visa is what you receive when you visit family or "snowbird" in the U.S. (See our companion book "The Canadian Snowbird in America" for more details)
- No application is required.
- No visa is issued.

- You don't typically receive a passport stamp.
- It is good for six months only.
- You are not eligible to work in the U.S.

C-1 Continuous transit: for aliens in transit passing through the U.S.
- No application is required.
- It is good for a maximum of 29 days.

C-2 United Nations diplomats: for those traveling to UN meetings in New York.

C-3 Foreign Government Official: Family members or personal assistants

C-4 See TWOV

D   Crew member: for sea or air crew members.

E-1 Treaty trader (importer/exporter): for a person who works for a Canadian-owned/controlled firm in the U.S., and the position involves abilities essential to operation of the U.S. firm.
- It is issued for two years.
- It is renewable for as long as you continue to qualify.
- It does not lead to a green card (non-immigrant visa).
- You typically file U.S. tax returns annually.
- It may include a spouse and/or child.

E-2 Treaty investor: for Canadians citizens with a substantial investment in a business to create U.S. jobs.
- It is issued for two years.
- It is renewable for as long as you continue to qualify.
- It does not lead to a green card.
- You typically file U.S. tax returns annually.
- It may include a spouse and/or child.

F-1/OPT Student: for students seeking an education in the U.S.
- You must prove you have sufficient funds to support yourself and your family for the duration of your studies.

- It is issued for each year of study; once studies are completed, you must return to your home country.
- It does not lead to a green card.
- You are able to work on campus without permission of the United States Citizenship and Immigration Services (U.S. CIS) and off campus in certain circumstances.
- You typically don't file U.S. tax returns.

Optional practical training: allows you to work and live in the U.S. on a temporary basis for training purposes only.
- It is an extension of the F-1 visa.
- Your work must be related to your field of study.
- It is issued for an additional 12 months after the F-1.
- It does not lead to a green card.
- You typically file U.S. tax returns annually.

F-2 Dependent: for the spouse and dependent children of an F-1 student visa holder.
- No work in the U.S. is permitted.

G-1 International organizations: for principal resident representatives of a recognized foreign government to an international organization such as NATO.

G-2 International organizations: for other representatives of a recognized foreign member government to an international organization.

G-3 International organizations: for representatives of a non-recognized foreign non-member government to an international organization.

G-4 International organizations: for international organization officers or employees.

G-5 Dependents: for attendants, servants, personal employees, or immediately family of G-1 through G-4 visa holders.

H-1B Specialty workers: typically for professionals who have a degree (or equivalent experience) and a job that requires that degree.

- It is issued for three years initially.
- It is renewable once for a total six-year stay.
- It is typically pursued when you can't qualify for a green card, but it can lead to a green card if the employer can demonstrate to the U.S. Department of Labor that there are no U.S. citizens or permanent residents qualified and willing to do the job.
- There is an annual quota of 65,000 that starts each October 1 (and is usually filled by March).
- You typically file U.S. tax returns annually.

H-1C Registered nurse: a temporary visa established by the Nursing Relief for Disadvantaged Areas Act of 1999 and expired in June 2005; it is currently under review by Congress to be extended.
- It is issued for three years initially, with no extensions, and comes with a host of restrictions, such as working in an impoverished area.
- A maximum of 50 H-1C visas are permitted per year in each state with a population of more than 9 million.
- A maximum of 25 H-1C visas are permitted per year in each state with a population of less than 9 million.
- Canadian nurses are better off entering the U.S. on a TN visa since it is less restrictive.

H-2A Seasonal farm workers: for a temporary worker performing agricultural services unavailable in the U.S.
- Labor certification is required to confirm there is a short supply.
- It is issued for one year.
- It is renewable for two additional terms (maximum of three years).
- It is expensive and rarely used.

H-2B Unskilled labor: for a temporary worker performing other services (non-farm workers) unavailable in the U.S.
- Labor certification is required to confirm there is a short supply.
- It is issued for one year.
- It is renewable for two additional terms (maximum of three years).
- It is expensive and rarely used except in some special circumstances by some hockey players.

H-3 **Trainees:** intended for those going to the U.S. to get on-the-job training and then return to their foreign countries.
- It is issued for one year (maximum).
- An extension is possible for two more years (maximum of three years).

H-4 **Dependents:** for the spouse or dependent child of any H visa holder.
- No work is permitted.

I   **Media:** for foreign media correspondents, representatives, employees, and their families (a popular visa during the World Trade Center tragedy).

J-1 **Exchange visitor:** for those in an approved exchange program for education, culture, or employment; it is used primarily by doctors, professors, or scientists studying in the U.S.
- It is issued for the term of the program (predefined).
- You don't typically file U.S. tax returns.
- It does not lead to a green card.
- You may have to return home for two years before being eligible to change to another status.

J-2 **Dependents:** for the spouse and dependent children of a J-1 exchange visitor visa holder; no work is permitted unless separate authorization is obtained.

K-1 **Fiancés/ées:** for those about to move to the U.S. and wed a U.S. citizen within 90 days of entry.

K-2 **Dependents:** for unmarried children under age 21 of K-1 fiancé/ée visa holders.

K-3 **Spouses:** for those moving to the U.S. with a U.S. citizen spouse while waiting for their immigrant visa to be processed.
- This is a new category created in 2001 to deal with the eligible spouses of U.S. citizens who were forced to live apart from their

U.S. spouses while their visas were being processed.
- It is issued for two years only.
- Work authorization is granted for two years only.
- You must continue the I-130 petition process or change of status application filed and active with U.S. CIS.
- It precedes an application for a green card.
- It is a temporary solution to the large backlog at U.S. CIS.

K-4 Dependents: for unmarried children under age 21 accompanying a K-3 spousal visa holder.

L-1 Intracompany transfer: for companies in both Canada and the U.S. that need to transfer executives, managers, or those with specialized knowledge between certain related companies in both countries.
- You must have worked in a country besides the U.S. for at least one of the past three years.
- It is issued for two years only but can be renewed for a total of seven years.
- It is considered a "shortcut" to a green card for executives and managers only (specialized knowledge excluded).
- You typically file U.S. tax returns annually.

L-2 Dependents: for the spouse and dependent children of an L-1 intracompany transfer visa holder.
- Work is permitted.
- You typically file U.S. tax returns with the L-1 visa holder.

M-1 Vocational/non-degree students: for those studying in the U.S. but not in a program leading to a degree.
- It is issued for one year, with annual extensions.
- One month of work for each four months of study is allowed after studies are completed.
- You typically don't file U.S. tax returns.

M-2 Dependents: for the spouse and children of an M-1 visa holder.

N   **Special immigrants:** for the parents and children of certain special immigrants.

NATO NATO representatives: there are NATO-1 through 7 visas for all representatives, staff, experts, support staff, and dependents related to NATO.

O-1 **Extraordinary ability:** for those with sustained national or international acclaim for displaying extraordinary ability in art, science, business, or athletics.
- It is issued for three years initially and then renewable for one year or the period of the event, whichever is less.
- It is used by well-known professional athletes coming from Canada to play in the U.S.
- There is an annual quota on this visa.
- You typically file U.S. tax returns annually.

O-2 **Accompanying support:** for support staff vital to O-1 visa holders.
- You typically file U.S. tax returns annually.

O-3 **Dependents:** for the spouse and dependent children of an O-1 visa holder.
- No work is permitted.
- You are typically included on O-2 U.S. tax returns.

P-1 **Performing entertainers and athletes:** for those with less acclaim than O-1 visa holders but still internationally recognized.
- It is issued for up to five years and can be extended to 10 years.
- There is a quota of 25,000 visas annually for all P categories.
- You typically file U.S. tax returns annually.

P-2 **Exchange program:** for those artists and entertainers in a reciprocal exchange program with a foreign country.
- You typically don't file U.S. tax returns.

P-3 **Unique abilities:** for artists and entertainers who are culturally unique.
- You typically don't file U.S. tax returns.

P-4 **Dependents:** for the spouse and dependent children of a P visa holder.
- No work is permitted.

Q-1 **Cultural exchange visitor:** for a participant in an international cultural employment exchange program run by the U.S. CIS.
- You must be engaged in business for at least two years.
- You must employ at least five people.

Q-2 **Irish exchange visitor:** for participants in the Irish peace process program.

Q-3 **Dependents:** for the spouse or child of a Q-2 visa holder.

R-1 **Religious workers:** for workers within a religious organization.
- You must be part of the same religious denomination for at least two preceding years.
- It is issued for a maximum of five years.

R-2 **Dependents:** for the spouse or child of an R-1 visa holder.

S-5 **International informants:** for certain aliens supplying critical information relating to a criminal organization or enterprise.

S-6 **International informants:** for certain aliens supplying critical information relating to terrorism.

S-7 **Dependents:** for qualified family members of S-5 or S-6 visa holders.

T **1 to 4:** for victims (and their families) of a severe form of trafficking in persons.

TN **Trade NAFTA visa:** a unique category based on the North American Free Trade Agreement (NAFTA) between the U.S., Canada, and Mexico.
- It includes a specific list of professions that are eligible (including medical professionals, scientists, engineers, computer professionals, architects, accountants, architects, and consultants).
- You must have a degree (unless a management consultant).
- It is renewable annually for an unlimited period of time.
- It usually does not lead to a green card.
- You typically file U.S. tax returns annually.

TD **Dependents:** for the spouse or child of a NAFTA professional TN visa holder.

TWOV Transit without visa.

U **U 1 to 4:** For victims (and their families) of certain crimes.

V-1 **Dependents:** for the spouses of lawful permanent residents of the U.S. waiting for more than three years for immigrant visas.
- This is a new category created in 2001 to deal with the eligible spouses of U.S. citizens and permanent residents who were forced to live apart from their U.S. spouses while their visas were being processed.
- You are able to work.

V-2 **Dependents:** for the children (under 21) of lawful permanent residents of the U.S. waiting for more than three years for immigrant visas.
- You are able to work.

V-3 **Dependents:** for the children (under 21) of the spouses of lawful permanent residents of the U.S. waiting for more than three years for immigrant visas.
- You are able to work.

Facts and Myths

There are both facts and myths surrounding immigration to and remaining in the U.S. for an extended period of time. Here are some common ones we have dealt with.

Myth: Special Circumstances Apply

No matter what, you must have a valid, approved visa to enter the U.S. Despite popular opinion, you can't remain in the U.S. unless you have a valid status to do so, even if one wasn't given to you at the border or your passport was not stamped. In one case, we talked to someone in California who had been in the U.S. for years on a visitor's visa (good for six months), had assumed an actor's name for acting pursuits, and ran a small business paying only California sales tax. The person simply stopped filing Canadian tax returns and has never filed a U.S. income tax return. The person has even gone back to Canada on occasion to visit family! Regardless, it is a game of roulette that will quickly come to an end as border crossings are more closely monitored with the events of 9/11.

Some immigration policies aren't so flagrantly broken. We have witnessed children bring an ill parent to the U.S. to live with them for an extended period of time because there was no other family in Canada. Unfortunately, the parent is still an illegal alien despite the good intentions of the family. Further, provincial and travel health insurance policies have finite time limits and limited coverage, so someone could get stuck with a huge medical bill that could devastate what has taken a lifetime to accumulate.

Myth: Buy a Rental Property

Many folks have asked us if they can buy a home in the U.S. to live in and another home to rent out to obtain a U.S. visa. The visa they are pursuing with this strategy is an E-2 treaty investor.

This strategy is rarely successful because it has come under severe scrutiny in past years. To begin with, this is not considered a "material, bona fide" investment (in time, effort, and money) to justify the issuance of an E-2 visa. However, if you own a couple of apartment buildings or are going to purchase substantive real estate, your chances increase. The investment for prospective purchases and development needs to be irrevocable (held in escrow), but a lot of it depends on the mood of the adjudicator that day and whether he believes you are meeting the issued guidelines for a "substantial" investment through "material participation" in the management of the real estate holdings. This is where an experienced immigration attorney should be brought onto the team to provide insights into what types and numbers of properties qualify and to help you meet the definition of material participation.

Fact: You Will Get Caught

Some people, with little regard for the laws of the land, have asked, "How will the government know?" or "How will I get caught?" Scrutiny in this area has increased significantly since the unfortunate events of 9/11. During his tenure, Secretary of State Colin Powell called for a policy of "secure borders, open doors." In the Enhanced Border Security and Visa Entry Reform Act of 2002, U.S. Congress mandated the use of biometrics with almost all U.S. visas. This law requires embassies and consulates abroad to issue "only machine-readable, tamper-resistant visas and other travel and entry documents that use biometric identifiers" (fingerprints of two index fingers and a digital photo) not later than October 26, 2004. For those traveling without a visa, passports must have a digital photo stored in a chip in the passport.

With passage of the Homeland Security Act in 2002, the Department of Homeland Security has made the establishment of an automated entry/exit system a top priority. The department was allocated a $380 million budget in 2003 to establish the U.S.-VISIT system (United States Visitor and Immigrant Status

Indicator Technology), and it is now functional (you may have seen the digital fingerprint machine at your border crossing). This system is intended to expedite the passing of legitimate travelers but to make it much more difficult for illegitimate travelers to cross the border. To achieve these goals, the department is creating, maintaining, and sharing a database of biometric identifiers using the latest in technology to identify the wrong people and prohibit them from entering the U.S. or overstaying their visas while enhancing traffic flow for those crossing the border for legitimate purposes. All visitors will have their two index fingers scanned and a digital photograph taken to verify identity at the port of entry. In fact, it is the department's intent to create a complete travel record on each individual entering or leaving the U.S., including complete name, immigration status, the date you crossed the border, citizenship, sex, passport number and country, U.S. visa number, et cetera. The Visa Waiver Permanent Program Act of 2000 (vwp) directed the collection of travel information from airline and cruise line travel databases, which are now combined with the U.S.-visit system. Further, the irs (part of the Department of Treasury) and the United States Citizenship and Immigration Services (U.S. cis, part of the Department of Homeland Security) are beginning to work more closely in this effort. They are combining tax slips with visa records to ferret out tax evaders and illegal aliens. Whatever you do, don't enter the U.S. illegally and overstay your visa boundaries. The likelihood of getting caught increases with each passing day.

Myth: Canada-U.S. Marriages Happen Quickly
With the advent of the Internet and increased Canada-U.S. travel, many Canadians are finding love in the U.S. Our firm has seen a large increase in inquiries (and horror stories) from Canadians getting married to U.S. citizens. Many of these people are in shock when they realize their wedding plans are in jeopardy due to the unanticipated long immigration processing

times. The difficulty starts when deciding where to get married.If you get married in Canada, you have two choices to emigrate to the U.S.: a green card or K-3 spouse's visa. The K-3 visa was introduced in 2001 to shorten the processing times because U.S. CIS was taking so long to process green cards. The problem today is the K-3 and green cards are taking about the same time to process (8–10 months depending which U.S. CIS office is processing your application). When you receive a K-3, you can emigrate to the U.S., begin working, and file a change of status for your green card. The problem is that, once you file for your K-3 visa or green card, you must stay in Canada until the processing is completed. If you want to be together as newly-weds, the U.S. citizen has to stay in Canada and risk becoming a Canadian resident for tax purposes, or the U.S. citizen has to return to the U.S. and wait for the Canadian's K-3 or green card to be processed, when they can be together again. The bottom line is you should be prepared to spend some time apart . . . not something newlyweds want to hear.

If you decide to get married in the U.S., the Canadian has to go to the U.S. border and answer the agent's questions before being allowed to enter the country. The agent will ask you about the purpose of your trip, and if you state your intention is to get married he will ask you for your K-1 fiancé/ée visa. If you can't produce one, you will be denied access to the U.S. because you won't be allowed into the U.S. under a B-2 visitor's visa (intending to visit) because your intention is to get married. It is important to be truthful since the agent may document the conversation, and if you are caught lying, you could be banned from entering the U.S. for five years or more. If you are caught illegally in the U.S., you could be banned for life and find yourself on the same list as Osama Bin Laden. One option, dual intent, has been fought successfully in the courts; with this option, you have two reasons for entering the U.S. but share only one of them, and the agent doesn't ask enough questions to expose the other. For example, if you are legitimately going to the U.S. to visit family and to get married, you are truthful in all aspects about your visit with family (staying at their house, length of stay, etc.), and you get married to your fiancée on the same trip, you can enter with a B-2 visitor's visa, get married, and remain in the U.S. when you file for a change of status to a green card. If the agent doesn't ask you if you have a girlfriend in the U.S., or whether you have any other intentions for your trip, you can achieve your immigration goals through dual intent. Again, it is important that you stay in the U.S. while your green card is being processed, which means you won't be able to return to Canada for a few months unless your attorney files for a traveling exemption as well. As you can see, the right immigration planning well in advance of your planned nuptials can help to make your dreams come true. Otherwise, you could be stuck in the kind of nightmare we have seen many times.

Immigrant Visas: Green Cards

The technical term for a green card is lawful permanent resident status. In fact, the term "green card" is derived from the original color of the card provided when you obtained lawful permanent resident status in the past. In fact, the card is no longer green because the U.S. CIS changes it slightly every year to stem false duplication. CIS now also requires biometric identifiers (a fingerprint of your index finger and a photo) to ensure the validity of the cardholder. Today there are about 2.5 million green cards issued annually, and the card contains your picture, an expiration date, your fingerprint, and other pertinent details, as illustrated in Figure 3.1.

Figure 3.1

The U.S. "Green Card"

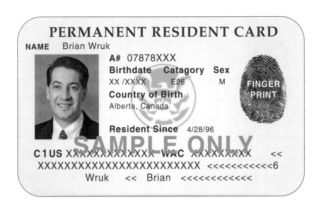

PERMANENT RESIDENT CARD

NAME   Brian Wruk

A# 07878XXX

Birthdate   Catagory   Sex
XX /XXXX   E26   M

Country of Birth
Alberta, Canada

Resident Since   4/28/96

SAMPLE ONLY

FINGER PRINT

C1US XXXXXXXXXXXX WAC XXXXXXXX   <<
XXXXXXXXXXXXXXXXXXXXXXXX <<<<<<<<<<6
Wruk   <<   Brian <<<<<<<<<<<

Once you have held a green card for five years (three years if married to a U.S. citizen), you are eligible to apply for U.S. citizenship. At my citizenship ceremony, I handed in my green card, and it was replaced with my Certificate of Naturalization. Any Certificate of Naturalization is a very valuable document and should be stored in a safe deposit box. When you apply for a passport, you will be required to provide your Certificate of Naturalization, but contrary to popular opinion you will receive it back when your passport is issued.

Many people are unaware of the regulations, duties, and responsibilities surrounding their green card until they go to the border and it is seized. Since holding a green card is considered lawful permanent residence, you must demonstrate to the U.S. CIS that you are actively using the right granted to you, or the "intent to abandon" rules may apply. Some of these duties include using your green card by living in the U.S. and filing U.S. tax returns annually. Leaving the U.S. for an extended period of time has been deemed abandonment of your green card. Many people are unaware of these regulations and are simply living in Canada with a green card in their pocket totally unaware that U.S. CIS may deem them to have "abandoned" it. (See our companion book

"The American in Canada" for more details.) This is typically determined too late, when the green card holder attempts to reenter the U.S. If you have a U.S. green card and you are residing in Canada, you need to "use it or lose it." If you lose it, you must start the green card application process all over again.

Unfortunately, the typical backlog at the U.S. CIS means that, no matter which immigration strategy is selected, there is typically a long wait ahead of you. In some cases, it can be as short as six to eight months, but we are aware of applications taking up to 10 or more years! As a result, the U.S. CIS has introduced the K and V visas (listed above) as a temporary solution. There are two ways of getting lawful permanent resident status (a green card) in the U.S.

1. Family Sponsorship

Family-based sponsorship is possible by U.S. citizens or green card holders. Landed permanent residence status is granted based on one of five "preferences" in the order listed below.

- *Immediate relatives preference:* for spouses, parents, and unmarried children (under the age of 21) of U.S. citizens only. There is no limit to the number of green cards issued under this preference in any particular year, and they are granted in order of preference as outlined below.
- *First preference:* for unmarried children over age 21 of U.S. citizens only.
- *Second preference:* for spouses and unmarried children under age 21 or unmarried children over age 21 of green card holders.
- *Third preference:* for married children of U.S. citizens only.
- *Fourth preference:* siblings over the age of 21 of U.S. citizens only.

2. Business or Professional Relationship

Lawful permanent resident status for business or professional reasons is also granted based on one of five "preferences" in the order outlined below.

- *First preference:* for priority workers who have risen to the top of their profession. At least 40,000 first preference green cards are issued annually. This category is broken into three employment-based classes of immigrants:

    o *EB1-A extraordinary ability:* for those with sustained national or international acclaim for ability in art, science, business, or athletics; Wayne Gretzky and Jim Carrey are examples.

    o *EB1-B advanced degrees:* for researchers and professors with exceptional ability and international recognition coming to the U.S. to conduct full-time research for a company or university.

    o *EB1-C skilled workers:* for executives and managers of multinational companies who have worked in a Canadian affiliate for one of the past three years, and now the U.S. affiliate is petitioning for permanent status.

- *Second preference:* priority workers whom the U.S. CIS views as benefiting the "national interest" (i.e., helping the economic, cultural, educational, or general welfare of the U.S.) if employed in the U.S. This is sometimes called the "national interest" waiver (a company or institution doesn't have to obtain labor certification, as described under the third preference below). At least 40,000 second preference green cards are issued annually. They are broken into the following two categories:

    o *EB2-A advanced degrees:* for professionals with advanced degrees (or equivalent experience) who display exceptional ability in science, business, or art. Proof of ability is not as strenuous as in the first preference category, but you must prove you are the only one qualified (or the most qualified person) for the position.

    o *EB2-B exceptional ability:* for those with more ability than ordinary folks in the areas of art, science, business, or athletics but who don't have the extraordinary ability of the first preference category. Defining ordinary versus exceptional versus extraordinary can be difficult.

- *Third preference:* for skilled and unskilled workers who don't fit into the first or second preference areas. At least 40,000 third preference green cards are issued annually, but no more than 10,000 are issued to unskilled workers. Each of the third preference categories requires labor certification under which the U.S. employer must demonstrate to the satisfaction of the U.S. Department of Labor that there are no U.S. citizens or permanent residents able and willing to do the job. There are three categories.

  o *EB3-A workers with degrees:* for professionals with a degree.
  o *EB3-B skilled workers:* for those with at least two years of experience or higher training and education.
  o *EB3-C unskilled workers:* for those with less than two years of experience or higher training and education.

- *Fourth preference:* for special immigrants, including religious workers or those who have worked for the U.S. government abroad for 15 years. At least 10,000 fourth preference green cards are issued annually.

- *Fifth preference:* since 1990, Congress has made available a fifth preference immigrant visa category known as an EB-5 investor green card or a "gold card." There are only 10,000 available per year, and the rules and regulations surrounding them are very specific (about 1,000 get approved annually, so don't do it yourself). An investor who establishes a business in the U.S. with an investment of $1 million ($500,000 if a U.S. cis "targeted employment area") can obtain a green card with conditions that last for two years. The U.S. cis wants the investment "locked in" for at least two years to ensure that it will benefit the U.S. economy and has directly or indirectly created at least 10 full-time jobs. Once filed, the investor's petition is normally approved by the U.S. cis within 60-90 days, so it is an unusually quick turnaround time. If approved, you move into the normal green card application process in which you get a physical and go through the interview process. Once the investment has been made, your "gold card" has been approved, and your entity has operated for two years, a petition can be filed to lift the restrictions from the "gold card," and you become eligible for an unencumbered green card. After holding the green card for an additional three years, you can apply to become a naturalized U.S. citizen. We have experience in getting the "gold card" (hard to find) and have experts available to assist you in implementing this complex but very convenient immigration strategy.

Applying for a Green Card

To apply for a green card, the starting point is filing U.S. CIS Form I-485 — Application to Register Permanent Status or Adjust Status along with the $395 filing fee for adults ($295 for minors) and two color photographs. There are other supplemental forms, such as the I-134: Affidavit of Support, that may be required, depending on your circumstances. Before undertaking this yourself, seek good counsel to save yourself a lot of time and to ensure you are filling out the right forms and submitting them in their entirety to the right location. If all of these requirements are not met, the U.S. CIS may reject your application, delaying the process significantly.

U.S. Citizenship

For many Canadians, the prospect of becoming a U.S. citizen is a terrifying thing, while for others it is the next most coveted nationality around. Millions of people around the world would welcome the opportunity to become a Canadian or U.S. citizen and be able to work and live anywhere in Canada or the U.S. Once again, there are many rules and regulations surrounding citizenship with which you must contend. U.S. citizenship is obtained in one of the following three ways.

1. Birth in the U.S.

In general, if you were born in the U.S. (legally), you are a U.S. citizen unless you effectively renounced your citizenship.

Loss of Citizenship

Before 1986, the U.S. Department of State involuntarily renounced your U.S. citizenship if you performed an "expatriating act" (became a citizen of another country, declared allegiance to it, enrolled in its military, or worked for its government). Many U.S. citizens residing in Canada received a Certificate of Loss of Nationality from the U.S. Department of State, but in most cases your citizenship can be reinstated. To regain it, you need to write to the U.S. Department of State and ask it to revoke the Certificate of Loss of Nationality. However, before you do so, realize that you become liable to file U.S. tax returns and be subject to U.S. estate taxes, among other things. Be sure you fully understand all the implications of reinstating your loss of citizenship and the negative consequences that may be involved.

Reinstating Citizenship

Given the seemingly constant backlog at the U.S. CIS, we recommend you "short-circuit" the process of reinstating your citizenship by first applying for a passport at the U.S. Department of State. You fill out Form DS-11 and submit it along with US$97 and two recent photographs of yourself. You will get an answer sooner this way and can determine the next course of action. Alternatively, you can file Form N-600 — Application for Certification of Citizenship with the U.S. CIS along with the US$255 fee and two photographs to apply for U.S. citizenship. This approach will take longer and will require more time and effort.

Renouncing Citizenship

Formally renouncing your citizenship has become a difficult, lengthy process because new rules make it very difficult to do so. The primary reason is that Congress is trying to stem the flow of people who are renouncing their citizenship and in turn no longer filing U.S. tax returns (remember, the U.S. taxes people based on citizenship and domicile, not physical presence). In particular, you will be subject to the expatriation rules if you have a net worth of us$2 million+ in 2007 or have paid an average of us$136,000+ in annual income taxes for the preceding five years. For those who have taken up citizenship in a tax-free island country with the intent of avoiding U.S. taxes, they may be in for a rude awakening. The rules state that, even if you have formally renounced your citizenship, you are still required to file U.S. income tax returns and pay U.S. taxes for the next 10 years! Further, you are not permitted to return to the U.S. However, under certain conditions you may be able to renounce your citizenship if you are returning to your "home" country (e.g., Canada).

2. Derivative Citizenship

Many people living in Canada, though they have never lived in the U.S., may be U.S. citizens and not even know it! The derivative citizenship rules provide that you may be a U.S. citizen depending on where you are in your family tree. You may be able to claim U.S. citizenship if one or both of your parents were U.S. citizens and/or resided in the U.S. Determining whether you are a derivative citizen is a bit complex because the rules have changed over the years. The following decision tree (Figure 3.2) should assist you in determining whether you are a derivative citizen of the U.S., but you should consult with an experienced immigration attorney to confirm your derivative citizenship.

Basically, if one or both of your parents were U.S. citizens and resided in the U.S. at some point, you may be a derivative citizen. However, in establishing derivative citizenship, it may be difficult to provide enough substantive evidence to the U.S. cis that your parents were U.S. citizens and/or resided in the U.S. for the required time periods. Birth certificates and proof of a U.S. address are typically required but often difficult to come by, particularly in small towns or counties. The rules surrounding derivative citizenship are complex, and you'll likely require the

Figure 3.2

Derivative Citizenship Decision Tree

services of a good immigration attorney to build your case before exercising your right to derivative citizenship. However, before doing so, you should recognize that you become liable to file U.S. tax returns, become subject to U.S. estate taxes, and so on, so ensure you fully understand all of the implications of exercising your right to derivative citizenship and what can be done beforehand to mitigate any negative consequences.

Applying for Citizenship

Again, given the current backlog at the U.S. CIS, you can "short-circuit" the derivative citizenship process by applying for a passport at the U.S. Department of State. You fill out Form DS-11 — Application for Passport and submit it along with US$97 and two recent photographs of yourself. You will get an answer sooner this way and be able to determine your next course of action. Alternatively, you can file Form N-600 — Application for Certification of Citizenship with U.S. CIS along with the US$255 fee and two photographs to determine your U.S. citizenship.

3. Naturalization

The primary method used to obtain U.S. citizenship by Canadian citizens is becoming a naturalized citizen through an American spouse (after holding a green card for three years, like I did) or after holding a green card for five years. It is a relatively easy process that requires you to file Form N-400 — Application for Naturalization with the U.S. CIS along with the US$400 fee and two photographs to get the process started. This form is onerous because you have to provide the details of every trip you have taken outside the U.S. since you received your green card, so start tracking them now!

Once the U.S. CIS receives the form, you'll be fingerprinted, an FBI background check will be completed, and you will have a personal interview with a U.S. CIS naturalization examiner. She will ensure you can both speak and write English and have a general understanding of U.S. history and government. Historically, there is a pool of 100 questions that the examiner will draw from for your interview and she will typically pick five to ten of these questions to test your speaking and writing abilities. However, U.S. cis began testing 140 new pilot questions in select cities across the U.S. in 2007. These new questions are intended to ensure applicants understand the meaning behind some of America's fundamental institutions rather than just memorize names and facts. The list will be narrowed to 100 and will be rolled out nationwide in early 2008 (see Appendix D for a list of the current and pilot questions).

Becoming a naturalized citizen of the U.S. can be a nerve-racking experience . . . you need to understand you are becoming a citizen of another country. My own experience was particularly difficult because I had an older, experienced examiner who'd been lured out of retirement for the second time to handle the caseload. In the verbal interview, he asked, "If we went to war with Canada, would you fight for our side?" After getting a lump in my throat, I nervously replied, "A war with Canada would never happen!" He immediately replied, "The question still stands." That is when I realized the gravity of what I was doing. In the written portion of the interview, the examiner asked me to "demonstrate your writing skills by writing 'the color of my new flag is red, white, and blue.'" This was sobering to say the least as I tried to keep my hand from shaking so the writing would be legible. Thankfully I passed and during my citizenship ceremony, exchanged my Green Card for my naturalization certificate (valuable document so store in a safe deposit box). My citizenship ceremony was a very interesting experience and I encourage you to participate in it (you don't have to). The most powerful part is generally the time people share their testimonies and how thankful they are to be U.S. citizens.

Pros and Cons of U.S. Citizenship

Table 3.2 presents some of the pros and cons you should consider before becoming a naturalized citizen of the U.S.

Table 3.2

Pros and Cons of U.S. Citizenship

Pros	Cons
• You can work and live anywhere in Canada or the U.S. (Including Canada, with its socialized medical health-care system.)	• You must file U.S. taxes for the balance of your life no matter where you live in the world (including Canada).
• You do *not* relinquish your Canadian citizenship.	• To avoid filing U.S. taxes as above, you must renounce your citizenship, which can be very difficult to do.
• You get the same estate planning benefits that U.S. citizens get.	• You do not get the unlimited marital estate tax deduction at the first spouse's death.
• There is unlimited gifting between married spouses on an annual basis.	• Gifting between spouses is limited to $125,000 annually in 2007.
• You can use the quicker-serving U.S. health-care system for the balance of your life.	• You still can't run for president of the United States.
• You can vote in the U.S. and help to shape the political landscape there.	• You may still be subject to Canadian income taxes on certain income.
• You can carry both a U.S. and a Canadian passport for traveling purposes.	
• You can run for municipal or state political office.	

Obviously, becoming a U.S. citizen is a very personal decision and needs to be considered seriously in light of the pros and cons above. Since our firm has direct experience with the entire process, we can certainly provide assistance in making this decision.

Facts and Myths

There are many facts and myths surrounding U.S. citizenship. Here are the most common ones we have seen.

Fact: Dual Canadian-U.S. Citizenship

I am living proof, and so are most of our clients. We have even worked with people who have moved from Australia to Canada to the U.S. and obtained citizenship in all three countries. Others have moved from the United Kingdom to Canada to the U.S., while still others have moved from Hong Kong to Canada to the U.S. and are citizens in all three countries. This is totally legal, and you do not have to give up citizenship in one country for that in another, but you'll find few immigration officials who admit to knowing about it. Dual citizenship comes about because the citizenship applications for both countries are separate. You do not apply for dual citizenship. You simply are a Canadian citizen applying for U.S. citizenship or a U.S. citizen applying for Canadian citizenship.

Since Pierre Trudeau declared his "Once a Canadian, always a Canadian!" policy in 1977, Canadians cannot lose their Canadian citizenship even if they take up citizenship in another country. This came up for debate in 2006 when tens of millions were spent to bring Canadians home from Lebanon and they aren't paying any taxes. Stay tuned because this is a hot political issue that could have far reaching effects. Some people incorrectly state that U.S. citizenship requires that you renounce your Canadian citizenship. If so, what proof does the U.S. cis ask for? Besides, who is the U.S. government to tell the Canadian government whom that government can deem a citizen? It just doesn't pan out. As a result, you can be a dual Canadian-U.S. citizen.

For Americans, becoming a Canadian citizen used to mean they automatically lost their U.S. citizenship. Before 1986, the U.S. Department of State involuntarily revoked your U.S. citizenship if you performed an "expatriating act," as outlined above. Many U.S. citizens residing in Canada received a Certificate of Loss of Nationality from the U.S. Department of State in such circumstances. However, in most cases, your citizenship can be reinstated. Refer to the section on "Loss of Citizenship" for information on how to get it back.

To us, dual citizenship is the ultimate in freedom since we can work and live anywhere in the two greatest nations in the world. In addition, what a heritage to pass on to your children! U.S. citizenship is not for everyone, though, so ensure you understand all that is involved before you make your decision.

If one or both of you are Canadian citizens and you have a child that is born or adopted after you have moved to the U.S., you should consider "invoking" their Canadian citizenship from abroad without having to become permanent residents of Canada. Your child will not take up tax residency and it will allow them quicker access to a Canadian passport or to return back to Canada for any reason. If your child is born naturally to you, you need to fill out Form CIT 0006 – Application for a Citizenship Certificate from Outside Canada (Proof of Citizenship) Under Section 3 along with the supporting forms and documentation (including a c$100 filing fee). It may take a while for your child's application to make its way through the government system and it is difficult to determine where you are in the process so we caution you now to exercise patience.

For adopted children, this opportunity wasn't available until May 15, 2006 when the federal government tabled Bill C-14, which amends the Citizenship Act to make children adopted abroad by Canadian citizens living abroad. Thankfully the restrictions placed on adopted children of Canadian citizens versus naturally born children has been removed and "invoking" Canadian citizenship is possible for both adopted and naturally born children using the same Form CIT 0006.

Myth: Green Card Lottery

The green card lottery is really called the Diversity Immigrant Visa Lottery, and it does happen annually. Once and sometimes twice a year the U.S. will make 50,000 green cards available through a lottery system. The intent behind this lottery is to equalize the immigrants entering the U.S. from around the world. Countries that do not get their "fair share," and where it is a political advantage for the U.S. to do so, will be put on the "list." Only those countries on the list will be eligible for the lottery. Unfortunately, Canada has its fair share of emigrants to the U.S., and since 1993 Canadians have been excluded from the lottery. However, if you have citizenship in another country, you may be able to enter the lottery using that citizenship.

Becoming a U.S. Resident

Once you have completed the transition to the U.S. and officially given up Canadian residency (but not citizenship!), there is a whole new set of items to consider.

Stay out of Canada

To demonstrate that you have severed your ties with Canada and established U.S. residency, it is best if you postpone any lengthy stays in Canada for at least two years and preferably three. Do not return to Canada for extended periods of time (e.g., six months), and if you do go to Canada be sure it is for short visits to family (it always helps to document your trips).

Review Your Estate Plan

As outlined in Chapter 7, now is the time to have your Canadian estate plan reviewed by a qualified U.S. estate planning attorney familiar with Canada-U.S. issues to determine its validity in the U.S. You need to ensure that your children are cared for and that all your financial affairs are managed according to your wishes in the event you become incapacitated. In addition, you need to ensure that your children have guardians and that your estate can be settled quickly (in both the U.S. and Canada) when you pass away. These are serious issues that need to be addressed immediately.

Register, Apply for, Subscribe

As outlined in the next chapter, you should register your vehicle in the state in which you are residing and get a valid driver's license (you typically have 30 days). You should also get the appropriate U.S. homeowner, auto, and liability insurance policies. See Chapter 2 for further details on these areas. A credit card is a must in the U.S., and you should apply for one upon your arrival. See Chapter 6 for the difficulties and solutions in building a credit rating in the U.S.

Cancel, Cancel, Cancel

This is the time to cancel your Canadian provincial medicare, driver's licence, vehicle registration, and credit cards to clearly sever your ties with Canada and indicate your residency in the U.S. It is usually best to mail them back to the issuing authority along with a letter stating that you are now a U.S. resident. If you don't do this, you risk these items being used to show you never really intended to leave Canada.

RRSPs/RRIFs

Provided you have a well-thought-out plan by a transition planner knowledgeable in Canada-U.S. matters, now may be the best time to withdraw some, or all, of your RRSPS/RRIFS/LIRAS. Chapter 5 gives you further insights into severing your ties with Canada and the taxation of your RRSPS. Chapter 10 addresses the issues in moving these accounts to the U.S.

Establish a US$ Investment Portfolio

Depending on your tenure in the U.S., you should establish a U.S.-dollar-based investment portfolio at a discount brokerage firm. Provided it is structured correctly, your portfolio can reduce your tax bill by consuming foreign tax credits while funding your future U.S.-dollar-based liabilities during retirement, U.S. expenditures, and so on. See Chapter 10 for more details in this area.

4

Moving Your Stuff

Take your flocks and herds, as you have said, and go. — Exodus 12:32

Despite the many tax, immigration, and estate planning issues you may encounter when making the transition to the U.S., moving your physical assets there is what garners most people's attention. In light of 9/11, Canada and the U.S. signed the Smart Border Declaration on December 12, 2001. The intent of this declaration was to outline an action plan to collaborate in identifying and addressing security risks without hampering the transfer of legitimate travelers and goods. The countries agreed to share information and intelligence to strengthen the coordination between both enforcement agencies in addressing common threats. However, there can still be much frustration in this process because, in our experience, when you contact U.S. Customs and Border Protection, the answer to your question is typically different every time you call. To that end, we suggest you document the time and date of each call along with the name of the agent. Call three times for any question; then take the best answer and be prepared to defend it with the documentation you have. You may still endure some inconvenience at the border, but you should get some marks with the customs agent for your efforts. Here are a few other things to consider when moving your physical assets to the U.S.

Automobiles

For some reason, most Canadians insist on taking their automobiles to the U.S. when they move. However, moving your automobile to the U.S. is a tricky proposition and should be avoided if at all possible particularly for long-term or permanent moves. Because of the reasons listed below, you will typically get a higher price in Canada when you sell than you would in the U.S., and trust us . . . it is a lot easier to move cash! You will have to fill out U.S. Department of Transportation Form HS-7 — Declaration and Environmental Protection Agency Form 3520-1 — Import Declaration. In addition, there are several other issues in trying to take your automobile to the U.S. that you should consider.

Kilometers versus Miles

The primary denomination of both the speedometer and the odometer are in kilometers, which means you have to pay to have them converted to miles, or your vehicle will be worth less when you sell the auto in the U.S. To convert your automobile from kilometers to miles in the U.S. costs approximately $800 provided the requisite parts for your make and model can be found.

Safety Standards

Your vehicle must pass the rigorous safety standards in the U.S., and it most likely will. These standards are enforced by the Department of Transportation, which has a say in whether your car meets the standards or not. If not, you could create some difficulties for yourself because you won't be able to register the vehicle until a safety certificate is issued.

Emissions Test

Your Canadian vehicle has a high likelihood of not passing the high (and ever-increasing) emission standards required in sunshine states such as California and Arizona. As a result, you will be required to invest the money to bring it up to standards or destroy/deport the car. It will typically not meet the emission standards if it was not originally manufactured to comply with the tough U.S. emission standards. We have witnessed people bring brand-new vehicles down to the U.S. assuming they would have no problem passing the emissions test, but in fact they failed it. The problem is the emission devices placed on the vehicles in Canada may not be approved by the Environmental Protection Agency in the U.S. Once you get an emissions test failure, you are unable to register the vehicle, which means you can't drive it until you produce a passed emissions test certificate. This is becoming a greater issue in moving to the U.S. because of the high levels of smog in most U.S. cities. As a point of interest, the American Lung Association cites the following cities as having the highest levels of smog in the U.S.: (1) Los Angeles (plus three other cities in California), (5) Houston (then another three cities in California), (9) Knoxville, (10) Dallas-Fort Worth, (11) Washington/Baltimore, (12) Philadelphia, (13) New York City, (14) Charlotte, (15) Cleveland, (16) Greensboro, (17) Pittsburgh, (18) Phoenix, and (19) San Diego. In Canada, the five highest smog levels are in Ontario: (1) Windsor, (2) Sarnia, (3) Toronto, (4) Hamilton, and (5) London.

Registration

In most states, you must register your vehicle within 30 days of taking up residency in that state since your provincial plates will be considered expired, and you could face fines for driving an unregistered automobile. However, be prepared because the state auto registration fees can be punishing ($400 or more) if they are based on the value of your vehicle (as in Arizona).

The good thing is a portion of your registration fees may be deductible on your U.S. tax return.

Duty

Depending on the year and make of your automobile, there may be duty to be paid at the border when you take your vehicle to the U.S. The idea behind duty is to prevent what was happening with prescription drugs . . . buying a newly manufactured car in Canada at lower prices (due to currency exchange, different manufacturing costs) and then moving it to the U.S. You should contact U.S. Customs and Border Protection well in advance of your move to research your particular vehicle and the applicability of any duties so you don't get a nasty surprise at the border. These duties are required at the time of your crossing, or the vehicle is impounded until you pay them.

Investigation

Be prepared for a lengthy stay at the border crossing . . . officials don't allow automobiles into the U.S. easily. The reason is to stem the flow of stolen vehicles from Canada being sold in the U.S. I watched as a customs agent checked every number inside and outside my car and compared it to the information contained in Customs' databases. There were countless questions on when the car was purchased, where, for how much, and so on. Be sure to have adequate documentation, bill of sale, title, et cetera to prove evidence of ownership to ease this difficult process.

Salt

Any autos from Canada are not viewed as favorably as local cars in the southern states because of the salt used in Canada during the winters and the toll it takes on vehicles. There is typically a large decrease in value, particularly in the sunshine states. Besides, you won't need the antirust undercoating and block heater in Florida.

Driver's Licence

Most states require you to obtain a local driver's license typically within 30 days of taking up residency in the U.S. Some states require extensive measures, such as writing the driver's exam, taking an eye test, a reaction test, and a road test. Others simply issue you a driver's licence when you present a valid provincial driver's licence (New York does this). The rules vary by state, so you should check with your local state authorities on what is required from you and the appropriate time lines before you move.

Household Goods

When you reach the border, you will need to file U.S. Customs and Border Protection Form 6059B — Customs Declaration, which requires a complete inventory of all the goods you are importing. You can make life easier by making a list of all the items (and their approximate values if known) as you pack. Per U.S. Customs and Border Protection, you should break your items into the areas outlined below.

- *Furniture:* tables, chairs, sofas, bedroom, home office, and living room furniture, desks, lamps, mirrors, etc.
- *Kitchenware:* silverware, glassware, chinaware, pots, pans, utensils, electrical appliances, etc.
- *Household goods:* linens, towels, rugs, toiletries, cleaning products, decorative articles, art, framed pictures, toys, strollers, crafts, holiday decorations, fans, washers, dryers, VCRS, TVS, stereos, records, collectibles, etc.
- *Sports equipment:* bicycles, weights, stationary equipment, skis, skates, surfboards, etc. (note that this doesn't include firearms).
- *Clothes:* for men, women, boys, girls, and infants.
- *Books/printed materials:* books, calendars, personal records, photo albums, etc.
- *Home office equipment/tools of trade:* computers (CPU, monitor,

printer, software, etc.), filing cabinets, shredders, fax machines, telephone equipment, calculators, books, etc.

- *Other personal effects:* items not covered by the categories outlined above should be individually described.

Be sure to have a full count available of the boxes or pieces you have enclosed in the moving container/truck/trailer to ease the process as well. If you intend to leave some of your goods in Canada, you need to file Form 3299 — Declaration for Free Entry of Unaccompanied Articles when you go to pick them up later to "enter" them into the U.S. You should create this inventory at the same time you are packing the rest of your goods to make things easier on yourself. However, we caution you on storing your personal goods (particularly valuables) in Canada for an extended period of time since doing so can be considered a tie to Canada for income tax purposes (see Chapter 5).

Pets

There are certain requirements in moving your pets to the U.S. First, you will need a health certificate from your pet's veterinarian proving your pet has a clean bill of health. Second, each pet will also need a letter from its veterinarian confirming that it is coming from a rabies-free zone. In lieu of this letter, you can show proof that your pets (dogs) have had valid rabies shots at least 30 days prior to entering the U.S. Depending on which border crossing you use when you enter the U.S., your pets may have to go through a preclearance process. Any unusual or exotic pets might be barred from entry to the U.S. As a result, you should call U.S. Customs in advance of your move to determine if there are any additional requirements.

Alcohol, Tobacco, Firearms

Bringing your own wine cellar or firearms with you to the U.S. is permitted when you move, but for obvious reasons the process is much more involved than those for your other belongings.

There are possible restrictions, duties to be paid, and licenses and permits to obtain not only at the federal level but also in the state where you enter, the state through which you will transport the goods, and the state where you will reside. The variety of situations is far too great to discuss here, so we encourage you to get answers to your specific situation by contacting the relevant government authorities, starting with the Bureau of Alcohol, Tobacco, Firearms, and Explosives — the ATF.

Monetary Instruments

When moving to the U.S., do not take any significant amount of cash (greater than c$10,000), traveler's checks, money orders, stock or bond certificates, or other negotiable instruments with you when you drive to the border. For amounts in excess of c$10,000, you must declare that amount at the Canadian border when you leave, and it just stands to reason that you will be detained and asked to explain the source of it all and why you are carrying it with you. You will need to fill out Form E677 — Cross-Border Currency or Monetary Instruments Report — Individual and file it with the Canada Border Services Agency. If the amount is greater than US$10,000, you will need to fill out U.S. Department of Treasury Financial Crimes Enforcement Network Form 105 — Report of International Transportation of Currency or Monetary Instruments and file it with U.S. Customs and Border Protection. This is just part of the Canadian and American attempts to stop money laundering and control the flow of money to criminal and terrorist organizations.

To avoid these complications, we recommend you transfer these items electronically through preestablished channels (wire from a bank) since these are traceable transactions and because the financial institutions fill out and file this myriad of forms for you. Note that the Canadian financial institution automatically reports any cash transactions (deposits or transfers) in excess of c$10,000 on Form E667 — Cross-Border Currency or Monetary Instruments Report — General to the Canada Border Services

Agency. Transactions in excess of US$10,000 are automatically reported by the U.S. financial institution on U.S. Department of Treasury Financial Crimes Enforcement Network Form 104 — Currency Transaction Report and filed with U.S. Customs and Border Protection. Now, we know what you are thinking . . . why not just move $9,900 in a series of transactions to avoid all this reporting? Because it is considered a crime called structuring, which is arranging to give or receive amounts of less than $10,000 to avoid the reporting rules. You may recall Rush Limbaugh in the U.S. (a prominent Republican radio talk-show host), whose representative at U.S. Trust suggested he do that; U.S. Trust then paid a $10 million fine. See Chapter 10 for more details on how to legally move your cash and other financial instruments to the U.S.

Hiring a Mover

When planning the move of your physical goods to the U.S., we don't recommend you flip through the *Yellow Pages*, close your eyes, and let fate decide which mover you are going to hire based on where you finger lands. We recommend you look for a certified mover through an organization such as the American Moving and Storage Association (www.moving.org). Its website is full of good information and gives you an opportunity for recourse in the event a move goes awry, because companies approved to use the trademark agree to a code of conduct providing complete disclosure, written estimates, et cetera. You can also contact the Better Business Bureau, but despite its great reputation our experiences have shown it is an unreliable source for finding trustworthy vendors. Our firm has been solicited by the BBB to join, but we have refused because it is willing to admit almost any financial planner who submits a form and a check without undertaking the due diligence required to determine if the planner is held to a suitability standard or a fiduciary standard.

Hiring a professional mover is the easiest and most expensive way to get your stuff to the U.S. A family of four with 8,000 pounds of stuff moving 1,200 miles will cost approximately $3,000 during the summer months, but you can usually save about 10% by moving during the off season (October to May). Be sure to deal with a reputable firm, or accompany the driver to the weigh station when the truck's weight is recorded when empty and again when full to ensure you are getting an accurate weigh-in of your goods. If you want to save some money, consider packing and unpacking all of your goods yourself, and buy your own packing boxes and tape from a discount retailer rather than from the moving company, since it will tend to mark them up 10–20%. If you want to save even more money, rent a truck through U-Haul, Ryder, or some other company. We had the good fortune of getting a new truck that U-Haul wanted to move from Calgary to Phoenix so it could be tested in the hot weather. As a result, we got a greatly discounted rate, and we got to drive a brand-new truck. Many new companies are now offering to do the driving for you. They drop off a crate or trailer at your home that you pack. When you are finished, they come and pick it up and drop it off for you at the address you specify. If you do some comparison shopping, you can see they are slightly cheaper than U-Haul and far cheaper than a fullservice mover. Remember to keep track of all your expenses, and keep your receipts because they may be deductible on your U.S. tax return in the year you move.

Visiting Canada

Once you have settled in the U.S. and begin making plans for your first trip back to "the homeland," consider the things listed below to make your trip easier.

Passport

Be sure to take your American passport with you if you have one or your Canadian passport, because as of January 23, 2007, the Department of Homeland Security requires a valid passport for Canadians and Mexicans entering the U.S. via air and as early as

January 1, 2008, by land or sea. You also want to take your American passport to ensure you have it on record when you left the country and when you returned. Some dual citizens believe it is better to show your Canadian passport when you enter Canada and your U.S. passport when you enter the U.S. again. It is really irrelevant because your U.S. passport clearly states your country of origin, so border agents already know you are a dual Canadian-U.S. citizen. However, if you have one passport going in and another on the way out, you increase your chances of inconsistencies showing up in your file, which could lead you to be detained for further questioning.

Gifts

You are permitted to take back to Canada gifts of c$60 per recipient tax and duty free. You are limited to 200 cigarettes, 50 cigars, and 1.5 liters of wine, 1.14 liters of liquor, or 24 cans of beer/ale.

Luggage

Be aware that most major airlines now charge a fee of US$50 or more if any of your bags exceeds 50 pounds. This is particularly true if you are planning on bringing back a lot of stuff from Canada. To protect yourself from this charge, do not buy the big suitcases on wheels that have expansion panels in them. Keep to the medium-sized suitcases, and pack a collapsible duffle bag in case you are over or want to bring more goods back than expected. Also be aware that most airlines will allow you one carry-on (which fits under the seat or in the overhead bin), one purse or similar item, and two pieces of checked luggage per person. If you exceed these amounts, you will face additional charges as well.

Food

A common question our firm fields is "Are there any prohibitions on any foods taken to Canada?" It has been our experience that, as long as the food isn't grown in Canada, border agents will typically allow it in with little or no difficulty. I have taken citrus, nuts, Arizona sweet onions, and freshly caught shrimp and fish through the Canada Border Services Agency with little difficulty. Just be sure to notify the customs agent you have it with you (or you risk a c$400 fine) and you know the source of each item. You can check out which items are permissible at www.beaware.gc.ca or call 1-800-O-Canada.

Bringing It Back

You are permitted to bring back to the U.S. us$400 per person duty free every 30 days. This amount applies to goods that are purchased or received as gifts and brought back with you when you travel (called "accompanied baggage"). You are also limited to 200 cigarettes, 100 cigars, and a liter of alcohol every 30 days. There may be restrictions at the state level as well, so you should check with the authorities in your state to ensure you don't violate their liquor transportation laws when you land. The value of alcohol and tobacco is included in your $400 duty-free exemption, but if you exceed this limit you will have to pay duty plus IRS taxes on the excess amount. All items must be for your own use and not for resale. Goods to follow via mail or courier are allowed duty free as long as they are valued at less than $200.

Visitor Tax Refund

Now that you are no longer resident in Canada for tax purposes, you are now eligible to apply for the Tax Refund for Visitors to Canada. However, purchases after April 1, 2007, will no longer be eligible for the refund since the federal government is eliminating it. Until then, you can still get a refund for the GST (6%) and the Harmonized Sales Tax (14% for the provinces of Nova Scotia, New Brunswick, and Newfoundland and Labrador). To qualify for a refund, you need to

- spend more than c$200 on certain goods and/or accommodations;

- take the goods out of Canada within 60 days of purchase (boarding pass required);
- submit *original* receipts (credit card slips are not acceptable); and
- each receipt must be in excess of c$50.

As of July 1, 2006, Canada Revenue Agency requires proof of export for individual items that cost in excess of $250 only, which means you must have the customs agent stamp your original receipts (except hotel receipts) with confirmation that the good(s) were brought back to the U.S. if you are traveling out of one of Canada's major airports (allow yourself extra time). There are certain items that you cannot get a GST refund on, such as alcohol, tobacco, meals and beverages, auto fuel, transportation, recreational vehicle rentals, campsite fees, general services (dry cleaning, hair dressing, auto repairs, entertainment), and goods consumed or left in Canada. We find it incredible that, up till now, the Government of Canada (the Quebec Sales Tax refund is no longer available) shifts this tax burden to its residents only rather than derives further benefit from its tourism industry. Also, take note of whether your application form is from the Canadian government (Form GST176 — Tax Refund for Visitors to Canada at www.cra-arc.gc.ca/taxnon-residents/visitors/menu-e.html) or from some for-profit firm that charges a "processing fee" and takes a percentage of your eligible refund. All the firm will do is fill out the form for you, which you can do on your own.

5

Double Taxes, Double Trouble

Is it right for us to pay taxes to
Caesar or not? — Luke 20:22

Of all the areas to consider in your move, taxes are by far the most complex yet potentially beneficial area. This is particularly true if the planning is done before making the transition to the U.S. Some advisors make the generalization that you will always pay less tax in the U.S. than in Canada, and many people use that as their sole reason to move to the U.S. In our experience, Canadians generally pay less income tax in the U.S. than they would in Canada if they are a retired couple. However, if you look at income and payroll taxes combined (and health care?), working Canadians may end up paying more income tax in the U.S. than they would in Canada (see the case studies in Appendices E and F). It depends a lot on your individual tax situation now, how it projects into the future, the state you are going to move to, the makeup of your family, your sources and types of income, and what both governments end up doing with their respective tax systems in the years to come. Paying less income tax is one of the things that appeals to most people when considering a move to the U.S. (along with the warmer weather). Generally, the evidence is there to confirm that thinking because in 2006 tax freedom day fell on April 26 for Americans (according to the Tax Foundation) versus June 19 for Canadians (according to the Fraser Institute). Income taxes are a large part of most everyone's budget, but with proper tax planning and then competent tax preparation to implement the planning, there are some tremendous opportunities to take advantage of before exiting Canada. This chapter outlines some of the key things you need to know in the area of taxes when making the transition from Canada to the U.S.

It is important to note the difference between tax planning and tax preparation. Tax preparation is purely a historical event. You simply take the tax slips recording the transactions from last year, input them into the tax software, and hit the calculate button. Based on the luck of the draw, you either get a refund or have an amount due. Tax planning, on the other hand, takes actions in the current tax year to use legal tax avoidance techniques to reduce your tax bill in advance of your tax preparation. It is also important to differentiate between tax avoidance and tax evasion. Tax avoidance employs techniques permitted by law to reduce your tax bill and ensure you pay the appropriate amount throughout the year. Tax evasion is the intentional defrauding of the tax authorities and what is legally due to them.

Interestingly enough, our firm receives the bulk of its calls from February to April of each year. That seems to be the time when people who have moved to the U.S. realize they should have done some planning because they are confronted with the harsh realities of filing their tax returns. We get questions such as "Do I need to file in Canada? What income do I declare? On which return?" To answer these complex questions, people typically turn to their reliable Canadian CA to get their Canadian return filed. Then, for the sake of convenience, the CPA geographically closest to them prepares the U.S. return. Everything is filed on time, and they take comfort in the fact that they have made it successfully through their first U.S. tax season. Unfortunately, it's a false sense of security because in our experience very few people know how to properly prepare these returns unless they are practicing regularly in this area.

What many CAS and CPAS don't realize is that RRSPS/RRIFS/LIRAS et cetera are fully taxable in the U.S. Many don't know how to coordinate the preparation of the Canadian and U.S. returns, they don't know how to properly apply the Canada-U.S. Tax Treaty, and they can't ensure that the necessary compliance issues are fulfilled in both countries. It is only a matter of time before one of the taxing authorities catches a compliance issue and the "hate mail" starts to fill your mailbox. More importantly, the potential overpayment of taxes paid to both CRA and the IRS can be significant, and the CA, CPA, and you will be none the wiser.

A recent example was someone who exited Canada, prepared his own Canadian tax return, and had a local U.S. accountant prepare the U.S. federal and state returns. Our firm reviewed the returns and noted numerous errors. An adjusted Canadian return was filed for an increased refund of c$17,000, and the U.S. return was amended to get him into compliance with the IRS and the appropriate state tax authorities (additional US$200 paid). The important thing to note is that this was not a high-income client! Needless to say, if a lack of planning prior to your departure results in an unexpected large tax bill in Canada and/or the U.S., our firm will not condone or participate in any techniques we believe to violate current income tax laws to reduce your tax bill (yes, we have been asked).

Tax Filing Requirements
Canada
Many people move to the U.S. and just stop filing Canadian tax returns because they believe that, since they no longer live in Canada, they don't have to file tax returns there anymore. They

are correct, Canada Revenue Agency taxes based on Canadian residency, but what these folks aren't aware of is the "departure tax" when leaving Canada. When you leave Canada, you have to file an "exit" return, which is one of the criteria you use to sever your tax residency with Canada (but not your citizenship). This doesn't mean you are completely done filing taxes in Canada, because, if you continue to have Canadian-source income in the future (e.g., interest, dividends, or rent), you will continue to have a tax obligation in Canada through withholding, filing to correct withholding, or filing a tax return to declare income.

Exit Return

CRA agrees to stop taxing you on your worldwide income when you leave — but not before it takes its "pound of flesh." Certain property you own worldwide is "deemed" sold and repurchased again (whether you actually do so or not), and any gains are declared on your final tax return (affectionately known as the "Departure Tax"). Items such as stocks, bonds, mutual funds, partnerships, income trusts, et cetera in regular brokerage accounts, U.S. real estate, and certain businesses must be declared on your exit return. This can mean potentially huge capital gains on your final exit return and a large tax liability owing before you are sent on your merry way. Items not taxed at your exit include all items the government can "attach" itself to (called "taxable" Canadian property). This includes the following:

- All registered plans (RRSPS, RRIFS, LIRAS, RCAS, Profit Sharing Plans, Pensions, Money Purchase Plans, et cetera)
- All Canadian real estate
- Property owned by a business but not the shares of that business
- Employee stock options granted while in Canada
- Life insurance policies or annuities
- Trusts, depending on a variety of issues

Note that this is not an extra tax you are paying; it is simply an early collection of tax because you are leaving Canada. What catches most people by surprise is the early collection of this tax because it is not anticipated. On top of the departure tax, you must declare your worldwide income (any wages, interest, dividends, etc.) that you received when resident in Canada. With the small brackets and high marginal rates, it doesn't take long to reach the top tax bracket of 45%+ when leaving Canada. One client we worked with recently had to pay in excess of c$55,000 in tax because she did not do the requisite planning before she left Canada! Her biggest frustration was that she didn't see it coming and had to come up with a large amount of cash on short notice or post security with the government. With proper planning before you leave Canada, you can use many techniques to mitigate your taxes significantly while reducing your U.S. income and estate taxes at the same time.

The exit return is filed on a T1 tax return, but you must fill in your departure date in the space provided. In addition, your basic personal amount is prorated based on the amount of time you spent in Canada up to the date of your departure. To ensure you are reporting the departure tax correctly, CRA requires Form T1161 — List of Properties by an Emigrant of Canada — to be filed along with your T1 tax return when the value of all your property exceeds c$25,000. This form lists all of the items subject to the departure tax and establishes the fair market value of each item on the date you departed from Canada. In addition, Form T1243 — Deemed Disposition of Property by an Emigrant of Canada provides a detailed record for CRA on how you are calculating your final departure gains. In certain situations, it may be worthwhile to file Form T1244 — Election under Subsection 220(4.5) of the Income Tax Act, to Defer the Payment of Tax on Income Relating to the Deemed Disposition of Property by posting security with CRA so you are not forced to come up with a large amount of cash up front. This strategy "freezes" your departure tax, but its applicability depends on your unique financial situation and the liquidity of your assets (e.g., shares of a small business).

For married couples who are leaving Canada at different times, CRA generally determines the exit date to be that of the spouse who leaves last. Exit date planning is a critical component of your transition to the U.S. and, done correctly, can mitigate your taxes significantly. Your exit return is due by April 30th of the year after the last spouse leaves Canada. This tax return is filed with the International Tax Services office in Ottawa (not with your local province), and your Notice of Assessment can take up to six months or a year to receive. It takes so long because CRA goes over these returns with a fine-toothed comb to ensure it is collecting every last bit of tax before granting you non-resident status. Remember, this is CRA's last chance to collect the resident income taxes owing at ordinary rates; after that, the appropriate tax withholding rates and non-resident returns must be filed, which are typically lower than the ordinary income tax rates on a T1 tax return. See the case studies in Appendices E&F for strategies to reduce the departure tax.

Part XIII

Once you are in the U.S., Canada retains the right to tax any Canadian-source income (dividends, interest, rents, etc.) according to the rates specified in the Canada Income Tax Act and adjusted per the Canada-U.S. Tax Treaty. If too much withholding is taken, you will be overtaxed, and if you are under-withheld you will begin receiving tax bills from CRA for the balance. You need to review all of your Canadian sources of income to ensure the correct withholding has been taken per the treaty or the Income Tax Act and, if necessary, prepare Form NR7-R — Application for Refund of Non-Resident Part XIII Tax Withheld to sort out your non-resident tax withholding refunds with CRA. This tax return needs to be filed by June 30th of the following year. For the correct withholding rates on various types of income, see "Withholding Taxes in the Canada-U.S. Tax Treaty" later in this chapter. Failing to file this return with CRA could be considered a tax residency factor by CRA.

T1 Non-Resident Return

Just when you think you have escaped the clutches of CRA and your need to file a T1 tax return, you realize to your chagrin that there are different types of income for which no withholding applies. As a result, you cannot file a Form NR7-R, and you are back to filing a T1 non-resident tax return. Canadian sources of income such as wages, exercise of vested stock options, and rents all must be filed on a T1 non-resident tax return. The problem is you don't get the personal amount or much of any deductions (see income-specific items below).

U.S.

Unlike Canada (which taxes its residents on worldwide income), the U.S. taxes its citizens and residents (including green card holders) on their worldwide income. This approach leads to difficulties because, if you are a U.S. citizen or a green card holder living anywhere in the world, you have a tax filing obligation with the IRS. Specifically, when Canadians take up tax residency in the U.S., they must file a U.S. "start-up" tax return and report their worldwide income. Doing so can lead to double taxation because you have to file a Canadian exit return declaring your worldwide income and then pay the appropriate withholding on any Canadian source of income after you exit Canada. There are different ways of filing your U.S. returns to minimize your tax liability, and depending on your situation several tax and compliance elections may need to be taken as well. These are complex tax returns to complete. Unfortunately, most U.S. CPAs have no idea how to handle Canadian issues on the U.S. return, and usually you end up being out of compliance with the IRS and your local state government from the very first tax return you file in the U.S. It is in your best interest to get the assistance of a professional who works regularly and consistently in the Canada-U.S. tax preparation arena to ensure you remain in compliance with the IRS, file the necessary exit return with CRA, and coordinate the preparation of both your U.S. and Canadian returns to minimize your tax liability in both countries. Further, there is a lot to be said for doing your initial filing correctly so you can have peace of mind and avoid having the IRS, your local state, or CRA turn on the "hate mail" machines because something is not filed correctly.

Your "start-up" U.S. tax return (and your applicable state return) are due by April 15th of the year after you take up tax residency in the U.S. (due to your presence in the U.S. or the issuance of a green card). One unique aspect of the U.S. tax system that confuses some people is the ability to file an extension. Many Canadians believe that, by filing IRS Form 4868 — Application for Automatic Extension of Time to File U.S. Individual Income Tax Return before the deadline, they can postpone paying their taxes. Nothing is further from the truth. An extension, if approved by the IRS, means "I am paying my tax now, and due to circumstances out of my control, my paperwork will follow later." If you choose not to pay your tax liability at that time, interest and penalties will accrue on that liability from April 15th until paid in full. Unfortunately, filing an extension still requires you to prepare a mock tax return using the information you have available to estimate whether you have a balance owing or not. You are allowed one extension after the April 15th deadline until October 15th (that's why you will see most CPAs so busy at that time of year).

You will also have to file a separate state tax return depending on your state of residence (like Quebec, they all collect their own income taxes). You will file a "part-year" tax return for your particular state and potentially a county or city tax return as well (as in New York). There are nine states with no income tax.

- Alaska
- Florida
- Nevada
- New Hampshire
- South Dakota
- Tennessee

- Texas
- Washington
- Wyoming

Severing Tax Ties with Canada

When making the transition to the U.S., you must ensure you properly sever your tax ties with Canada so you are not subject to the higher Canadian rates and deemed a resident of Canada for tax purposes. If done improperly, you can create untold complexities, paperwork, and double taxation. The Canadian courts have held "residence" to be "a matter of the degree to which a person in mind and fact settles into or maintains or centralizes his ordinary mode of living with its accessories in social relations, interests, and conveniences at or in the place in question." Therefore, the key to severing your ties with Canada is to ensure you move your community of interest, vital interests, family and social relations, cultural and other activities, place of business, and place of property administration clearly from Canada to the U.S. The CRA does not look at any one item in particular but at an accumulation of things together to determine your residency, as outlined in Form NR73 — Determination of Residency Status. There is no obligation to file this form, and we don't recommend you file it unless specifically requested to do so. CRA uses this form to "determine" if you are still a resident of Canada for tax purposes. It is intentionally tricky, so get competent assistance in filling it out since you may not have many options later if CRA determines you are still a resident for tax purposes. To sever your ties with Canada, you should review the checklist below for those items that pertain to you.

❑ Move your spouse and children at the same time you move where possible.

❑ Sell your principal residence.

❑ Take all your personal possessions with you, especially expensive and cherished items.

❑ Terminate all memberships to churches, civic leagues, clubs, and cultural and other religious organizations.

❑ Terminate memberships to all professional associations.

❑ Close all checking and savings accounts except those for convenience only, and ensure they are converted to a non-resident account with your U.S. address on it.

❑ Sell or "wind up" any business interests (except as needed for your immigration strategy).

❑ File a Canadian exit return.

❑ Terminate all family allowance or child tax benefit payments.

❑ Terminate all Canadian credit card accounts.

❑ Mail in your provincial driver's license (may be difficult to do).

❑ Terminate your Canadian auto insurance and provincial auto registration.

❑ Mail in your provincial health-care card (may be difficult to do).

❑ Notify the post office of your address change in the U.S.

❑ Close all post office boxes and terminate any other addresses in Canada. Do not have any mail addressed to you delivered to a Canadian address, including those of family!

❑ Close all safe deposit boxes.

❑ Terminate all subscriptions to magazines and newsletters or inform them of your address change (there may be a surcharge).

❑ Notify all financial institutions of your U.S. address.

❑ Terminate all utility services (electric, water, sewage, trash collection, cell phone, telephone, Internet access, cable, etc.).

❑ Do not make frequent or regular visits to Canada or remain there for an extended period of time. Try to remain outside Canada for as long as possible after you initially leave.

❑ Establish ties in the U.S. by ensuring you do the reverse of all the items above, such as getting a state driver's license, registering your automobile, opening up bank accounts, starting up memberships, and generally moving your community of interest to the U.S.

Becoming a Tax Resident of the U.S.

Nothing can be more confusing than knowing when you have left Canada as a tax resident and when you have become a tax resident of the U.S. Knowing this requires a thorough understanding of the U.S. residency rules and how the Canada-U.S. Tax Treaty overrides them in some circumstances. Again, properly planning your Canadian exit date with your U.S. entry date can provide many benefits and simplify your tax-filing situation. Whatever you do, try to avoid "straddling" the border unless your unique tax situation warrants it and the appropriate advice is sought. In our experience, people trying to maintain tax ties in both countries generally haven't done much planning before leaving Canada and are playing a dangerous game of "Russian Roulette" that could have many unintended negative consequences. The risk you run is, if the Canada-U.S. Tax Treaty "tiebreaker" rules need to be used to determine your residency and you end up having closer connections to the U.S., you could be deemed a U.S. tax resident by the Canadian authorities and automatically subject to the departure tax, when planning is restricted or no longer can be done. We encourage you to do your planning before you go — and don't try to straddle the border.

Substantial Presence Test

Overall, the rules for determining when you become a tax resident of the U.S. are generally a black-and-white proposition due to the substantial presence test the IRS uses. Generally, if you reside in the U.S. for more than four months per year for three consecutive years, you will be considered a tax resident for U.S. purposes (unless Form 8840 is filed and accepted, as referenced below). What is interesting about this is you don't need any form of working immigration status to become a tax resident for U.S. purposes! This creates an interesting conundrum: a B-1 or B-2 visitor's visa allows you to remain in the U.S. for up to six months, but neither allows you to earn wages in the U.S. However, you are substantially present in the U.S. (and considered a tax resident for U.S. purposes) if you have been in the U.S. for 183 days or more in the current year or over the past three years based on the following formula in Table 5.1.

Table 5.1

Substantial Presence Test

Days present in the U.S.	Multiplier	Total
Current year (t)	1	# days x 1
Previous year (t-1)	1/3	# days x 1/3
Year before that (t-2)	1/6	# days x 1/6
Grand total		**??**

- If less than 183 days, you are not a U.S. tax resident.
- If 183 days or more, you are a U.S. tax resident (or must file Form 8840). (See our companion book "The Canadian Snowbird in America" for more details.)

Some further clarification of definitions is needed. You must count a day in the U.S. when you are physically present in the U.S. (even if you visit just to fill up with gas, shop, and return to Canada). It is important to note that the days don't have to be consecutive — any day you are in the U.S. counts toward the substantial presence test. Finally, a year is considered a calendar tax year, January 1st through December 31st inclusive. As with any government rules, there are always exceptions. If you are in the U.S. for less than 31 days in the current year, the substantial presence test does not apply in this year no matter how many days you were in the U.S. previously. There is a commuting exception as well. Exempt individuals (e.g., students, professional athletes, and foreign government representatives) can reside in the U.S. and not have any of those days count. Likewise, if you are in the U.S. for less than 24 hours when in transit between two places outside the U.S., it does not count (e.g., flying from Aruba to a Chicago stopover and on to Edmonton, like I did on my honeymoon). Finally, if you develop a medical condition in the U.S. that prohibits you from leaving, those days will not count toward the substantial presence test either. For those "snowbirds" who end up exceeding 182 days, they must file IRS Form 8840 — Closer Connection Exception Statement for Aliens to demonstrate that they have closer tax ties to Canada than to the U.S. to avoid being deemed a U.S. resident and having to file a U.S. tax return. Failing to file can lead to a long list of IRS penalties.

Green Card Test

Currently, there are thousands of people with U.S. green cards who have since moved back to Canada to live for an extended period of time. The bad news is the IRS considers you a resident for tax purposes if you are a "lawful permanent resident" (green card holder) at any time during the calendar year under the "green card test." This means that, if you are given the privilege of residing permanently in the U.S. as an immigrant, you are considered a resident for tax purposes and must file the requisite U.S. tax returns annually. However, the good news is the Canada-U.S. Tax Treaty can exempt this IRS rule, and you won't have to file U.S. tax returns except to declare U.S. sources of income. One note of caution: if you choose to use the treaty and not file U.S. federal and state tax returns as a green card holder, the U.S. CIS will likely rule that you have abandoned it (see Chapter 3).

Dual Status

Generally, you are a dual-status tax filer if you are both a resident alien and a non-resident alien of the U.S. in the same tax year (typically in the year you move into or out of the U.S.). Different U.S. rules apply to that part of the year you resided in Canada versus the time you resided in the U.S. Generally, you will have to file a 1040NR and declare any U.S. source income for the period of time you resided in Canada. For the time you were considered a tax resident of the U.S., you have to file a 1040 tax return and declare your worldwide income for that portion of the year.

To simplify things and reduce your tax liability, you may want to take the full-year residency election per IRC §6013(g), which allows you to be declared a U.S. tax resident for the entire calendar year. This election can simplify your U.S. "start-up" return filing and offer some tax advantages. Determining whether to use this election to file your tax returns depends on your individual circumstances and on the reduction of your overall tax liability. If you take the full-year residency election, one interesting provision in the Internal Revenue Code permits you to exclude up to US$85,700 in wages earned in 2007 while residing outside the U.S.

Another election you can take is IRC §6013(h), which allows you to file a married filing joint return with a non-resident alien spouse remaining in Canada. This election allows you to avoid filing "married filing separately" and can lower your tax liability, particularly if you have a low-income spouse. The catch is you have to declare your spouse's worldwide income on your U.S. tax return along with your own, so you should analyze this election to see if it is in your best interest as well.

The Canada-U.S. Income Tax Treaty

To resolve some of the complications citizens create in moving back and forth, Canada and the U.S. have negotiated the Income Tax Convention between the United States of America and Canada. Put simply as the Canada-U.S. Tax Treaty (or the treaty), the most substantive change was negotiated and signed on September 26, 1980. Since then the treaty has been revised only four times: June 14, 1983; March 28, 1984; March 17, 1995; and July 29, 1997. Compared with the U.S. Internal Revenue Code or the Canadian Income Tax Act, it is evident that treaty changes occur infrequently. The purpose of the treaty is to prevent the double taxation of Canadian and U.S. residents on the same income, provide mutual assistance between the authorities in the collection of taxes, and authorize the sharing of information to improve compliance.

The Canada-U.S. Tax Treaty "overrides" certain areas of the Canadian Income Tax Act and the Internal Revenue Code in the U.S. to afford protection from, among other things, double taxation in both countries. An example may help. If you are residing in the U.S. and you generate c$100 in interest from a Canadian bank account, Canada retains the right to tax this income as "Canadian source" income. However, as a U.S. resident, you are required to declare your worldwide income on your U.S. return, including the c$100 from Canada. Without the Canada-U.S. Tax Treaty, the Canada Revenue Agency takes a 25% default withholding tax on the interest (c$25), while the U.S. taxes the interest at your ordinary income tax rate (assume 25% or c$25). In total, you have now paid c$50 on c$100 of income (see the detailed example later in the "Foreign Tax Credit Planning" section of this chapter). This is one of the issues the Canada-U.S. Tax Treaty attempts to resolve. As you can see, tax preparation of this nature requires a thorough understanding of the treaty coupled with the experience in knowing how to apply it optimally to your unique situation. The key provisions of the treaty are outlined below.

Determining Tax Residency

Once you or the government authorities have determined you meet each of their respective residency laws and are deemed a tax resident of both the U.S. and Canada, the treaty "tiebreaker" rules are used to sort out in which country you are resident. The tiebreaker rules are generally applied in the order they are listed in the treaty:

1. the location of your permanent home (principal residence);
2. your center of vital interests — where your personal and economic relations exist;
3. the location where you "habitually" reside;
4. where you are a citizen; and,
5. if none of the above can determine your residence, the Canadian

and U.S. competent taxing authorities will agree between themselves who gets to tax you.

Sharing Information

To catch those who might evade taxation on income from one country while resident in the other, both countries agreed in the last treaty negotiations to share tax information on you with each other. In fact, the treaty allows either tax authority to ask for your complete tax file (electronic, paper, or otherwise) from the other country's tax authority. This means that, if you have a Canadian source of income that is not taxed in Canada (e.g., OAS or CPP) or an NR4 designated as U.S.A. and you don't report it on your U.S. return, your chance of the tax authorities catching it has increased significantly. Based on our experience, it appears that real estate transactions, dividends, interest, and in particular government pension payments are exchanged electronically on a regular basis. Further, the two countries have agreed to allow each other to collect each other's taxes. This means that CRA can use the IRS's "long arm of the law" to collect Canadian taxes in the U.S. As you can see, your chances of getting caught evading income or tripping up on a compliance issue are more pronounced than most people believe. To stem the tax evasion occurring in foreign accounts, CRA has modified the T1 tax return to require disclosure of accounts outside Canada and is signing tax treaties with countries around the world to allow them to exchange tax information to ferret out those not declaring income.

Foreign Tax Credits

The IRS allows taxes paid to Canada as a foreign tax credit against that income on the U.S. return to avoid double taxation. Using the example above, you would take the C$25 you paid to Canada, convert it at the prevailing exchange rate, and use it as a foreign tax credit on your U.S. return. The treaty allows you to take the taxes paid to Canada and use them against any tax liability that income generates on the U.S. return. See the "Foreign Tax Credit Planning" section of this chapter for more details.

Exempt Certain Income

The treaty sorts out what income is taxed in which country as well as exempts certain income altogether. For example, it provides direction on where capital gains are taxed and exempts some self-employment income earned in one country from being taxed in both countries. It also contains specific provisions to eliminate double taxation between the two countries should it occur.

Withholding Taxes

The treaty specifies the various withholding rates for the various types of income sourced out of that country. In the example above, the withholding on interest income is reduced to 10% rather than the default 25% withholding for non-treaty countries as outlined in the Canadian Income Tax Act. For Canadian sources of income accruing to those in the U.S., the current treaty withholding rates are as follows.

- Interest — 10%
- Dividends — 15%
- Government interest — 0%
- Canada Pension Plan — 0%
- Old Age Security — 0%
- Company pension — 15% (excluding RRSPs)
- Periodic RRIF/LIF withdrawals — 15%
- Rental income — 25%

Taxation of RRSPs, RRIFs, et Cetera

The most frequent question our firm fields from U.S. CPAs, Canadian CAs, and those who have moved to the U.S. is "How are RRSPs or RRIFs (or any other registered plans) in Canada taxed in the U.S.?" These registered plans are so misunderstood in the U.S. and the complexities so diverse that a competent Canada-U.S. transition planner should be sought before starting tax preparation (ideally, you did the requisite planning before you took up tax residency in the U.S.). For a review of the issues in moving these accounts to the U.S., see Chapter 10. Listed below are the key myths and facts about the taxation of Canadian registered plans in the U.S. To simplify things, we refer to RRSPS, but generally we are referring to all types of registered plans in Canada, including the following.

* RRIFS — registered retirement income funds
* LIRAS — locked-in retirement accounts
* LIFS — life income funds
* LRIFS — locked-in retirement income funds
* RCAS — retirement compensation arrangements
* DPSPS — deferred profit sharing plans
* RPPS — registered pension plans (e.g., a money purchase RPP)

Fact: RRSPs/RRIFs/LIRAs Are Taxable in the U.S.

Few people (including most CAs and CPAs!) realize that the IRS does not recognize the tax-deferred status of RRSPS like CRA does. In fact, the IRS considers them nothing more than a regular brokerage account with all interest, dividends, and capital gains being taxable on your U.S. return. This means that, if you have even one dollar in an RRSP, any "simple return" is complicated exponentially. If you leave your registered accounts in Canada, you can get yourself into a huge tax liability as well as endure a pile of IRS paperwork. The reason for this complexity is the IRS has various reporting requirements that, if not fulfilled, could subject you to varying fines of US$10,000 (or 5% of the value of your RRSP). The income inside these registered accounts needs to be declared as income annually and taxed accordingly.

If you decide you don't want to declare this income, there are two ways of deferring it. First, a treaty election to defer the income can be taken on IRS Form 8833 — Treaty-Based Return

Position Disclosure in a timely manner (when you file your return). Next, in any year you make contributions to or withdrawals from your registered plan, you may be required to file IRS Form 3520 — Annual Return to Report Transactions with Foreign Trusts and Receipt of Certain Foreign Gifts and Form 3520A — Annual Information Return of Foreign Trust with a U.S. Owner. The second and simpler alternative for some plans may be the new IRS Form 8891 — U.S. Information Return for Beneficiaries of Certain Canadian Registered Retirement Plans issued in March 2005. There are other tax filing requirements as well, including reporting these foreign accounts on Form TD F90-22.1 — Report of Foreign Bank and Financial Accounts each year. Finally, to properly account for and use any foreign tax credits generated at withdrawal, you will need to file Form 1116 — Foreign Tax Credit.

Determining the taxable amount of your RRSPs et cetera in the U.S. is a complex undertaking, and — with the recent changes brought by the American Jobs Creation Act on October 22, 2004 — most Canada-U.S. tax experts we correspond with have varying opinions. Exactly how RRSPs are taxed is open to debate, and the Canada-U.S. International Tax Council we co-chair with the IRS is trying to push the matter with the IRS and the Department of Treasury to get some concrete answers. Until recently, IRS rules stated that your original contributions were returned to you tax free so it is best to consult with an experienced Canada-U.S. tax expert to understand the risks, take a position and be prepared to defend it in the unlikely scenario the IRS challenges it. Despite popular opinion, you do not get an automatic "step-up in basis" when you take up tax residency in the U.S. To further complicate things, you must take into account the appropriate exchange rates in establishing the "cost basis" of your RRSP for IRS purposes because there may be currency gains or losses that need to be accounted for as well. Therefore, before you take up tax residency in the U.S., it is best to "step-up" the basis in your RRSPs.

The next issue to contend with is taxation at the individual state level. The IRS has one set of rules and forms to deal with RRSPs, but the states don't necessarily follow along. Some states don't have an income tax, while others do. Some states don't recognize the IRS treaty election to defer the income inside the RRSP, so the income needs to be reported each year and state income taxes paid even though the IRS allows the deferral! Some states will allow a foreign tax credit against the income, and some will not. As you can see, each situation needs to be dealt with on a case-by-case basis.

In summary, you have only three options to consider regarding your RRSPS.

1. Collapse the registered plan, withdraw all the money, and pay the withholding tax to Canada and the applicable income tax to the IRS and your state of residence. Take the appropriate foreign tax credits or deductions as applicable to avoid some, or all, of the double taxation. This is not guaranteed, since your foreign tax credits or deductions could be limited or unavailable depending on your unique tax situation.

2. Leave the registered plan in Canada and declare the income on both the federal tax return and the state return as applicable.

3. Leave the registered plan in Canada and take the treaty election to defer the income on the federal tax return; if allowed by the state, defer the income on your state return as well until distributed.

To determine the best course of action for your registered plan depends on your individual circumstances and what you are trying to achieve (see Chapter 10 for details on moving these accounts to the U.S.). You may be focused on getting your registered plans out of Canada, but what are you going to do with the funds once withdrawn? Good RRSP planning considers how your funds are invested, the best means of collapsing it (lump-sum or staged), and the best use of the funds once collapsed. Some non-working spouses may be able to get their RRSPs out of Canada tax free depending on their circumstances. As you can see, the complexities surrounding these decisions require a thorough understanding of your unique financial situation accompanied by much thought and analysis.

Fact and Myth: Withdraw Your RRSP Tax Free!

We have seen advertisements and other pronouncements that declare "Withdraw your RRSP tax free or close to zero tax from Canada!" This has misled some people into thinking this is a regular occurrence, and therefore you should hire those making such pronouncements. It is possible to withdraw an entire RRSP tax free from a Canadian perspective with certain financial situations, and our firm has succeeded in doing so when the requisite planning, tax preparation, and investment management are all coordinated. However, this shouldn't be considered the norm. With proper planning and tax preparation, it's possible to pay a rate lower than the 25% lump-sum withholding rate mandated by CRA. A lot depends on your individual financial circumstances and what you will do with the money once your RRSP has been collapsed and the funds moved to the U.S. The other important component is ensuring the appropriate tax preparation is done. The most effective tax planning in the world won't amount to much if it is not properly implemented on your tax return. This is where comprehensive planning and a competent Canada-U.S. transition team come into play.

Myth: Roll Your RRSP into a U.S. IRA

Many people believe they can simply maintain the tax-deferred status of their RRSPs by rolling them into an individual retirement account (IRA) in the U.S. This cannot be done. The only way you can make a contribution to a regular IRA is with cash. This means you have to collapse your RRSP, pay the requisite taxes in both Canada and the U.S., and then move the cash into an IRA if eligible. Sometimes there is confusion surrounding transfers into a "rollover" IRA that can come from a U.S. qualified plan such as a 401(k), 403(b), et cetera, not a Canadian registered plan (see Chapter 8 for more details on these plans). The only way to maintain the tax deferral in your RRSP while living in the U.S. is to take the appropriate elections on your U.S. tax return each year, as outlined above (or declare the income every year on some state returns . . . you simply have no choice).

Myth: Lump-Sum RRSP/RRIF Withdrawals Have a 10% Withholding
People have often told us we were wrong on the withholding of lump-sum RRSP withdrawals because the financial institution told them 10% needs to be withheld instead of the Income Tax Act mandated 25%. In fact, the confusion lies with the financial institution that processed the withdrawal, because for residents of Canada the following rates apply (see Table 5.2).

Table 5.2

RRSP/RRIF Withdrawals

Withdrawal	Canada	Quebec
C$0–5,000	10%	5%
$5,001–15,000	20%	10%
$15,000 +	30%	15%

The usual reason the institution withholds 10% is because there is still a Canadian address on the account — your financial institution hasn't been told you moved to the U.S. and are no longer a resident of Canada for tax purposes. According to the Canadian Income Tax Act, the correct withholding on lump-sum withdrawals is 25%, and you are required to submit the remaining 15% through a Part XIII tax filing. Likewise, our firm has filed Form NR7-R for clients who have a 5% refund coming because their financial institution took the default withholding of 30% on lump-sum withholding in excess of C$15,000.

Myth: Withholding Tax Can Be Paid from Outside the RRSP

Often an RRSP may contain nothing but investments that you may not want to sell (deferred sales charges, etc.). As a result, you may want to keep all the investments intact and pay the withholding tax by a separate check so that nothing has to be sold. Unfortunately, the withholding (hence the term) must come from within the RRSP account. This means you will be forced to sell enough investments (and incur any deferred sales charges, etc.) to pay the required withholding before you can collapse the RRSP.

Taxation of Interest and Dividends

Interest

Both Canada and the U.S. tax interest as ordinary income subject to your marginal tax rate. For U.S. residents, interest from a Canadian bank account is subject to a 10% treaty withholding tax at source. Sometimes we have seen a 0% withholding because there is still a Canadian address on the account. Yet you still owe the 10% and must pay it by filing a Part XIII tax return to correct the withholding in Canada. This interest income must also be reported on your U.S. tax return, resulting in the potential for double taxation because you are required to report your "worldwide income" on the U.S. return. There is no withholding on interest from Canadian government obligations such as treasury bills, Canada Savings Bonds, et cetera, but they are taxable in the U.S. and must be reported as income.

Dividends

In comparing the Canadian versus U.S. taxation of dividends, Canada provides a 145% gross-up and the ensuing 18.97% tax credit. In the U.S., qualified dividends including those from U.S. corporations and major corporations in a foreign jurisdiction the U.S. has a tax treaty with are taxed at a flat 15% tax rate (5% if in the 15% marginal tax bracket or below). Non-qualified dividends including those from real estate investment trusts, dividends from commodity mutual funds, money market or bond funds, corporations in countries the US. does not have a tax treaty with are taxed at your ordinary marginal income tax rates (as high as 35%). The rules surrounding qualified and non-qualified dividends from Canada are complex so competent Canada-U.S. tax assistance should be sought.

For residents of the U.S., Canadian dividends are subject to a 15% treaty withholding tax at source. Again, because no withholding was taken does not mean there is none, and you have to file a Part XIII tax return and remit the 15% as stipulated in the Canada-U.S. Tax Treaty. Like interest, this income must be reported on your U.S. return as part of your "worldwide income," resulting in the potential for double taxation. As with interest income, proper planning and tax preparation can recapture some or potentially all of this 15% tax on your U.S. return.

Taxation of Capital Gains

In comparing the taxation of capital gains between Canada and the U.S., Canada includes 50% of the total gain in taxable income. This means that, if your marginal rate is 39% in your province of residence (assume Alberta), your capital gains rate is essentially 19.5%. The U.S. capital gains rate depends on how long you have held the investment and what your marginal tax bracket is. For investments held one year or less, the capital gains are taxed as ordinary income, just like interest. For investments held greater than one year, a maximum 15% capital gains rate applies (5% for those in the 15% or lower marginal tax bracket). For those making the transition to the U.S., capital gains are typically reported in the country of residence only, but it depends on the type of investment you are selling and if you are a U.S. citizen or green card holder. For example, CRA reserves the right to tax Canadian real estate, business interests, and trusts, and the IRS will tax that transaction as well. This is another reason you should use caution when a Canadian investment firm manages your investment portfolio. Be sure it has a thorough knowledge of the U.S. tax rules; otherwise, you could receive an unnecessarily large tax bill.

Taxation of Pensions

Company Pension Plan

In Canada, your employer's pension is fully taxable but is offset with a $2,000 non-refundable tax credit. However, when you move to the U.S., your Canadian company pension plan is subject to a 15% treaty withholding tax at source and must be reported on your U.S. tax return as part of your "worldwide income," resulting in the potential for double taxation. Proper planning and tax preparation can recapture some or all of this 15% on your U.S. return.

Here again, the Canada-U.S. tax experts we correspond with regularly have varying opinions on how these pensions are taxed in the U.S. Previously, your contributions to the plan would be considered tax-free in the U.S. but the new rules passed as part of The American Jobs Creation Act of 2004 cast significant doubt on that. Therefore, it is best to seek competent Canada-U.S. tax assistance to understand the risks, develop a position and be prepared to defend it in the unlikely scenario the IRS challenges it. Even so, your Canadian withholding can still be used as a foreign tax credit in the U.S. to eliminate the double taxation.

One strategy that may save you some Canadian withholding tax on your pension is using a Section 217 tax filing that taxes you more favorably as if you were resident in Canada. The rules for this are complex but if your annual pension income (including RRSPS or RRIFS) is around C$10,000 to $20,000 and you have virtually no other income from outside Canada, this tax filing will allow you to claim the personal amount (along with a few other non-refundable credits) against pension type income. You will still have the 15% withholding at source but you get some or all of it refunded when you file your tax return by June 30th of the following year. If you think you are going to qualify for a Section 217 filing in the next tax year, you can file Form NR5 — Application by a Non-Resident of Canada for a Reduction in the Amount of Non-Resident Tax Required to be Withheld with CRA by October 1. Once approved by CRA, your employer will be authorized to reduce the withholding at source.

U.S. Social Security
In the U.S., Social Security benefits are partially taxed on the U.S. return. The first 15% of your benefits are tax free no matter how much money you make. If your income is between US$32,000 and $44,000 ($25,000 and $34,000 if filing single), 50% of your benefit is taxable. Income in excess of $44,000 ($34,000 if filing single) means the maximum 85% of your benefit is taxable. Interestingly enough, the Canadian tax return allows this 15% tax-free benefit for those living in Canada collecting U.S. Social Security.

Old Age Security
In the U.S., OAS is taxed similarly to U.S. Social Security in that the first 15% of your benefits are tax free, and the remaining 85% may be taxable (at the lower U.S. rates) depending on your income. One of the most compelling reasons for moving to the U.S. is that the OAS recovery tax (the "clawback") no longer applies to U.S. residents. This means that Canadians with an income of more than C$63,511 in 2007 no longer lose any of their OAS due to the clawback (15% of the difference between the threshold and your income is clawed back, which means you lose it all in 2007 when your net income exceeded C$101,118, adjusted quarterly). Even more good news, not only can you begin collecting up to an additional C$5,846.19 annually (adjusted quarterly for the CPI) per person in 2007 if you move to the U.S. because of the elimination of the clawback, but also there is no withholding on your OAS by CRA.

Canada Pension Plan/Quebec Pension Plan

According to the last treaty negotiations, your CPP/QPP is no longer subject to any Canadian withholding but is fully reportable on your U.S. tax return as part of your worldwide income. Like OAS, your CPP/QPP is taxed like U.S. Social Security benefits at the lower U.S. rates, with the first 15% of your benefits being tax free and the remaining 85% taxable depending on your income. Also be aware that your CPP can affect your Social Security benefits through the windfall elimination provision, discussed in Chapter 8.

Taxation of Rental Properties

For some valid reasons, many Canadians insist on keeping their home in Canada to rent it out. We have seen this done numerous times, but what people aren't prepared for is the potential tax, estate planning and paperwork nightmare that comes with having a rental property in Canada. This complexity needs to be considered in your overall decision to rent out your current home in Canada along with consideration of this tax tie to Canada.

Canada

Even if you live in the U.S., CRA retains the right to tax all Canadian-source rental income or capital gains on real property, and you are required to appoint an agent in Canada to ensure taxes owing are paid. If you don't pay the tax, your agent residing in Canada must do so. This way, CRA has assets and people it can attach itself to for any claim of taxes owing. To appoint an agent, you need to file Form NR6 — Undertaking to File an Income Tax Return by a Non-Resident Receiving Rent from Real Property or Receiving a Timber Royalty each year with CRA. Once approved, this option allows you to remit 25% withholding tax on the net income each month (if any) when rent is collected. If you don't file an NR6 in a timely fashion, you are subject to a 25% withholding tax on the gross rental income, which could lead to a significant cash outflow problem. You must also file a Section 216 tax return each year to properly account for your expenses against any rental income, which may result in a refund or a balance owing.

When you sell your rental property, you are subject to even more complexity. As a non-resident of Canada selling Canadian real property, you are subject to a flat 25% withholding tax on the gross sales price. This means if you sell a property in Canada for c$200,000, $50,000 will be withheld and remitted to CRA by your attorney. However, if you file Form T2062 — Request by a Non-Resident of Canada for a Certificate of Compliance Related to the Disposition of Taxable Canadian Property, you can reduce the amount withheld to 25% of the net gains only. This means if you get an approved T2062 from CRA before the sale of your real property, you would only have to remit c$200,000 less c$100,000 original cost of the property = c$100,000 gain multiplied by 25% = $25,000. That is why it is important to get a formal appraisal of your property to establish its fair market value when you leave Canada or convert it to a rental property.

Finally, if capital cost allowance is taken on the Canadian return, there could be a nasty "recapture" upon the sale of the property that you should be sure you plan for. Recapture is the taxation of the cumulative capital cost allowance taken on the property over the years all in the year of sale. All of this is captured on a T1 non-resident tax return where the final tax liability is determined.

U.S.

Since you are required to report your worldwide income on your U.S. return, the rental income you derive from Canada must be reported on your U.S. return after converting everything to U.S. dollars. This income gives rise to the potential for double taxation because of the 25% withholding paid to CRA. Proper tax planning and preparation can recoup some of the tax paid to Canada as a foreign tax credit on your U.S. return. Interestingly enough, you must depreciate the rental property on your U.S. return even though claiming capital cost allowance is optional in Canada. Again, when it comes time to sell the property, there is the "recapture" of the depreciation on your tax return in the year of sale, and it can lead to a nasty tax surprise. Proper tax planning can make this a much easier transaction.

Social Security Number/ITIN

Social Security Number (SSN)

Similar to the Social Insurance number (SIN) issued in Canada, the U.S. issues a Social Security number, but note that they are two completely different numbers for two different countries! Your SIN is of no use in the U.S. except in getting a credit rating, as noted in Chapter 6. Do not attempt to give your SIN to a U.S. bank or use it on a U.S. tax return; you will cause yourself no end of grief because the IRS will not recognize your SIN and kick out your tax return. Besides, it can be considered fraud if you try to pass off your SIN as an SSN!

Once you have taken up residency in the U.S. and are permitted to work via a valid visa or green card, you are required to apply for a Social Security number using Form SS-5 — Application for a Social Security Card. Once you have it completed, file it with the Social Security Administration, not the IRS! You need an SSN because income paid to you from an employer, interest from a bank account, or a dividend from a mutual fund at a brokerage firm needs to be tracked to a SSN for income tax purposes. Likewise, any wages and payroll taxes need to be tracked to your SSN to ensure you establish the necessary coverage to qualify for U.S. Social Security and Medicare. It is interesting to note that the first digit of your SSN indicates which state it was issued in (Arizona is "6").

Individual Taxpayer Identification Number (ITIN)

Dependent family members of valid visa holders residing in the U.S. but ineligible to work are still eligible to claim on your taxes to get the ensuing tax benefits. To do so, each family member must have an ITIN (generally starts with a "9"), or the IRS will deny any tax benefits for your dependents. To obtain an ITIN, you must fill out and submit Form W-7 — Application for IRS Individual Taxpayer Identification Number and provide the required documentation to the IRS (not the Social Security Administration), which will issue an ITIN in approximately eight to 12 weeks. Unfortunately, recent rule changes have led to the IRS being more stringent in issuing ITINs, and they now require a demonstrated need to have an ITIN. As a result, you need to fill out the form appropriately and submit all of the required documentation. Once you or your family member receives authorization to work, an SSN will be needed to replace the ITIN. To do so, just fill out Form SS-5 outlined above and submit it to the Social Security Administration. (SSA) There is a spot on the form to provide your ITIN, and the SSA will ensure it is replaced in the IRS system with your new SSN.

Please note that sometimes a spouse ineligible to work will be issued an SSN, but stamped across it will be "Not eligible for employment." In this case, do not file an ITIN, since you will have two tax numbers to identify yourself, causing untold confusion among the U.S. government authorities.

Foreign Tax Credit Planning

By far the most complex, least understood, yet potentially beneficial area in your move is that of foreign tax credit planning. Foreign tax credits are a dollar-for-dollar credit allowed by the IRS and the treaty to eliminate the double taxation of the same income by both the U.S. and Canada. The aim is to alleviate the U.S. taxpayer of taxes owed in the U.S. when taxes are required on the same income in Canada (or any other country). Despite its good intentions, the IRS makes it difficult to completely avoid being double taxed on the same income because

- the IRS limits the amount of foreign tax credits you can use

in any one year by a ratio of your U.S. income to your total
world income

- foreign tax credits are thrown into two different "buckets"
  depending on the type of income they are derived from: passive or general limitation; and
- foreign tax credits are given a "life" of the current year when
  generated, one year back, and 10 years to carry forward. If
  they are not used up in the specified time frame, they expire.

The key to good foreign tax credit planning is having a
well-designed withdrawal strategy of your assets in Canada, a
properly structured investment portfolio in the U.S. to generate
foreign income, and competent tax planning and preparation.
Any income generated by the portfolio goes on your U.S. tax
return, but the tax liability associated with that income is paid
by the taxes withheld in Canada (which is much better than
having to pay them out of pocket). This is where an experienced
Canada-U.S. investment manager should be brought onto your
transition team.

The degree to which you are able to reduce your effective
Canadian withholding rate is dependent on many factors, such
as the timing of your RRSP withdrawals, the size of your investment portfolio, and the amount of other foreign income you
have. Foreign income can be generated within your investment
portfolio, but the amount is dependent primarily on your risk
tolerance and the performance of financial markets. That's why
you need to be cautious of claims to "remove your RRSP from
Canada at no or very low tax." In either case, the key is not to let
the "tax tail wag the investment dog."

A Simplified Example
Assumptions:
- You have C$10,000 in a Canadian mutual fund in a taxable
  brokerage account.

- The Canadian mutual fund pays a 5% dividend (c$500).
- The prevailing Canada-U.S. exchange rate is c$1 = US85¢.
- You have exited Canada and are a U.S. resident and taxpayer.

Canadian tax:
- According to the Canada-U.S. Tax Treaty, the withholding on dividends is 15%.
- Therefore, c$500 x 0.15 = c$75 is remitted to CRA.

U.S. tax:
- c$75 x 85¢ = us$63.75 in passive foreign tax credits on your U.S. tax return.
- Declare c$500 x 85¢ = us$425 as ordinary dividend income on your U.S. return.
- Assuming the dividend is non-qualified in the U.S. and you are in the 25% tax bracket, us$425 x 0.25 = us$106.25 tax liability.
- Use us$63.75 in foreign tax credits to offset us$106.25 in tax.
- Net out of pocket us$106.25 - us$63.75 = $42.50 U.S. tax out of pocket.

If not for the foreign tax credits, you would pay 25% + 15% = 40% tax on your dividend (us$170) versus 25% alone in the U.S. ($106.25). As you can see by this simple example, without proper understanding and accounting of the foreign tax credits, double taxation is inevitable. We have seen many people who went to their local CPA (unfamiliar with foreign tax credits) and ended up paying far more taxes than they were legally obligated to pay.

Key Tax Differences
Following are some of the key differences in the tax systems between Canada and the U.S (see also Table 5.3).

- For married couples in the U.S., you can choose married filing jointly or married filing separately when filing your tax return

- In Canada, each person files his or her own tax return, while in the U.S. you have several filing statuses, including single, head of household, or qualifying widow.
- In Canada, common-law marriages are accepted as a filing status, but for the U.S. federal return you must be legally married. Individuals living common law must file single at the federal level or jointly in the states where common-law marriages are recognized, as listed below.
    - Alabama
    - Colorado
    - District of Columbia
    - Idaho
    - Iowa
    - Kansas
    - Montana
    - Ohio
    - Oklahoma
    - Pennsylvania
    - Rhode Island
    - South Carolina
    - Texas (no state income tax)

- In Canada, your deductions are calculated as a credit against your tax liability.
- In the U.S., you deduct the higher of the basic standard deduction the government gives to you or your "itemized" deductions (add up your mortgage interest, state income or sales taxes, property taxes, auto registration, charitable giving, etc.) from your income before arriving at your taxable income.
- In the U.S., separate tax returns are filed with the IRS and the applicable state, while in Canada you file these tax returns together and send them to the federal government (except in Quebec).

Table 5.3

2007 Federal Tax Brackets

Canadian taxable income ($)	Per return	U.S. taxable income ($)	Filing single
0–37,178	15.5%	0–7,825	10%
37,179–74,357	22%	7,826–31,850	15%
74,358–120,887	26%	31,851–77,100	25%
120,888+	29%	77,101–160,850	28%
		160,851–349,700	33%
		349,701+	35%

2007 deductions	Canada ($)	U.S. ($)
Standard deduction/	8,929	5,350
Spousal amount/personal exemption	7,581	3,400
Mortgage interest	x	✓
Property taxes	x	✓
Auto registration	x	✓
Provincial/state or sales taxes	x	✓
Medical expenses	3% threshold	7.5% threshold
Charitable contributions	75% of income	50% of income
Contributions to political parties	✓	x
Safe deposit box	✓	✓
Tuition and education	✓	✓

2007 credits	Canada ($)	U.S. ($)
Child tax credit	x	1,000 per child
Foreign tax credit	✓	✓

Now let's compare one of the most expensive tax states in the union (California) with the cheapest tax province in Canada (Alberta) with the latest data available (see Table 5.4).

Table 5.4

2007 State/Provincial Tax Brackets (EST.)

Alberta taxable income ($)	Per return	California taxable income ($)	Filing single
0+	10%	0 – 6,319	1%
		6,320–14,979	2%
		14,980–23,641	4%
		23,642–32,819	6%
		32,820–41,476	8%
		41,477–999,999	9.3%
		1,000,000 +	10.3%

2007 (EST.)

Deductions	Alberta	California
Standard deduction/ personal exemption	14,899	3,254/ 87
Mortgage interest	x	✓
Property taxes	x	✓
Auto registration	x	✓
Provincial/state taxes	x	✓
Medical expenses	3% threshold	7.5% threshold
Charitable contributions	75% of income	50% of income
Contributions to political parties	✓	x
Safe deposit box	✓	✓

When you move to the U.S., you should familiarize yourself with the tax slips and forms in Table 5.5 so you are better prepared when it comes time to file your first tax return.

Table 5.5

Tax Slips and Forms

Tax slip	Canada	U.S.
Wages/bonuses/commissions	T4	W-2
Self-employment	T4(A)	1099-MISC
Interest	T3, T5	1099-INT
Dividends	T3, T5	1099-DIV

Tax Slip (cont'd)	Canada	U.S.
U.S. Social Security	T4A(P)	SSA-1099
Canada Pension Plan	T4A(P)	NR4
Old Age Security	T4A(OAS)	NR4(OAS)
Company pension	T4A	1099-R
RRIF	T4RIF	NR4
RRSP	T4RSP	NR4

Tax Form	Canada	U.S.
Personal tax return	T1	1040
Changed personal return	T1-ADJ	1040X
Capital gains/losses	Schedule 3	Schedule D
Dividends/interest	Schedule 4	Schedule B
Charitable donations	Schedule 9	Schedule A
Corporate tax return	T2	1120
Partnership tax return	T5013	1065 or K-1
Trust tax return	T3	1041

To see how these tax systems work in comparison to each other, see the comprehensive case studies in Appendices E and F of this book.

Alternative Minimum Tax

Both Canada and the U.S. have an alternative minimum tax system. In the U.S., the AMT system was brought into the tax code in the 1960s to prevent high-income people with lots of deductions from zeroing out their tax liability. The intention was to force these people to pay some tax into the system (similar intention in Canada). However, for higher-income taxpayers moving to the U.S., there is a looming tax nemesis you need to be aware of as tax planning brings your ordinary income down. In the U.S., when your taxes are prepared, your tax situation is run through the normal 1040 tax return, and your "regular" income tax liability is calculated based on your itemized deductions, personal exemptions, and so on. This amount is compared with the amount you had withheld during the year, and a refund or balance owing is calculated. What most folks don't realize is that their tax situation is also run through Form 6251 — Alternative Minimum Tax — Individuals at the same time, and they pay the higher of their regular income tax or the affectionately known "stealth tax." The problems with the AMT system (and there are many) are listed below.

- You don't get all of the deductions under the regular income tax system (namely, state income taxes and property taxes).
- With higher-income taxpayers, the basic AMT exemption for 2007 of $62,550 (for married couples)/$42,500 (for singles) is phased out.
- The exemption amount has not been increased with inflation or in conjunction with the exemptions, et cetera, given in the "regular" tax system. As a result, more and more U.S. taxpayers are getting caught in the net of the AMT.
- AMT rates are 26% on the first $175,000 of AMT income for married couples ($87,500 for singles) and 28% thereafter (essentially a flat tax).

Despite the popularity of the recent tax cuts by President Bush, the unspoken truth is that they applied only to the "regular" 1040 tax calculation and indeed lowered the regular tax liability. However, what will blindside most taxpayers is the AMT system that left the basic exemption virtually unchanged (read not indexed) since the late 1960s. Unfortunately, there is very little that can be done to "plan" around or reduce your AMT. In the annual taxpayers' advocacy report delivered to Congress in 2003, 2004, 2005, and again in 2006, the AMT was the number one issue to be resolved. The reason is that many people will complete their regular 1040 tax returns with no inclination that they also need to fill out a 6251 AMT return and pay the higher of the two taxes.

Payroll Taxes

Often the savings in income taxes become the focal point in justifying a move to the U.S. For retirees, this move has many advantages, as outlined in Chapter 8. However, if you are moving to the U.S. to resume work, you must be aware that payroll taxes in the U.S. are much higher than in Canada and can potentially challenge your premise for moving to the U.S. In Canada, payroll taxes consist of Canada Pension Plan and Employment Insurance. For 2007, the Canada Pension Plan contribution is 4.95% on a maximum amount of c$43,700 in "pensionable earnings" less the basic yearly exemption of c$3,500. As a result, the maximum Canada Pension Plan contribution is c$1,989.90. The Employment Insurance contribution rate is estimated at 1.80%, with maximum insurable earnings of c$40,000, leading to a maximum contribution of c$720. Combined, there is a maximum payroll tax of c$2,709.90 for 2007.

In the U.S., the first $97,500 of your wages in 2007 are subject to the Social Security contribution of 6.2%. That equals a payroll tax of $6,045 annually. You are also subject to the Medicare contribution of 1.45% with no limits. If you earn $97,500 in U.S. income in 2007, you would pay a total of $6,045 + 1,413.75 = US$7,458.75 compared with a maximum of c$2,709.90 in Canada. However, the benefits differ between the systems, as outlined in Chapter 8. In summary, Canadians are eligible for a maximum CPP benefit of approximately c$10,365 annually in 2007 plus a maximum OAS benefit of approximately c$5,903.16 annually for a total maximum benefit of c$16,268.16 per person. Adding the OAS for a non-working spouse, the maximum CPP and OAS benefits could be as high as c$22,171.32 for a married couple. In the U.S., the maximum Social Security benefit you can receive is $25,392 in 2007, and your spouse automatically qualifies for half of your amount even though nothing was paid into the system. This means the maximum Social Security benefit for a married couple in the U.S. could be as high as $38,088. As you can see, you pay more — but you may get more!

In the U.S., it is more common to control the amount of income tax you want withheld from your paychecks. Through Form W-4 — Employee's Withholding Allowance Certificate, you are able to increase or reduce the amount of income tax withheld. The idea is to allow you to pay in the amount you are required without being forced to overpay, essentially giving the IRS an interest-free loan. Alternatively, having too little withheld (violating the "safe harbor" rules) could result in underpayment penalties being assessed. The IRS wants its money when you make it; otherwise, everyone would reduce his or her withholding to zero and pay it all on April 15th (if they have it). There is no way the government could function under such a regimen. If you reside in a state that also has an income tax, it will have a form similar to the W-4 to enable you to adjust your state withholding as well. In Canada, Form TD1 — 2006 Personal Tax Credits Return is used to accomplish the same thing as a W-4, but its use is generally reserved for when you change employers, get divorced, or face some other circumstances.

As explained earlier, the level of Social Security taxes payable in the U.S. is significantly higher than the Social Security taxes payable in Canada on the same level of income. For individuals moving to and working in the U.S. on a short-term assignment (not greater than five years), there can be the opportunity to opt out of paying U.S. Social Security taxes on their U.S.-source employment income. By filing CRA Form CPT56 — Certificate of Coverage under the Canada Pension Plan Pursuant to Article V of the Agreement on Social Security between Canada and the United States, an individual sent to the U.S. by his or her Canadian employer can continue to be covered by Canada Pension Plan and Employment Insurance as opposed to U.S. Federal Insurance Contributions Act (FICA) and Medicare taxes during the assignment in the United States. To claim this exemption, the Canadian employer files Form CPT56 and requests a Certificate of Coverage from the Ottawa Tax Services Office, CPP/EI Rulings section. The U.S. employer's payroll department then maintains the approved certificate. The Canadian employer files a T4 each year indicating CPP contributions with a footnote on the T4 that should read "Filed for purposes of the Canada-U.S. Totalization Agreement." It is also recommended that if you are eligible for this exemption you attach a copy of the approved Form CPT56 with your U.S. Form 1040 on an annual basis. Please note that this exemption is available only for U.S. assignments through a Canadian employer for no longer than five years. If you are moving to the U.S. with a new or unrelated Canadian employer, this exemption is not available to you. You will lose the opportunity to qualify for U.S. Social Security and Medicare benefits, but you will be contributing to a bigger benefit in Canada, where you plan to remain. If there is a chance you may return to the U.S. at some point in the future, you may want to pay into the Social Security system in the U.S. to qualify for Medicare and Social Security.

Sales Taxes

Another factor to consider in your move is state sales taxes. In Canada, there is the recently reduced Goods and Services Tax of 6%. There may also be a provincial sales tax (except for Alberta), which can easily add another 8%. This is a total of 14% in additional sales taxes on most items purchased. Believe it or not, most folks residing in the U.S. end up paying more taxes to their local government than they do to the federal government. When you take into account property taxes (generally lower in the U.S.), sales taxes (gas, alcohol, tobacco), licence fees (motor vehicle, hunting/fishing), and income/estate taxes, you typically end up paying over half of your tax bill to your local state. In the U.S., there is no federal sales tax like the GST, but most states have a sales tax that is typically from 4% to 6%, similar to most provinces. In addition, most municipal governments have a sales tax that typically ranges from 0% to 7%. The amounts of these taxes depend on what state and county you reside in when you move to the U.S.

6

Show Me
the Money

He took his purse filled with money and will not be
home. — Proverbs 7:20

You will have to face moving your loonies to the U.S. at some
point. This chapter aims to clear up some of the misconceptions
about exchanging money and to provide some insights into
overcoming a seemingly difficult issue for most folks. The technical term, cash management, deals specifically with matters
related to your net worth (assets less your debts), currency
exchange, and cash inflows/outflows. In our experience, assets
on both sides of the border lead to a lot of complexity and
inconvenience, so we generally recommend that you try to consolidate all of your assets on the U.S. side of the border. There
can be some other hidden landmines in keeping assets in
Canada, particularly if they remain in Canadian loonies. Here
are some items to consider in the area of cash management
when making the transition to the U.S.

Currency Exchange Facts and Myths

Ask most Canadians, and they can tell you within a penny or two what the Canadian-U.S. exchange rate is. In our opinion, some Canadian's national pride rises and falls in relation to the exchange rate of the Canadian dollar to the U.S. dollar. In our experience, nowhere have we dealt with more confusion or deliberation of decisions than the area of currency exchange. It appears the record high closing rate for the Canadian dollar occurred on August 31, 1957, and again on October 31, 1959, at $1.05485, with the record low closing set on January 18, 2002, at $0.61989. This section aims to clear up some misconceptions and confusion so you can begin to move forward with confidence in this area.

Myth: You Lose Money When You Convert

One of the biggest misconceptions out there is you "lose money when you exchange Canadian loonies for U.S. dollars." Nothing could be further from the truth. The thinking goes, if you lose money during currency exchange, there must be ways of making money during it too! On one day in 2006, the following exchange rates were observed:

$1 Canadian
= $0.898 U.S.
= $6.99 Hong Kong
= $29.36 Taiwan
= $91,122 Zimbabwe.

The first thing to notice is that all of these countries use the "dollar" as the name for their currency, and therein lies the problem. Because the currency has the same name, people assume it should have the same value. It does not. This is because they are different currencies, from different countries, with a different value associated with each one. A Polish zloty is different from a U.S. dollar, which is different from the Euro, which is different from an Italian lira, which is different from a Canadian loonie. Different currencies from different countries (even if they have the same name) have different values ascribed to them by the supply and demand of a particular country's currency in the world. If you stop thinking about Canadian dollars and start calling them Canadian loonies — doing so will help you to start dealing with the currency exchange issue.

To further illustrate the point, suppose you exchange one Canadian loonie into one U.S. dollar. According to the example above, you will receive US$0.898 for your Canadian loonie. People believe that, since they are getting 10.2¢ less, they have "lost" money. If that argument holds true, then take your Canadian dollar and exchange it into Zimbabwe dollars, and you will "gain" $91,121! If you exchange 100 Canadian dollars, you could become a millionaire in Zimbabwe! But we all know a Zimbabwe millionaire is a lot different from a Canadian millionaire, who is different from an American millionaire. Consider as well that, if you were to convert your US$0.898 right back into Canadian loonies the next day, how much would you receive? You're right, pretty much one Canadian dollar (less any transaction fee), so where did you lose money in the currency exchange? And where did you gain money?

The real issue is the difference in living expenses that you will incur in the U.S. versus Canada. If the expenses (food, shelter, taxes, gas, autos, health care, etc.) are lower in the U.S. and your currency conversion leaves you with fewer "dollars" in your pocket, then the currency exchange may be inconsequential because you have lower living expenses in the U.S. for the same lifestyle. We all know it is cheaper to live in Zimbabwe, but you would have to look at the other aspects of the lifestyle to get some insights into whether becoming a millionaire in Zimbabwe is worthwhile.

The other factor that comes into play is the fluctuation in exchange rates over time. For example, if you have a fixed Canadian pension, you could face a loss of purchasing power in the U.S. if the Canadian-U.S. exchange rate declines, particularly if your Canadian pension is your primary source of income.

Myth: Someone Knows Where the Exchange Rate Is Going

We don't know how many times people have asked for our opinion on where the Canadian-U.S. exchange rate is going. The resounding answer is we have no idea, but in our view "A bird in the hand is better than 1.01 birds in the bush." First, as seen in the graph below, waiting for a better exchange rate has been the wrong thing to do for the majority of the past 33 years, until of late. Second, in 1971, who knew that this would be the case? Research has shown that even the most prudent currency traders, economists, and investment managers can't make successful predictions over any extended period of time. If they could, they wouldn't tell you, and they would no longer need to make predictions — they would have more money than they had ever dreamed of getting.

Figure 6.1

Canada-U.S. Exchange Rates, 1971–2006

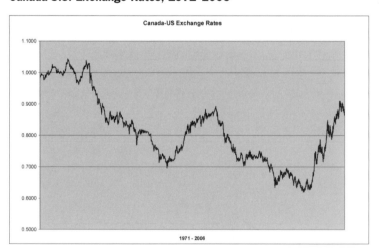

A number of factors influence Canadian-U.S. exchange rates and make it impossible to predict where the rate is going over the long term with any consistency. The causes of currency exchange fluctuations are what economists love to talk about at parties. We have limited knowledge in this area and offer you the following key factors that the experts agree influence the Canadian-U.S. exchange rate:

- the difference in inflation rates between Canada and the U.S.;
- the difference in productivity performance;
- the tax system and the tax burden imposed on the citizens of each country;
- the difference in interest rates;
- the difference in non-energy commodity prices;
- the difference in trade and current account balances;
- the difference in fiscal balances;
- the economic growth prospects of each country;
- the political issues and political stability in each country; and
- the need to borrow money by each government.

Despite all of this economist jargon, the bottom line is, whichever currency is more desired by the world, that currency will enjoy a higher exchange rate. It is simple supply and demand, and unfortunately the world wants U.S. dollars more than it wants Canadian dollars at this time (although that has been changing as of late). Canadian economists have often theorized about how to fix the problem, including abandoning the floating currency and adopting the U.S. currency wholesale, "pegging" the Canadian dollar to the U.S. dollar, or forming a North American "dollar" with the U.S. and Mexico. We will leave all of this to the economists, but the question to ask is "What do we do now?"

If you have a need for U.S. dollars in the future, be sure you have U.S. dollars available, and put the "currency speculating" aside. Likewise, if you need Canadian dollars in the future, be sure you keep some Canadian dollars to meet that need. We have seen folks devastate their U.S. retirement plans because they decided to currency speculate and leave their money in Canadian dollars when they had an ongoing permanent need for U.S. dollars. They watched their retirement nest eggs decline significantly and kept hoping for the Canadian dollar to bounce back. This unintended overconsumption of their Canadian-dollar retirement assets can have long-term effects on their financial security.

Even though we don't know where the currency rate is going, we do know the Canada-U.S. exchange rate fluctuates about 100 basis points every day. If you need to exchange currency at some point in the future, be aware that there are some currency exchange tools available that you may want to consider using to take advantage of the normal fluctuations in the exchange rate. For example, if you have a purchase you need to make in the short-term but want to buy at the lower-end of the daily fluctuation, you may want to make a "currency bid" with your currency broker. A currency bid is an agreement to purchase a certain amount of foreign currency at a fixed price sometime in the future. This will allow you to avoid the current spot rate and make a bid to purchase the currency at the lower end of the daily fluctuations. The problem with this is if the currency exchange is in a upward pattern, your bid may never get filled. A currency bid can be put out for a maximum of 30 days and cancelled or amended at any time with no penalty. Another tool available is a forward contract, which is an agreement to purchase a certain amount of foreign currency at some point in the future at a rate set today. This is for those that know they are going to need foreign currency in the future to fund a purchase and want to lock in the exchange rate now. The motto "a bird in the hand is better than two in the bush" is accomplished with a forward contract because they can be set for up to a year in advance. The drawback is there is an expense in the currency rate you receive the further out you want the contract to go.

The bottom line is nobody can predict the future, and it is really our emotions that are driving the decision . . . and this spells trouble. For example, when we ask "What rate does the exchange have to achieve for you to convert?" we typically get an off-the-cuff answer. Sure enough, when that exchange rate arrives, the decision to wait for an even better rate is made, and the tendency is to ride the exchange rate back down again. Soon your life revolves around the currency exchange section of the newspaper, and your mood for the day is dictated by what happened in currency exchange markets overnight. Is this any way to live? What a way to spend your golden years . . . glued to the newspaper watching the exchange rates (or the stock market, for that matter).

Myth: Wait to Convert

Often people struggle with deciding when to convert their Canadian loonies into U.S. dollars, and "waiting for a better exchange rate" is the game they decide to play. The typical thinking is you can do better if you wait. What many don't realize is they have just made a prediction: the exchange rate will improve by the time you need to exchange loonies into dollars. You have now entered the realm of currency speculation, and frankly there are better ways of speculating on the currency exchange direction, such as buying currency futures contracts. Besides, there are currency traders with millions of dollars and all kinds of equipment monitoring global currency markets in the hope of conducting currency transactions to pay their bills. If there is money to be made in currency speculation, we would suggest there are many others that will make it ahead of you. So how do you determine when to convert?

The decision to convert should be determined by what you are trying to achieve (your personal goals and objectives). If you are moving to the U.S. permanently to retire, never to return to Canada, you will have an ongoing need for U.S. dollars, and it may make sense to convert your money now because you know with certainty what the exchange rate is today and how much you'll end up with. If the current exchange rate is sufficient now and the long-term projections of your financial situation in the U.S. show a high probability of your assets lasting your lifetime, why not exchange now, avoid any currency speculation, and get on with your life? Why not just do it now and avoid the other issues that come with leaving assets in Canada — such as the potential for double probate, double estate and income taxes, et cetera — as outlined in the other chapters of this book? At a minimum, understand the sensitivity of your financial situation to currency exchange fluctuations and make an informed decision. A prudent, deliberate, ongoing strategy of currency exchanges over a period of time may make the most sense in your situation. Your financial plan provides the guidepost for your decision making because, without it, important decisions such as exchanging your loonies are driven by emotions, not sound financial reasons. The time to exchange your assets is when you can achieve your desired lifestyle per your financial plan. This approach allows you to remove the currency fluctuations from your retirement projections. This analysis should be one of the criteria you are looking for in your Canada-U.S. transition planner and whether he or she can assist you with this important decision.

Exchanging your Canadian loonies for U.S. dollars can be a very emotional experience, but our firm can provide assistance in this area and help you to make the decision that is right for you. It is worth noting that you want to avoid currency exchange whenever possible because you have to pay the currency exchange broker or bank (see below). Therefore, it may make sense to leave some funds in a Canadian bank account if you plan on making regular trips to Canada for the summer, to visit friends and family, and so on. As long as you leave a nominal amount for convenience purposes only, it shouldn't be considered a "tax tie" by CRA.

Fact: How to Calculate Exchange Rates
Another misconception we often run into is confusion over the calculation of exchange rates. Typically, when C$1 = US85¢, folks

think that C\$1.15 = US\$1, which is simply not the case. Here is how currency exchange calculations work:

- If C\$1 = US85¢, you have to take 1 divided by 0.85 to find the reverse currency. Specifically, 1/0.85 = \$1.176, which means when C\$1 = US85¢, US\$1 = C\$1.176.

To make it easier on yourself, take the price of an item and divide it by the appropriate exchange rate to determine how much it will cost in your desired currency. For example,

- A hat at the outlet mall in Casa Grande, Arizona, costs US\$11: 11/0.85 = C\$12.94.
- A toque at West Edmonton Mall costs C\$11: 11/1.176 = US\$9.35.

Fact: There Is an Expense to Converting

Although, as we previously discussed, you don't lose money when you "convert" Canadian loonies into U.S. dollars, there is a transaction expense that you need to be aware of. Financial institutions "shade" the "spot" rate of the Canadian-U.S. exchange rate and use it as another source of profit for shareholders. The way you can tell is to compare the exchange rate online or in the newspaper (the spot rate in the market) with those posted at your local bank or at the "currency exchange carts" at the airport. The difference can be significant. In some cases, using your Canadian credit card in the U.S. for purchases in U.S. dollars may be better or worse. By shading the exchange rate on your purchases in the U.S. or applying additional fees, the credit card companies make a small fortune, and you may have no idea. The next time you get your credit card statement look for any additional fees or the rate the company exchanged your purchase at, and then locate the historical rate — you may grimace. We encourage you to be informed beforehand.

Here are some things you can do to reduce the expense of

converting your Canadian loonies into U.S. dollars.

- Ask your currency exchange provider to give you a rate as close to the current spot rate as possible (don't deny them from making a living, but make sure you aren't getting gouged). The spot rate is what the market is paying at that moment when the currency exchange is not shaded at all.
- Accumulate your loonies together and convert them in one lump sum rather than make several smaller transactions because bigger transactions generally get a better exchange rate.
- Determine the expenses associated with using your Canadian-dollar credit card for U.S.-dollar purchases and if prohibitive, avoid using your Canadian-dollar credit card at all; find a credit card company that issues U.S.-dollar cards instead so you can control the exchange rate better rather than take the prevailing rate the credit card company decides for that day.
- Avoid using your bank unless you have a good relationship with it; then ask your banker to give you the spot rate or something as close to it as possible.
- Avoid the currency exchange carts in airports or be sure to compare their rates to a discount currency broker or the spot rate in the newspaper or online whenever possible.
- Avoid converting cash, since doing so is more expensive. Consider traveler's checks, bank drafts, money orders, or personal checks instead.
- Make sure you do comparative shopping, particularly if you are exchanging large sums.
- If you have an account at a Canadian brokerage firm, it may offer you competitive exchange rates as part of its customer service to you, particularly if you already have a U.S.-dollar account.
- U.S. casinos typically provide excellent exchange rates in the hope you will leave some of your money in their machines or

at their tables.

- Unless you go to the casinos, don't typically wait until you get to the U.S. to exchange your currency. Most U.S. banks will not convert your Canadian loonies. However, banks owned by a Canadian bank are more inclined to offer this service to their clients.

- Leave sufficient U.S. dollars in the U.S. to meet your currency needs each year or, as mentioned previously, enough Canadian dollars in Canada to meet your needs there.

(Thanks to the discount currency broker Custom House Currency, private client team, for their contributions to this section.)

Mortgages

There are huge differences in mortgages between Canada and the U.S., and they clearly favor the U.S. Since buying a home is typically the single largest purchase you will make in your lifetime, getting the right mortgage should be of primary consideration as well. Our firm has helped numerous clients in making the transition to the U.S. get the right mortgage with the right terms from the right (read honest) mortgage broker.

Amortization

In Canada, the typical mortgage is amortized over 25 years, while it is 15 or 30 years in the U.S. Taking a 30-year mortgage will obviously lower your monthly payments from a 15-year mortgage, but which mortgage you select in the U.S. depends on your individual circumstances. There are a number of other loan options (e.g., adjustable rate) to consider besides these conventional loans that may better suit your goals and objectives.

Fixed Interest Rate

In Canada, the typical mortgage fixes your interest rate for up to 10 years, and then it is adjusted to the prevailing rate at that time. You are required to bear the risk of any interest rate changes. This is where a U.S. mortgage has a big advantage over those in Canada, because you can fix your interest rate for the full 15- or 30-year amortization — the bank bears the interest rate risk. This can make a huge difference in stabilizing one of your largest debts over the long term. The other nice thing with mortgages in the U.S. is if rates decline significantly at any point, you can refinance your mortgage and lock it in for another 15 or 30 years at an even lower rate, lowering your monthly payments even further. In addition, mortgages in the U.S. use simple interest calculations, while in Canada interest is compounded semi-annually. This means you will pay more interest in the U.S. if you make the minimum payment for the entire term of the mortgage, but you will pay less if you ever get in arrears because there is no interest on the interest, as there is in Canada. Likewise, U.S. lenders will typically charge a late fee for payments made in arrears, while these fees are typically prohibited in Canada.

One thing we have noticed many times with Canadians moving to the U.S. is they justify a much larger mortgage than they otherwise would consider because it is "deductible." Indeed, mortgage interest in the U.S. is deductible if your individual tax situation permits it (your itemized deductions aren't phased out), but be sure you understand exactly how it works. If you have a 7% mortgage and you are in the 25% marginal tax bracket, it means that for every $1 you give to the bank in interest the IRS gives you 25¢ back. Notice that you are still out of pocket 75¢. We have an even better deal: you give us $1, and we'll give you 99¢ back. We'll do that all day long, but who will end up with all of your money? Your mortgage is still an out-of-pocket expense to you.

Another justification we see is instead of paying off your mortgage you will invest it to get a better return. Your after-tax mortgage rate can be calculated as $7 \times (1 - 0.25) = 5.25\%$. The argument goes "I should be able to do better than 5.25% in the markets, so I'll get a bigger mortgage, make the minimum payments, and maximize my investments. The flaw in this argument is you can do better than 5.25% in the markets. If your money goes into a tax-deferred vehicle, the benchmark is 5.25%. But what if your money is in a taxable brokerage account and you get a return of 7%? You will have to pay taxes on the interest earned, so guess what — you are no further ahead. If you invest the money for capital gains, which can be taxed more favorably (flat 15%), you have to remember that markets don't go straight up. If you take a bigger mortgage so you can watch your portfolio go up, your business case falls apart if the markets go down (we saw this with the popping of the tech bubble in 2000 and more recently the real estate bubble).

Prepayments

Here is another area that makes U.S. mortgages far superior to Canadian mortgages. Most U.S. mortgages have no prepayment penalties, while Canadian financial institutions typically impose penalties for prepayments, restrict them to the loan anniversary, or simply do not allow any prepayments at all. In the U.S., you can send in as much additional money above your monthly mortgage payment as you wish, and it all gets applied to the principal. This means you can pay off your mortgage whenever you have the funds to do so (be wary and make sure you get a conventional mortgage). Many Canadians often want to set up biweekly payment schedules on their U.S. mortgages because it is an effective strategy in Canada to pay off your mortgage sooner. In the U.S., you have to be careful: U.S. financial institutions are often happy to oblige because there are many hidden costs and fees, and this approach typically doesn't make sense because you can accomplish the same thing by making an extra payment on your mortgage per year.

Down Payment

To purchase a home in Canada, you are required to put 25% or more down to avoid paying for mortgage insurance from the Canada Mortgage and Housing Corporation (CMHC). In the

U.S., the requirement is only 20% to avoid paying for mortgage insurance from the Federal Housing Authority (FHA) or a private insurer such as Fannie Mae. Depending on your situation, there are ways of structuring your mortgage to avoid the mortgage insurance while putting less than 20% down.

Closing Costs

It has been our experience that closing costs in Canada are typically higher than those in the U.S. In particular, lender fees in the U.S. are around US$400 versus C$1,000 in Canada. In addition, legal fees and land title fees are seen in the closing costs in Canada but not in the U.S. However, you typically don't need a termite inspection fee in Canada! The other difference when closing on a house in Canada is that you typically use an attorney to handle the transaction. In the U.S., you use a title company almost exclusively to complete the transaction, and title insurance is a good thing. You should note that realtor commissions are generally higher in the U.S. In Canada, the typical commission is 6% on the first $100,000 and then 3% on the balance. In the U.S. it is typically a flat 6%. This is why there are many firms popping up that will help you sell for a flat fee or a reduced rate.

Points

You will see points only in the U.S., and they can offer substantial benefits if planned correctly. There are three types of points: discount points, loan origination points, and seller paid points. Discount points allow you to "buy down" the interest rate on your mortgage. A point is typically 1% of the loan amount and can reduce your interest rate by one-eighth or so. This gives you more flexibility in creating a mortgage that works for you. Origination points, on the other hand, are fees charged by the lender for the evaluation, preparation, and submission of your mortgage loan application (typically "junk" fees). There are also seller paid points to provide an incentive to buyers by offering a discount of a certain percent on the sale of a home. The important thing to note is that points may be deductible on your U.S. tax return, so some careful planning here can provide an added benefit to you in getting the house you want with terms beneficial to you.

Impound (Escrow) Accounts

Impound accounts are another item seen only in the U.S. There the mortgage lender will automatically roll your homeowner insurance and property taxes into your monthly payment so they can be "precollected." The insurance company or local government sends the bill directly to the mortgage company, which pays the money out of your "escrow/impound account." The rationale behind these accounts is that, since the mortgage company owns 80% or more of your home, it can legally ensure the property taxes are paid and the home is protected in the event of fire or some other catastrophe. The company collects the money for these items in advance as part of your monthly mortgage payment and earns interest on it until the money is due. Overall, if you have more than 20% equity in your home, these accounts are generally a bad deal for you because it is like making an interest-free loan to your mortgage company. Interestingly enough, the company doesn't discuss this with you or give you the option beforehand, so ask some questions and be wary before accepting these impositions.

Applying

In qualifying for a mortgage, things can get a little tricky (see "Establishing a Credit Rating" below). First, be sure to provide copies of your RRSP statements and other investment accounts you have in Canada (or the U.S.) to your mortgage broker, who should take this into account in the underwriting process. It helps to have a letter of introduction from your banker in Canada that outlines your mortgage and credit line history with the bank and your history of repaying borrowed amounts. You should also have a letter typed up by your mortgage broker outlining your Social Insurance Number in Canada and your Social

Security Number in the U.S. so he or she can match up the two records. In the letter, request the broker to contact the Canadian credit agencies to get a full credit report from Canada. If the broker is successful, your Canadian credit rating should satisfy the U.S. mortgage underwriter and result in a favorable interest rate and mortgage terms for you. Thankfully, some Canadian banks have bought banks in the U.S. that can better handle your needs for a mortgage (see Canadian-friendly companies later in this chapter).

Establishing a Credit Rating

Many Canadians with an excellent credit rating in Canada move to the U.S. and are shocked when utility companies want payment in advance before starting service or they can't get a U.S. credit card or they can't qualify for a mortgage. Don't take it personally, this is commonplace because you don't have any kind of credit rating tied to your Social Security Number with the U.S. credit agencies. To resolve this problem, there are some things you can do in anticipation of your move.

FICO Score

FICO stands for Fair Isaac & Co., the Minnesota-based firm that created this scoring system in the early 1950s. These scores typically range from the 300s to the 900s and gauge the level of your credit risk (the higher the score, the less risky you are to extend credit to, and the lower the interest rate offered). A score under 620 is considered high risk or "subprime," and it's likely you won't be extended any credit. The score is created by giving different weights to the various criteria in your financial situation and is comprised of the following:

- 35% — your payment history (paying your bills on time);
- 30% — amounts owed (your total debt outstanding);
- 15% — length of credit history (yours will be short);
- 10% — new credit (recently applied for or issued debt);

- 10% — the type of credit used (mortgage versus auto loan versus credit card).

In the 1990s, mortgage lenders started using the score to rate prospective customers, and then in 1999 California passed a law requiring the lenders and the three national credit bureaus (Experian, TransUnion, and Equifax) to disclose your credit score to you. Today your credit score is used by most lenders to make instant decisions on extending credit to you, but this has led to increased credit-reporting errors that have negatively impacted innocent people's credit scores. As a result, the federal government recently mandated all three credit-reporting agencies to provide a free credit report annually upon request, and we recommend you take advantage of it to review and monitor your credit rating.

Before You Apply

Before you start the process of establishing a credit rating in the U.S., you need to have a Social Security Number, which you will need for every credit application you complete (see Chapter 5 on how to obtain one). Note that an Individual Taxpayer Identification Number (ITIN) will not do since it is viewed as a temporary number not typically eligible for credit purposes.

In desperation, some folks start applying for credit cards at every bank, department store, or gas station, anywhere to get some form of credit. What they don't realize is they may actually be damaging their credit rating. Each credit application you make is reported to the credit-reporting agencies in the U.S. and reduces your credit rating (new credit component). They think you are getting desperate for money and are applying wherever you can to keep yourself afloat. If your applications are subsequently rejected, your credit rating will sink even lower. This means that, when you are approved for a mortgage, for example, you will have to pay a higher interest rate because you are perceived as being a higher credit risk (i.e., your FICO score is low).

Table 6.1 shows how your FICO score can affect your monthly payments for a $216,000 fixed rate mortgage for a 30-year term (on one day in 2006).

Table 6.1

FICO Score

FICO score	Interest rate	Monthly payment
760–850	6.14%	$1,315
700–759	6.36%	$1,346
680–699	6.54%	$1,371
660–679	6.76%	$1,402
640–659	7.19%	$1,464
620–639	7.73%	$1,545
	1.59% difference	**$2,760 difference annually**

Transfer Your Credit Rating

We have seen some success in transferring a credit rating to the U.S. by using your current Canadian credit card to apply for and secure a new credit card with the U.S. subsidiary of the same company. I did this with American Express in 1996 when I moved to the U.S. from Canada. However, you should prepare yourself because this tactic will typically take many phone calls to both the Canadian and the U.S. sides of your credit card company before you are successful in moving your credit rating and membership rewards points (exchanged at the prevailing exchange rate) to the U.S. The beauty of this strategy is it allows you to get an instant credit rating with your desired credit card in the U.S. based on your credit rating established in Canada, and you don't lose any of your membership points.

Applying for a Credit Card

When you apply for a credit card, we recommend you do so in person with an officer at the bank of your choice. The bank may tell you it isn't necessary since this is a routine process, but tell the bank you are new in the country and have an established credit rating in Canada it will need to obtain. At this meeting, be prepared to provide the following.

- *Letter of reference:* get a letter of reference signed by your bank manager in Canada that lists all of your credit transactions with that bank (mortgages, credit lines, etc.) and your history in paying on time, never defaulting, et cetera. This letter carries a lot of weight in the process, especially since the U.S. institution can call the bank manager in Canada and verify everything.
- *ssn/sin:* have original Social Security and Social Insurance cards available. Instruct the loan officer to use your Social Insurance Number to contact the Canadian credit-reporting agencies to obtain a Canadian credit report. Equifax and TransUnion (see below) are credit-reporting agencies located in both Canada and the U.S., but their systems are separate, and it has been our experience that they rarely, if ever, talk to each other.
- *Identification:* be sure to provide an original passport or birth certificate to verify who you are.
- *Credit card:* take your current Canadian credit card with you so the institution can make copies and verify your existing credit history.
- *Pay stubs:* if applicable, take both your Canadian pay stubs and your current U.S. pay stub if you have one. You should also take your offer letter, stating your starting salary in the U.S., along with you.
- *Deposit:* it helps a lot if you have a U.S. bank draft for some amount that you are ready to deposit into your bank account when opened. You will typically get a higher level of service because the loan application officer is more motivated if you have money deposited with the institution. We have heard of cases where the money can actually be used as collateral if deposited in a certificate of deposit or money market account to secure a bank credit card.

- *Company credit union*: if you move to the U.S. to work with a large employer, it will typically have its own credit union set up (e.g., the Motorola Employees' Credit Union). This may be a good starting place to establish credit since credit unions tend to view you more favorably since you are an employee of a large, established employer and therefore a better credit risk.

You will need to fill out the standard credit card application with the bank to start the process. Be sure a copy of all the information above is attached to the application along with a letter signed by the loan application officer requesting a Canadian credit bureau check be done as well. This letter should clearly outline your Social Security Number and Social Insurance Number so that the appropriate match is made when your credit reports come in. Also ensure your previous Canadian address(es) are on the application form and in the letter. All of this information should allow the bank to issue a credit card to you with a healthy limit and low interest rates. As you begin using it, be sure to pay off your balances in a timely fashion to start establishing a credit rating in the U.S. You should obtain a copy of your U.S. credit report at least annually from the three primary credit-reporting agencies for the first few years to confirm that your credit rating is getting established in the U.S.

Canadian-Friendly Companies

It has been our experience that there is more success with American Express (call New Accounts — Special Handling at 1-800-453-2639) than with Visa and MasterCard when transferring your credit card to the U.S. subsidiary. We have also confirmed that First National Bank of Omaha (Customer Service 1-800-688-7070) has figured out there is a market for Canadians moving to the U.S. First National appears to know how to obtain a Canadian credit report and is willing to issue a U.S. credit card even while you are still in Canada. When moving to the U.S., just inform First National of your new address; your account and credit rating already exists with them in the U.S. Many of the Canadian banks, such as Toronto Dominion (which owns TD Waterhouse Bank in the U.S. and more recently bought Bank North Group), Bank of Montreal (bought Harris Bank), and Royal Bank of Canada (bought Centura), are good starting places for Canadians to obtain a credit card or secure a mortgage. These companies, because they have locations on both sides of the border, tend to have a better idea of how to get a Canadian credit report and give it its due weight in the underwriting process. There are two Canadian credit-reporting agencies they will need to contact: Equifax Canada (1-800-465-7166, 514-493-2314, or www.econsumer.equifax.ca) and TransUnion (1-800-663-9980 or www.tuc.ca). If you have a Canadian-friendly company you have dealt with, please let us know (book@transitionfinancial.com), and we will be sure to include it in the next edition of this book or on our website at www.transitionfinancial.com/us

7

Till Death Do Us Part

Man is destined to die once and then
the judgment. — Hebrews 9:27

By far the most neglected area we see with folks making the transition to the U.S. is will and estate planning. Unfortunately, the judgment of your estate plan won't come to light until after you can no longer do anything about it. In Canada, a simple will can accomplish many things at death. In fact, many Canadians mistakenly believe they should get their Canadian wills updated before their move to the U.S. However, when moving to the U.S., wills and estates become much more complex, particularly when property spans both countries and non-U.S. citizenship issues are added. We received a call from a desperate estate planning attorney in California. A man of substantial wealth living in the U.S. had suddenly passed away, and his widow, living in Canada, had no access to any funds to pay the family's bills. The man had a simple Canadian will, but most of the accounts had been frozen in both Canada and the U.S. because they were in his name only. Needless to say, it was a difficult situation at an already stressful time. In our opinion, estate planning is the most important area of planning you can do for yourself and your family, think about the following questions.

- Is your Canadian will valid in the U.S.?
- What would happen to your spouse and dependents if you died suddenly in the U.S.?
- Would your spouse be able to get access to any funds to meet the family obligations?
- What taxes would you pay in the U.S. and/or Canada in the event of your death?
- What would happen to your assets in Canada? Those in the U.S.?
- Can your heirs in Canada receive any of your assets?
- Who would care for your children if you and your spouse died simultaneously?
- Who would file your taxes, pay your bills, or care for your children in the event of your incapacity?
- In the event you end up in a coma, would you want the "plug pulled"? How would that be communicated?
- Would you want your body buried or cremated? In Canada or the U.S.?
- If you inherit assets from Canada, are they taxed? Where?

Estate planning is all about how much control you want in a variety of circumstances, including death and incapacity. A secondary consideration is saving every court cost, attorney's fee, and tax possible. Sometimes we hear "If I'm dead, I'm dead. What do I care?" If you do not want to determine the course of events in the situations listed above (don't want to spend the money to get an estate plan), your state of residence (or province where the asset is located) has default laws called intestate laws (*intestate* literally means to "die without a will") that will decide for you along with the attendant costs and delays that come with having no control. However, most people, when presented with the options, are not content to let anybody but them decide what to do with what has taken a lifetime to accumulate, their bodies, or their health-care decisions. A U.S. estate plan is needed. You just need to consider the cost of a U.S. estate plan as part of the overall expenses of moving to the U.S.

Estate planning for Canadians relocating to the U.S. can be extremely complex. It deserves much more attention than this book can provide because some areas have been tested in U.S. courts, there are some gray areas, and some scenarios have yet to be played out. We recommend you use a qualified Canada-U.S. estate planning attorney to get the appropriate counseling to determine what estate planning documents you need to achieve the level of control you want. How much counseling will you get with a downloaded do-it-yourself will or trust kit? In our experience, the majority of U.S. estate planning attorneys have no idea of the complexity of Canada-U.S. estate planning. The estate planning attorney drafts the documents; once they are completed, most folks sit back, let out a sigh, and take comfort that their estate plans are done. Unfortunately, it's a false sense of security because there is much to do in implementing your estate plan. Assets need to be retitled, documents need to be filed where they can be retrieved easily, and those having a role in your estate plan need to be briefed on your intentions. In our biased opinion, a team approach with an experienced Canada-U.S. transition planner as the quarterback is generally your best option.

Taxes at Death
Canada
Many people wrongfully assume there is no estate or death tax in Canada. They simply are not aware of the "deemed disposition tax" in Canada, which occurs at one's death. Similar to the departure tax when you leave Canada, this tax kicks in when you die in Canada and applies to your worldwide assets. At the first

spouse's death, things such as RRSPS/RRIFS can be rolled over to the surviving spouse to continue their tax deferral (provided the surviving spouse is named as the beneficiary on the RRSP/RRIF account). However, at the second spouse's passing, you must report the full value of your RRSPS, the capital gains in all investment real estate (including the U.S.), stocks or bonds, shares of your small business, plus any other income realized in the year of death on your final Canadian T1 tax return. Needless to say, with Canadian income tax rates reaching 48% or more, this can be a significant tax burden, particularly if you have illiquid assets. In addition to the federal tax burden, the provinces get their share of the proceeds plus a variety of additional probate fees that they levy individually (although they are fairly nominal and are coming under some legal scrutiny as of late). Probate fees alone aren't that expensive, but when an attorney is brought in to sort out the complexities, the expense can go up significantly, particularly since the probate process can last a year or more in certain provinces.

Once you are in the U.S. and a non-resident of Canada, the Canadian death tax situation changes a bit. Unfortunately, you are still subject to the deemed disposition at death, but it is at Canada Income Tax Act or Canada-U.S. Tax Treaty rates and is only on your Canadian assets, not your worldwide estate. For example, RRSPS/RRIFS are subject to a flat 25% withholding tax per the Income Tax Act because they are distributed at the second spouse's death. Canadian investment property is deemed disposed of as well, and a T1 tax return must be filed to declare any capital gains and ensuing income taxes paid to CRA.

U.S.

For anyone moving to the U.S., the myriad of taxes at death needs to be considered carefully. There can be up to five different taxes at your death, including estate taxes, gift taxes, generation-skipping transfer taxes, state death taxes, and federal/state income taxes. Most of these are cumulative taxes and, without the proper forethought and estate plan in place, could result in the loss of the bulk of your estate. As you can see in Table 7.1, with no or improper estate planning, these taxes can be more punitive than the deemed disposition tax at death in Canada.

Table 7.1

Estate Depletion of the Rich and Famous

	Gross estate	Settlement Costs	Shrinkage
Walt Disney	$23,004,851	$6,811,943	30%
Alwin C. Ernst, CPA	$12,642,431	$7,124,112	56%
J.P. Morgan	$17,121,482	$11,893,691	69%
Elvis Presley	$10,165,434	$7,374,635	73%
John D. Rockefeller, Jr.	$160,598,584	$24,965,954	16%

The settlement costs include the estate taxes, court fees, legal and accounting fees, probate fees, and so on that go into settling these estates after death. Your first line of defense in taking control of your financial affairs no matter what happens to you (death or incapacity) and reducing the settlement costs is a full "trust-centered" estate plan, which is discussed below. Even though John D. Rockefeller's estate was the largest, he was able to keep more of his estate through proper estate planning and by including charitable gifting as part of his plan. A brief discussion of each of these five potential taxes at death is outlined below.

1. Estate Taxes

The current estate tax regime has endured a number of changes over the last number of years, and it appears that Congress will continue tinkering with it for years to come. Congress is trying to balance the difficulties the estate tax causes in situations where assets are illiquid (family business, real estate, a farm) with the need to make up for lost revenues over the past few years. Under current rules, the estate tax is slated to remain as it is now until 2010 (with a rising exemption in 2009), when the current rules will be repealed and a "deemed disposition" (with generous exemptions) will be implemented similar to that in Canada. Then in 2011 the rules revert back to the rules used in 2001. The future estate tax picture will look a lot different than it does today, particularly since there will be one more presidential election during this time frame.

The IRS manages the estate tax system, and you have to understand that your worldwide net worth is included in the estate tax calculation. This includes items such as the following:

- life insurance proceeds payable to the estate or policies owned by the deceased; or policies transferred out of the estate three years prior to death;
- any gifted assets (exceeding any applicable gift tax exemptions) transferred out of the estate;
- your house(s), automobiles, RVs, boats, household and personal goods, furniture, fixtures, appliances in the U.S., Canada, and anywhere else in the world; and
- annuities, RRSPS/RRIFS, IRAS, and company-defined contribution plans like 401(k) plans, profit-sharing plans, and money purchase plans.

To report all of this at your passing, the IRS kindly provides Form 706-United States Estate (and Generation-Skipping Transfer) Tax Return. For those who prepare these forms (it should be a good estate planning attorney with a tax designation or an accountant who prepares them on a regular basis), it is clearly understood that you do not mail them to the IRS in an envelope — they are in a box. The documentation (including copies of your wills and trusts), schedules, evaluations, appraisals, and so on required by the IRS make this tax return a major undertaking.

Estate tax rates start at 18% and rise to 45% at just US$1.5 million in net worth. Everything above $1.5 million is taxed at the flat 45% tax rate. Specifically, the estate tax is calculated in Table 7.2.

Table 7.2

2007 Estate Tax Rates

taxable estate ($)	Tax rate	Cumulative tax owing ($)
0–10,000	18%	1,800
10,000–20,000	20%	3,800
20,000–40,000	22%	8,200
40,000–60,000	24%	13,000
60,000–80,000	26%	18,200
80,000–100,000	28%	23,800
100,000–150,000	30%	38,800
150,000–250,000	32%	70,800
250,000–500,000	34%	155,800
500,000–750,000	37%	248,300
750,000–1,000,000	39%	345,800
1,000,000–1,250,000	41%	448,300
1,250,000–1,500,000	43%	555,800
1,500,001+	45%	555,801+

To protect some (or potentially all) of your estate, Congress gives you a gift tax exemption amount (a "coupon") that can be used during your lifetime or an estate tax exemption that can be used at your death (you don't get both). The gift tax exemption is currently fixed at $1 million over your lifetime (unified credit of $345,800), but the estate tax exemption is higher, as outlined in Table 7.3.

Table 7.3

Estate Tax Exemption

Year	Estate tax exemption ($ millions)	Maximum tax rate	Unified credit
2007	2.0	45%	$780,800
2008	2.0	45%	$780,800
2009	3.5	45%	$1,455,800
2010	Repeal	Repeal	–
2011	1.0 ?	50% ?	$345,800?

It is important to note that, in order to make maximum use of the estate tax exemption for both spouses, a proper U.S. estate plan is required (see the figures below). Note that estate taxes are in addition to any professional fees, court costs, and probate fees that could consume another 3-10% or more of the value of your estate. The complexity and time required to settle an estate via probate are different for every state. Some states and provinces have a very streamlined probate process that is very inexpensive to settle even with an attorney, while other jurisdictions are much more complex and lengthy.

2. Gift Taxes

To prevent you from avoiding estate taxes entirely at your death by gifting away your estate on your deathbed, Congress instilled the gift tax. In general, any gift is a taxable gift unless it meets one of the exclusions. See the "Gifting" section below for more details.

3. Generation-Skipping Transfer Taxes

To ensure the government gets paid its estate taxes at every generation, it instituted generation-skipping transfer taxes to prevent you from passing your estate too far down the "family tree." The Generation Skipping Transfer Tax (GSTT) kicks in at the highest marginal estate tax rate (currently 45%) on any amounts that pass directly from you to your grandchildren and is in addition to any estate taxes above. Once again, the government is kind enough to allow you to exclude $2 million from the GSTT to pass to the next generation. This means that, without the proper planning, for every dollar in excess of $2 million that is passed, 45¢ must be paid to the IRS in GSTT. Since you are in the 45% estate tax bracket as well, you could see 90¢ in taxes for every dollar transferred to the next generation!

4. State Death Taxes

In general, there can be up to three different death taxes paid to your state of domicile. They include pick-up taxes, inheritance taxes, and estate taxes. The pick-up tax is called such because the state simply gets a portion of the federal estate tax bill up to the amount allowed as a credit by the federal government. This meant the deceased's estate wasn't out any more money. The 2001 Economic Growth and Tax Relief Reconciliation Act commenced the elimination of the federal credit and, as a result, the state pick-up tax. Many states are still deciding what to do with the complete elimination of the pick-up tax in 2005, and states in dire need of those revenues are installing their own estate or inheritance tax. Inheritance tax is levied on the right to receive property by inheritance and is in addition to federal estate taxes. The beneficiaries are typically divided into classes according to their relationship to the deceased, and different tax rates/ exemptions are applied to each class. Some states have their own "stand alone" estate taxes that operate like the federal estate tax system but are in addition to federal estate taxes. Overall, only one thing is guaranteed: the estate tax system at both the federal and the state levels will undergo change for years to come. This is why it is important to hire a competent estate planning attorney (see Appendix C or our website for sources) who can draft your documents to take into account these changes so you don't need to redraft the documents later.

5. Income Taxes

As in Canada, the U.S. deceased person's estate is required to file a final federal Form 1040 and the appropriate state income tax return to report any income in the final year. If not structured properly, things such as individual retirement accounts might have to be declared on your final return along with the taxable portion of your RRSPS. In addition, you will have to declare any interest, dividends, or realized capital gains in the year up to the point of death as well. These federal income taxes (don't forget state taxes as well) are in addition to any federal (or state) estate taxes owing.

As you can see, the total taxes owing at one's death can be unbelievable if the requisite planning hasn't been done. A recent case in New York had an American widow with settlement costs that were 102% of her $10 million estate! The time to plan is now because, if your estate is big enough and you just want to leave it to your heirs, you automatically cut in the government for a piece of your estate whether you want to or not. In our experience, most of our clients desire greater control over their estates than a game of "Russian Roulette" with the IRS or CRA.

Death of Non-U.S. Citizens

In the U.S., a non-citizen couple is not given the same estate planning benefits as U.S. citizens. For example, U.S. citizens can receive all of the spouse's assets at the first death tax free. However, non-citizens are not given the same "unlimited marital deduction" because the U.S. government fears the surviving non-citizen spouse could flee the country with the assets without paying any taxes otherwise due at the first spouse's passing. As a result, tax is typically due at the first death unless the government has some way of "attaching" itself to the assets. To avoid taxation at the first death in these circumstances, you should incorporate Qualified Domestic Trust (QDOT) provisions in your will or living trust. A QDOT provides estate tax deferral at the first spouse's death because the trust is resident in the U.S., and the government can require the trustee of the trust to pay any taxes owing (attach itself). When the assets are withdrawn or the second spouse passes away, the estate tax is paid at that time. Note that this strategy is simply a means of deferring the estate tax, not eliminating it.

Using the following fact pattern, here is a simplified example of how the U.S. estate tax system works:

- Canadian citizens only;
- US$6 million worldwide estate owned jointly between spouses;
- move to the U.S., permanently hold green cards, and reside in the U.S.;
- 2007 estate tax rules apply, and both spouses perish in 2007.

Figure 7.1

Without An Estate Plan

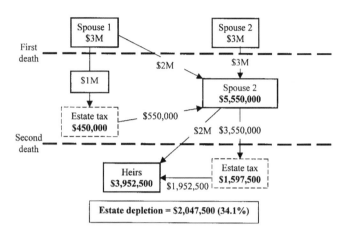

Figure 7.2

With An Estate Plan

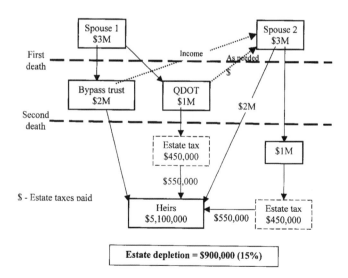

Table 7.4

Estate Tax Summary

	Estate taxes	$ Passed to heirs	Depletion
Canadians without an estate plan	$2,047,500	$3,952,500	34.1%
Canadians with an estate plan	$900,000	$5,100,000	15%
Savings	$1,147,500	$1,147,500	19.1%

As Table 7.4 illustrates, paying just a few thousand dollars to get an estate plan will pay off in hard savings, never mind the peace of mind that will come from knowing that what has taken a lifetime to accumulate will pass to your heirs according to your wishes. Once your basic estate plan is in place, other estate planning strategies and techniques can be employed to potentially bring your estate tax liability down to zero. It depends a lot on your unique situation (heirs in both Canada and the U.S.) and your wishes (passing your estate outright or protecting it with a trust). Further, if you do the requisite planning before you leave Canada, there are strategies to keep your assets out of your estate for U.S. estate tax purposes but still have access to them as needed. These strategies can bear an enormous amount of fruit if you do the requisite planning well before you move.

For Canadians residing in the U.S. with assets remaining in Canada, there is the potential for double taxation at death on some assets. First, for example, you are subject to Canada's withholding tax at death on any RRSPs/RRIFs and the deemed disposition on real estate. In addition, you may be subject to estate and/or income taxes in the U.S. on the same assets.

Fortunately, there are provisions in the Tax Treaty that allow a credit against income, profits and gains paid on Canadian real estate or other appreciated assets as a credit for U.S. estate taxes even though the two taxes are different – an estate tax versus a capital gains/income tax. Until recently, it was unclear if this provision of the Treaty applied to the 25% withholding on RRSPs and other similar plans at the second spouses death. A prominent Canada-U.S. estate-planning attorney we work with raised this issue initially in tax court and won. Then, the issue was raised again under Article xxvi of the Canada-U.S. Treaty where Competent Authority assistance can be sought when double taxation results. The issue was raised with the U.S. Competent Authority who consulted with the Canadian Competent Authority and based on their ruling, it now appears a full credit would be available for the 25% withholding on rrsps against any U.S. estate taxes.

However, you may not be out of the woods yet on the double taxation issue because the governments may still be able to double dip. You still may be subject to double income tax on your final irs tax return because it is highly doubtful you could use the same Canadian withholding twice against both your U.S estate and income taxes owing on the rrsp. In addition, you may be subject to estate and/or income tax by your state of domicile as well because the Treaty provisions and Competent Authority ruling don't apply. There may also be "Income in Respect of the Decedent" (ird) as well depending on your circumstances. Needless to say, there are many grey areas that have yet to play out in tax court. One thing you can do for estate planning purposes in both Canada and the U.S. is be sure you review the beneficiaries on your rrsps and other registered plans in Canada to ensure they pass according to your wishes or collapse them and move them to the U.S. (see Chapter 10). The other is to hire a competent, experienced Canada-U.S. estate planning attorney to draft your estate plan taking into account these assets in Canada.

Of equal importance is the fact that the irs does not recognize common-law or same-sex marriages in the U.S. estate tax system. These situations typically require additional sophisticated planning to ensure your wishes are implemented while ensuring court costs, attorney fees, and taxes are mitigated wherever possible.

The Trust-Centered Estate Plan

To garner the most control of your estate, we typically recommend a full trust-centered estate plan. There are typically four documents that make up a "trust-centered" estate plan.

Revocable Living Trust

A living trust provides instructions to the person(s) of your choice (your trustee) on how to handle your financial affairs in the event of your death or incapacity. While you are alive, you and your spouse can be the trustee(s) of your living trust, and you can change the trust at any time (it is revocable). However, at the first death, the surviving spouse continues as trustee, but the trust generally becomes irrevocable and may be limited in what can be changed. A living trust becomes a "receptacle" for all of your assets and governs how this portion of your estate is administered during your lifetime and how it is to be passed on to your heirs at your death. This document outlines in detail your wishes in a variety of events and circumstances that could befall you. Overall, a living trust offers you the following benefits.

- It allows you to avoid the probate process with its corresponding costs and delays.
- It allows you to take full advantage of the U.S. unified estate tax credit ($780,800), which is equivalent to exempting $2 million in assets at each death, for a total of $4 million ($1,561,600 in estate taxes) per married couple (from 2007 and 2008).
- It allows you as much, or as little, control as possible over your estate in a variety of circumstances.
- Your estate is kept private and does not become a matter of public record, reducing the likelihood of it being challenged in court by an ex-spouse or discontent heir.
- While you are non-citizens of the U.S., the QDOT (qualified domestic trust) allows you to defer any estate taxes until the second death.
- It eliminates the need for a court hearing to determine who

is to administer your estate in the event of your death or incapacity (with its attendant costs and delays).
- It alleviates your heirs from making difficult decisions about your money at an already difficult time.
- May provide some level of asset protection.

There are three key roles in any living trust.

1. The *grantor* puts the assets into the trust (also known as the *settlor, trustor* or *trust maker*).
2. The *trustee* governs the trust and manages the assets.
3. The *beneficiary* receives the income and assets from the trust as dictated by the terms of the trust.

When you are alive, you generally occupy all three roles in the trust because you put the assets into the trust, you manage it, and any income or distributions from the trust go to you. However, in the event of death or incapacity, the person you have specified steps in to manage your assets as trustee and to distribute the assets to the beneficiaries you have specified.

For most Canadians, a living trust is a new, potentially frightening topic because the use of trusts in Canada is not near what it is in the U.S. The primary reason is that in Canada trusts are taxed as a separate entity and are subject to the punishing Canadian trust tax rates (top marginal tax rate on the first dollar of income while you are alive). Further, there is a deemed disposition when assets are moved into, or out of, a Canadian trust. In the U.S., the taxation of revocable trusts is much different because they are "flow-through" entities that are taxed at your personal rates. This makes them much more popular and effective as an estate planning tool in the U.S., but if you moved to the U.S. in the past five years, you have to be careful of the Canadian non-resident trust rules and how they may apply to your situation. This is where a competent Canada-U.S. transition planner to coordinate your estate planning is critical.

Last Will

A last will and testament provides instructions to the person of your choice (your executor or personal representative) on what to do with your financial affairs in the event of your death. If you make your will part of an overall trust-centered estate plan, your Canadian will would simply be replaced with a "pour-over" will that would "pour" any assets left accidentally or intentionally out of your trust into the trust to be settled by its terms.

Many people have asked us if their Canadian wills are valid in the U.S. To be valid in U.S. probate court, your will simply needs to be presented and be properly signed and witnessed. However, if the provisions in your will are unclear, missing, or violate U.S. law, it may be valid, but the provisions may not be executable in the U.S. For example, there are differences in domestic law in who takes custody of your children or the disinheriting of heirs. Further, despite popular opinion, a will does not avoid *probate* (which means "to prove") and so is more easily challenged by ex-spouses or children from a previous marriage. As long as they can create doubt that your intentions were not as articulated in your will, they can cause long delays in court and incur thousands in legal fees. During this time period, accounts can be frozen, leaving the survivors in a position where it is difficult to meet daily living expenses. In Canada-U.S. situations, you can have double the problems because you may have to settle Canadian "situs" investments such as real estate (a summer home in Canada).

General Power of Attorney

This document outlines your wishes in managing your financial affairs in the event of your incapacity and gives the person of your choice (your agent or attorney-in-fact) the power to implement your wishes. Such powers may include the ability to pay your bills, vote on corporate stock, file your tax returns, open your mail, care for your pets, conduct routine banking, converse with your financial or legal advisors, and so on when you are unable to do so. Given that these documents are unique to most states, we typically recommend your Canadian POAs be replaced with properly drafted documents in your state of domicile.

Health-Care Directives

Typically, these documents include your living will, health-care, and mental power of attorney documents. Your living will outlines your wishes regarding your health care to physicians and other health-care workers, your family, and the courts in the event you are unable to communicate such wishes because you are brain dead, unconscious, under the influence of analgesics, or terminally ill. This document provides as much or as little control in how far you want life-prolonging procedures to go, specifies which medical procedures you want administered in which circumstances, and alleviates your loved ones from having to make these difficult decisions in such tragic circumstances.

A health-care/mental power of attorney gives the person of your choice (your agent or attorney-in-fact) the power to implement your health-care wishes as outlined. Likewise, if you go to the U.S. with Canadian health-care directives, you should have them replaced with documents suited to your state of domicile.

Estate Plan Implementation

As mentioned earlier, getting the estate plan documents drafted and executed is only the beginning. You must implement your estate plan properly if your wishes are to be followed. Unfortunately, a spouse does not automatically have the legal authority to undertake these actions on behalf of the incapacitated spouse on his or her solely named account (this is where proper implementation of your estate plan is important). You must fund your trust, and unless you carry your POAs in your back pocket wherever you go, filing them with a digital retrieval service is recommended. This is important so they are available as necessary for any medical staff to implement your wishes at the time they are needed.

There are a few things to consider in the "titling" of your

assets. In the U.S., there are several ways to hold property, including sole and separate property, joint tenancy with rights of survivorship, tenancy in common, tenancy by the entirety, community property, et cetera. How your assets are titled can have an effect on your estate plan because, with certain titling, your assets pass by law versus your estate plan. For example, joint tenants with rights of survivorship means that such a titled asset passes automatically to the surviving tenant at the first person's death. There are also community property states versus separate property states in the U.S. Separate property states have fewer income tax advantages at the first spouse's death than community property states, so the appropriate counsel should be sought in your state of domicile. The community property states in the U.S. are the following.

- Arizona
- California
- Idaho
- Louisiana
- Nevada
- New Mexico
- Texas
- Washington
- Wisconsin

Gifting

Most Canadians are completely unaware of the rules surrounding gifting in the U.S. In Canada, Canadians can gift cash or assets to spouses, children, or others with no gift tax repercussions because that form of tax does not exist in Canada. There are other Canadian tax rules such as the income tax "attribution rules" when gifting to spouses or children in lower tax brackets and the deemed disposition when gifting to a trust. You should familiarize yourself with the information below before arbitrarily making any gifts once a tax resident in the U.S.

Gifting to a Non-Citizen Spouse

If you and/or your spouse are not U.S. citizens, specific gifting rules apply. U.S. citizen spouses have an "unlimited" gifting exemption between them, which means that, during their lifetimes, they can transfer assets back and forth between themselves with no gift tax consequences. However, for non-U.S. citizen spouses, there is an annual limit of $125,000 in 2007 (adjusted for inflation), as outlined below.

$125,000

Non-citizen spouse <————> Non-citizen spouse

Unlimited

U.S. citizen <———— Non-citizen spouse

$125,000

U.S. citizen ————> Non-citizen spouse

If this limit is exceeded, the IRS has again kindly provided for your convenience Form 709 -United States Gift (and Generation-Skipping Transfer) Tax Return and using up some of your lifetime exemption or paying an attorney to devise other legal means of remaining in compliance. These gifts can occur very innocently, so care must be taken in coordinating your transfer of assets from Canada to the U.S. For example, if you collapse and withdraw your RRSP from Canada and deposit the funds in a joint account in the U.S., you may have just made a gift.

Gifting to Others

As mentioned previously, the IRS also has a gift tax of which many Canadians are unaware. U.S. residents are able to gift up to US$12,000 to any one person annually in 2007 (indexed annually for inflation but in $500 increments). Any gifts in excess of this amount require taxes to be paid or a portion of your $1 million lifetime gift exemption to be used up (e.g., giving an automobile) as filed on Form 709. The reason behind the gift tax is to prevent U.S. residents with large estates from giving away all of their estates during their lifetime or on their deathbeds to avoid estate taxes. The gift tax often catches many Canadians by surprise because of interest-free loans they may have given to children or associates. You need to determine up front if it is a gift or a loan. If it is a gift, it must be below the annual exemption or Form 709 must be filed. If it is a loan, the IRS deems an "imputed interest rate" to the lender at prevailing interest rates required on any amount lent. This must be realized as "phantom income" on your tax return even if no cash is received (interest is gifted to the child using the annual exemption). If the interest exceeds US$12,000 annually in 2007, a gift tax return has to be filed to pay the gift tax or "split" the gift with your spouse. One final point: the gift is not considered income to the recipient, so you don't have to worry about handing a big income tax bill along with your gift.

Receiving an Inheritance or Gift From Canada

We have received countless calls and e-mails from people desperately thinking that they would lose the inheritance they just received from a Canadian relative due to U.S. income or estate/gift taxes. Nothing could be further from the truth. A gift or an inheritance is exactly that; it isn't "earned income," so it is exempt from U.S. income tax. Further, as long as the requisite deemed disposition taxes were paid in Canada when the estate was settled, the inheritance should pass to you free of any Canadian or U.S. death taxes. However, there is one caveat: you should understand the impact of taking possession of the inheritance on your own estate if you live in the U.S. at your passing. Otherwise, you may want to disclaim any inherited amounts to keep them out of your estate. You will also need to report the inheritance to the IRS on Form 3520 — Annual Return to Report Transactions with Foreign Trusts and Receipt of Certain Foreign Gifts if the gift or inheritance exceeds $100,000. Note that this is not a taxable event but simply a reporting requirement of the IRS. Depending on your situation, there are strategies that can be employed using trusts, disclaimers, or other techniques to ensure the inheritance is kept out of your estate.

Taxation of Trusts

With the increased use of trusts in the U.S. for estate planning purposes, the following will allow you to familiarize yourself with the differences in the taxation of trusts between Canada and the U.S. In the U.S., the taxation of a trust depends a lot on whether the trust is revocable (changeable) or irrevocable (not changeable). If it is revocable, it is simply a "flow-through" entity and taxed at your personal income tax rates. If it is irrevocable, it is a stand-alone entity that must obtain its own Employer Identification Number (EIN) and is required to file Form 1041 — U.S. Income Tax Return for Estates and Trusts. Trusts are subject to the following tax rates (Table 7.5).

Table 7.5

2007 U.S. Trust Tax Rates

Taxable income ($)	Percentage
0–2,150	15%
2,151–5,000	25%
5,001–7,650	28%
7,651–10,450	33%
10,451+	35%

In Canada, trusts are always taxed as a stand-alone entity whether you are alive or not. Each trust has its own trust account number and is required to file a T3 trust tax return. If the trust income is retained within the trust, the taxation is simple: all of it is taxed at the highest marginal rate (29% federal plus that of your province, which can total up to 48%+). If the trust income is distributed to its beneficiaries, it is declared on the beneficiaries' tax returns and is subject to their marginal Canadian income tax rates.

The use of trusts in Canadian departure and U.S. pre-entry planning is common and, depending on your circumstances, can produce great income, estate, and gift tax savings. It is complex and should be undertaken only by attorneys and advisors well versed in Canada-U.S. transition planning.

8

Financial Freedom

And I'll say to myself, "You have plenty of good things
laid up for many years. Take life easy;
eat, drink and be merry." — Luke 12:19

In our firm, we use the term "independence planning" in place of the more common term "retirement planning" because of the connotations associated with the term "retirement." We are all saving so we can become financially independent, but the question becomes "Independent to do what?" Retirement is often thought of as stopping work and pursuing an unscheduled life of whatever your heart desires that day. In fact, we view retirement not as the closing of a book but as a turning of the page to a new chapter in life. Fortunately, that chapter is blank, and we encourage you to write it so that it is exciting, vibrant, and energizing for years to come.

A big part of our transition process is aimed at determining when you might become independent of work and helping you to understand what you want to do for the balance of your life. This approach creates excitement about the future and enables you to sacrifice now in order to achieve the goals you have set for your future. For you to gain these insights, any transition planning firm should spend ample time understanding what your current and future lifestyle looks like and then determining the cost of that lifestyle on an inflation-adjusted basis over your life expectancy. The analysis should incorporate the various sources of income you have, make a number of conservative assumptions, add the volatility of returns in financial markets, and then determine how your unique financial situation projects into the future once you are residing in the U.S. From there, you can begin to make these critical decisions based on numerical insights, not on opinions, conjecture, or notions.

In Canada, the primary vehicle used to become financially independent is the RRSP. Unfortunately, this is the last major savings vehicle left in Canada. It allows Canadian taxpayers to contribute up to 18% of their past tax year's salary up to a 2007 maximum amount of $19,000 (less any pension amounts made by an employer). Other savings alternatives include Registered Pension Plans, which allow $20,000 in contributions in 2007. The questions we are most often asked are "How do we save for our future in the U.S.?" and "Will we still qualify for some form of Canadian government or company pension when we are living in the U.S.?" These questions can be perplexing because you may have short earning histories in both Canada and the U.S. because of your move, which may mean you do not meet the minimum work history in either country to qualify for any government benefits at all. Once again, proper transition planning can set you on a course that will maximize your benefits because you lived in both countries. Following are some of the independence planning issues you should consider in making your move to the U.S.

Canada Pension Plan/Old Age Security

Many people have contacted us concerned that if they move to the U.S. they will lose their Canadian government pension benefits. If you qualify for benefits, you will receive them simply by applying for them no matter where you live in the world. In fact, the Canadian government can deposit your CPP/QPP or OAS benefits directly into your U.S. checking account if requested to do so. The exchange rates used are competitive, and the convenience is tough to beat. For the taxation of CPP/QPP and OAS in the U.S., see Chapter 5.

Qualifying for CPP/QPP

If you have made contributions into the system, you qualify for CPP/QPP at age 60 at the earliest (full benefits are received at age 65). You can obtain an estimate of your future CPP/QPP benefit by asking the Social Development Canada branch in your province of residence for a statement (1-800-277-9914). In 2007, the maximum CPP payment you can receive is C$863.75 per month (C$10,365.00 annually) at age 65 (adjusted every January for CPI).

Qualifying for OAS

To qualify for full OAS benefits at age 65, you must have lived in Canada for at least 40 years after reaching the age of 18 (till age 58). In 2007, the maximum OAS payment per person is C$5,846.19 annually (adjusted quarterly for the CPI) per person. But what happens if you make the transition to the U.S. before age 58? You still qualify for partial OAS benefits, but you must have lived in Canada for at least 20 years after reaching the age of 18 (till age 38). If you left Canada without living 20 years after reaching the age of 18 (left before age 38), the Canada-U.S. Social Security (Totalization) Agreement comes into play and qualifies you for benefits. For each year you live in the U.S., it counts as one year of eligibility toward OAS in Canada. Your benefits are based on the actual amount of time you spent in Canada, but you are now eligible for some benefits instead of losing them altogether because you decided to move to the U.S. There is a two-step process at work here: first, determining if you are eligible for any benefits at all; second, determining what your benefit amount is.

The Totalization Agreement is an executive agreement between the U.S. and Canada signed on August 1, 1984. An executive agreement is different from the Canada-U.S. Tax Treaty because it does not require the formal approval of Congress. The purpose of the Totalization Agreement with Canada is to provide employers and employees with relief from double payroll taxes and to "totalize" the payroll taxes you paid in both Canada and the U.S. in order to receive partial benefits in both countries for which you may not otherwise qualify. The U.S. currently has totalization agreements with 17 other countries.

Be aware of the difficulty in proving you lived in Canada to qualify for OAS. With CPP, the government has a record of how much you paid into the system and can calculate what you qualify for. OAS, however, does not require payment into the system — it is simply based on the amount of time you have lived in Canada. To keep people who do not qualify for OAS from defrauding the system, the proof of residency standards have increased. In one case, we had a stay-at-home mother who applied for benefits but couldn't prove she had lived in Canada. We helped her to gather some further documents so she would qualify. Some things you may want to consider using as proof include

- your spouse's tax returns (if divorced) since they will have your name and SIN;
- old passports showing exit from and entry to Canada;
- driver's license records;
- utility bills/records that have your name on them; and
- property tax bills that have your name on them.

U.S. Social Security

In making the transition to the U.S., you may wonder if you are eligible for any U.S. Social Security benefits. The initial answer is "no" unless you establish the necessary "quarters of coverage" that make you eligible. Since you are splitting your earning years between Canada and the U.S., it is rare that you will qualify for the maximum Social Security benefits. However, similar to CPP/QPP, if you pay into U.S. Social Security, you will receive some benefits. For the taxation of U.S. Social Security, see Chapter 5.

One of the political "hot potatoes" being juggled in the U.S. is what to do with Social Security. Based on the latest projections, the U.S. Social Security system is set to run out of money around 2042. President Bush made a number of attempts to change the system to sustain it (including private Social Security accounts that could invest in stocks) but in the end, the outcry was too great and it has since been put on the "back burner" of the political stove. However, some subtle changes have been made to extend the life of Social Security that the American public find more palatable. Until 2001, the age when you could receive full retirement benefits was 65. Now, the full retirement age is based on the year you were born as outlined below.

Table 8.1

Social Security Full Retirement Age

Year of Birth	Full Retirement Age	% Benefits Reduced if Collected at Age 62
1937 or before	65	20.0
1938	65 and 2 months	20.8
1939	65 and 4 months	21.7
1940	65 and 6 months	22.5
1941	65 and 8 months	23.3
1942	65 and 10 months	24.2
1943 to 1954	66	25.0
1955	66 and 2 months	25.8
1956	66 and 4 months	26.7
1957	66 and 6 months	27.5

Year of Birth	Full Retirement Age	% Benefits Reduced if Collected at Age 62
1958	66 and 8 months	28.3
1959	66 and 10 months	29.2
1960 or later	67	30.0

Your benefits are reduced by 5/9 of 1% for each month you collect Social Security before your full retirement age. As the table above illustrates, extending the full retirement age had the effect of penalizing folks in our year of birth by 30% if we collect early. The general consensus is that both the Medicare and Social Security systems in the U.S. need significant change to make them sustainable for the next generation. As outlined in Chapter 2, Medicare Part B moved to a "means tested" premium in 2007 (the more you make, the more you pay). We believe a "means tested" Social Security benefit is on its way similar to the OAS clawback in Canada where the more you make, the less you'll get. In addition, we expect the contributions into the system will be increased as well.

To qualify for Social Security retirement benefits, you must have established at least 40 quarters of eligibility in the U.S. To establish four quarters of eligibility, you must have earned income of US$4,000 in 2007. If you earn the minimum income amount for at least 10 years, you will have established the 40 quarters of eligibility and can begin collecting U.S. Social Security. The question then becomes "What if I can't establish the 40 quarters?" This is where the Canada-U.S. Totalization Agreement can get you qualified for benefits provided you have at least six quarters of eligibility established in the U.S. For each year you lived in Canada, it counts as one year toward U.S. Social Security. Your benefits are still based on the amount you paid into the U.S. Social Security system, and this amount will be nominal given your short earning history in the U.S. In 2007, the maximum Social Security payment you can receive is $2,116 per month ($25,392 annually).

Unlike Canada Pension Plan, Social Security offers a spousal benefit. If only one spouse qualifies for a Social Security pension benefit, the other spouse receives half of the spouse's pension benefit automatically (the reward for the stay-at-home parent). Some effective planning can be done with those moving to the U.S. whereby one spouse pays into the Social Security system and qualifies for benefits while the other spouse automatically qualifies for half of the amount without having contributed one nickel to the system.

Windfall Elimination Provision

When it comes time to apply for your Social Security benefits, you may be surprised to find out that, because you are collecting CPP, your U.S. Social Security benefits will be reduced due to the "Windfall Elimination Provision" (WEP). This is a confusing set of rules that can affect your benefits, but it depends on your individual circumstances. Here's how it works. To calculate your Social Security benefit, Social Security uses a percentage of your average earnings over the past 35 years. Since most Canadians moving to the U.S. have a much shorter earning history in the U.S., they qualify for a smaller Social Security benefit (because a number of your 35 years have zero as your earnings amount because you were in Canada). Now here's the rub: the smaller your average earnings over your 35-year history, the more Social Security aims to replace those average earnings (the smaller your average earnings, the more Social Security benefits will replace them). On average, lower-paid workers get a Social Security benefit that equals about 55% of their pre-retirement earnings, while the average replacement rate for highly paid workers is only about 25%. You, however, will have unusually low average earnings for U.S. Social Security purposes because you did not contribute for most of the 35-year "look back" period. Why? Because you were working in Canada and contributing to CPP and getting qualified for CPP benefits. CPP aims to replace about 25% of pensionable earnings on which your contributions are based. Again, CPP will drop about five of your lowest years in calculating your average contributions. As a result, the Social Security administration calls this a "windfall" that accounts for the fact you are getting full CPP benefits and are not entitled to the more generous Social Security benefits provided for those with lower average earnings over the 35-year period (some don't think this is fair treatment but we have to disagree). The Social Security agent then declares the Windfall Elimination Provision and reduces your Social Security benefits to take this "rub" into account (see Figure 8.2).

However, before accepting the agent's declaration, there are a few things you should know to make sure the Windfall Elimination Provision is properly applied to your situation. First, the provision was written for U.S. federal government workers and some state workers (e.g., police officers) who did not have to contribute to the U.S. Social Security system (it was voluntary). Even though it was written for these folks, like it or not it has broader application to those who work abroad, so the Social Security Administration will apply it as we believe is fair. Second, the provision does not apply if you use the Canada-U.S. Totalization Agreement to qualify for either CPP or Social Security benefits. Section 215 of the Social Security Act contains this rule, which is little known among frontline Social Security staff. In fact, for most agents, your application may be their first (and last) to take into account CPP benefits (but not OAS or any other company pensions!). You need to ensure the proper application of this rule to your situation, or you could find your benefits unnecessarily reduced. One way to ensure the rules are being applied properly to your situation is to file for Social Security benefits using Form SSA-2490-BK — Application for Benefits under a U.S. International Social Security Agreement. This form will be routed through the Office of International Programs and ensure a higher level of processing. At this writing, the form wasn't available online, so you will have to call the Social Security Administration or visit a local office to obtain a copy. Finally, if you fully qualify for CPP benefits in Canada and Social Security benefits in the U.S., the Windfall Elimination Provision applies, and only your U.S. Social Security benefits will be reduced. Take heart, however; you still come out ahead of someone who qualifies in either the U.S. Social Security system or the Canada Pension Plan system because both systems aim to replace more of the lower earner's wages . . . another advantage for those moving to the U.S.

Figure 8.2

How the WEP Rules Apply

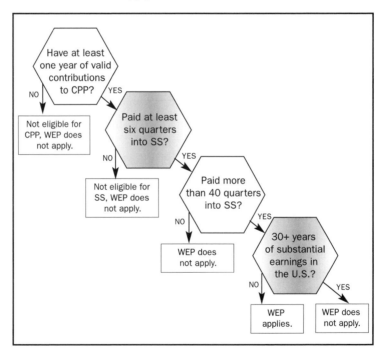

Individual Retirement Accounts (IRAs)

In the U.S., the closest thing you will find to an RRSP is an IRA. Do not mistake them for RRSPs, because the latter are treated differently from a tax standpoint in the U.S. Many clients are asked by their U.S. accountants what an RRSP is, and the typical response is "It's like an IRA." The accountant then wrongly assumes that it is an IRA and as a result does not prepare your tax return correctly, thereby creating tax and compliance issues with the IRS and potentially your state of residence as outlined in Chapter 5.

There are several types of IRAS, and which one to use depends on your unique situation and what you are trying to achieve (your goals and objectives). Traditional plans may be deductible or non-deductible depending on your adjusted gross income. There are SEP-IRAS and SIMPLE IRAS for those who have self-employment income and Rollover IRAS for those who are leaving their U.S. employers. One of the most welcomed plans in recent years is the Roth IRA that resulted from the 1997 Taxpayer Relief Act and the efforts of Senator Roth. This plan allows you to put away after-tax dollars and withdraw them tax free after age 591/2 (note: this is tax free versus tax deferred).

The rules surrounding these plans are complex and must be carefully considered before choosing the plan that is right for you. There are rules on how much you can defer each year, additional catch-up amounts if you are over 50, and penalties if you take them out too soon. There are other rules on when you must start taking funds out (age 701/2 compared to age 69 for the RRSP) and different rules that apply in the event of your death. There are even more rules on when you can make contributions and when the time has passed (typically you have to contribute by the time you file your tax return on April 15th versus RRSPS at the end of February). There are ways of passing your IRAS on to your heirs and allowing them to continue the tax deferral for the balance of their lives as well. Of course, all of this requires the appropriate planning based on what you are trying to achieve.

Following (Table 8.3) are the maximum contributions you can make to a traditional or Roth IRA.

Table 8.3

Contributions to an IRA

Year	Maximum contribution ($)	"Catch-up" amount ($)	Total contribution ($)
2006	4,000	1,000	5,000
2007	4,000	1,000	5,000
2008	5,000	1,000	6,000

Canadian Company Pensions

Many people ask us how a move to the U.S. will affect their current company pension plans. Again, if you have paid into the plan and are eligible for benefits, you do not suddenly become ineligible (unvested) for benefits because you move to another country. Your pension benefit amount remains, and in fact you may even get it paid directly into your U.S. bank account if you wish. The taxation of this pension is discussed in greater detail in Chapter 5. The problem with these "defined benefit" pensions is they are paid in Canadian loonies and may not be adjusted for inflation. You are thus exposed to a couple of risks. First, you face currency risk because, when you move to the U.S., you need U.S. dollars to fund your retirement expenses. Since your Canadian pension is paid in Canadian loonies, your pension amount will fluctuate based on the currency exchange rate. Some of our clients have had their pension incomes drop significantly when the loonie was worth US$0.6199 in January of 2002 and rise again, as it has to the time of this writing. Second, you face inflation risk since many defined benefit pensions are not adjusted for inflation (they pay the same fixed-dollar amount or only partially adjust it to inflation), and you will see a gradual decline in your spending power over your lifetime. By the time it starts to affect you, you are generally too elderly to return to work to supplement it.

U.S. Retirement Plans

In the U.S., there is a proliferation of "qualified" plans (versus "registered" plans in Canada) available for you to save toward your financial independence. These plans are typically governed by the Employee Retirement Income Security Act of 1974 (ERISA plans for short). The rules surrounding these plans are amazingly complex, and we have experts who deal with nothing but setting up and administering these types of plans. There are rules on how much you can defer each year and penalties if you take it out too soon. There are rules on when you must start taking funds out and different rules in the event of your death. Which plan you use depends on your individual goals and objectives and what you are trying to accomplish. You can contribute to an IRA in addition to the qualified plans listed below, which means you may be able to put away more pretax money in the U.S. than in Canada. Following is a brief description of the most popular plans.

401(k) Plan

This is by far the most popular retirement plan in the U.S. Its unusual name is due to that section of the Internal Revenue Code that permits these plans. They are used by most corporations and are considered a "defined contribution" plan because it defines how much you can put in (you bear the investment risk versus a defined benefit plan — see below). These plans allow you to defer some or all of your salary pretax up to the IRS specified limits (see the table below), and your employer may match a portion of it. If you leave your employer, you are able to roll your 401(k) plan into a Rollover IRA or another employer's 401(k) plan, but you should seek advice before doing so since it can be tricky, and there are some opportunities available to you. It is important to note that contributions to a 401(k) (and the plans listed below) are on a payroll basis only. You cannot go at year end and make a contribution to your employer's 401(k) plan; contributions must be withheld from your paycheck.

403(b) Plan

These plans are similar to 401(k) plans but are used exclusively by non-profit organizations (e.g., some hospitals and schools). The administrative expenses associated with these plans can be higher, but they still offer a good opportunity to defer income in a tax-deferred environment. Again, the unusual name is due to the particular section of the Internal Revenue Code that permits these plans.

457 Plan

They are used exclusively by state or federal government employees. There is usually some form of matching by the state, but it varies by state.

The maximum contributions you can make to the 401(k), 403(b), or 457 plans are as follows (Table 8.4).

Table 8.4

Contributions to 401(k), 403(b), and 457 Plans

Year	Maximum contribution ($)	"Catch-up" amount ($)	Total contribution ($)
2007	15,500	5,000	20,500
2008+	Indexed	in 500 increments	Indexed

Defined Benefit Plans

Unlike the plans outlined above that define the amount you contribute to the plan each year (you bear the investment risk), defined benefit plans specify how much must be contributed to produce a defined benefit at a certain age. Recent changes in law have made these plans very attractive in small business situations because they allow large amounts of income to be deferred each year. However, these plans have become less popular for major corporations with the recent changes in law. Overall, these used to be the plans of choice for most large corporations, but over the years they have dwindled (about 17% of employees in 2006) in favor of defined contribution plans because of the cost of funding, administering, and maintaining them. Further, many defined benefit plans had a cost of living allowance on the benefit that has all but been eliminated (it is seen more often in Canadian plans).

SEP-IRA, SIMPLE Plans

These plans are available for self-employed individuals who don't have the opportunity to shelter their net income with one of the other plans because of the expense to set up and administer them. These plans are easy to set up and inexpensive to administer and can be arranged at most discount brokerage firms.

Employee Benefit Plans

Several employee benefits may be available to you if you leave Canada to work with a larger employer in the U.S. Similar to Canada, the U.S. has stock option plans and deferred compensation arrangements. We provide a brief discussion below so you can familiarize yourself with them.

Stock Options

Stock options are a common form of compensation for employees in both Canada and the U.S. because they allow employees to participate in the movement of the employer's stock without having to commit any of their own funds. The taxation of these options is complex when crossing the border and beyond the scope of this book because each situation is unique. Following are a few general insights into stock options that may be helpful.

In Canada, stock options are allowed a 50% deduction of the amount between the exercise price and the fair market value of the stock at exercise. This means only half of the gain is taxed at the higher Canadian personal tax rates. In the U.S., there are two types of stock options, and the difference between them is related to how they are taxed in the U.S.

- *Non-qualified stock options (NQs):* the primary difference from the incentive stock options below is when the NQ is exercised, the difference between the exercise price and the fair market value of the stock is considered ordinary, wage income.
- *Incentive stock options (ISOs):* these stock options offer some terrific tax opportunities if circumstances permit. When the ISO is exercised, the difference between the exercise price and the fair market value of the stock is considered ordinary, short-term capital gain income if the stock is sold within a year of exercising. However, if the ISO is exercised and the stock is held for longer than one year, all of the gains are considered long-term capital gains and are taxed at the long-term capital gains rate of 15%. However, you have to be careful of the Alternative Minimum Tax (AMT) because the exercise of an ISO is considered income for AMT purposes. This means you could owe a boatload of tax even though you haven't sold a single share of stock. We highly recommend you exercise options with great caution, or you could cause devastating tax effects.

It is important to note that stock options granted to you for employment in Canada are generally taxable back in Canada even after you move to the U.S. Combined with the complications of the different options listed above, this warrants a cautious approach to exercising them because, if you are resident in the U.S., you will have to declare the stock option income on your U.S. return as well. Depending on your circumstances, it may be better to exercise all of your options in Canada at the lower tax rates before taking up tax residency in the U.S. Stock options have come under legal and regulatory scrutiny since the tech bubble of the late 1990s and as a result are coming increasingly under fire for their reporting on company financial statements. Many companies, including Microsoft and Intel, are moving away from these plans and instead instituting restricted stock programs to reward and retain their employees.

Deferred Compensation/Retirement Compensation Arrangements

Deferred comp plans, for short, are usually offered to senior-level executives to allow them to defer a portion of their salary (in addition to any retirement plans the company may have) into a plan they can collect after they retire from the company. The idea is to reduce the amount of taxable income now, when the executive is in a high tax bracket, until later, when the executive is assumed to be in a lower tax bracket. There are different types of deferred compensation arrangements in the U.S. depending on the company and its objectives for the plan. Most have the executive pay the payroll taxes up front, and when the plan distributes the income it is taxed just like wages, but these plans may be subject to the company's creditors, so there are some risks associated with the tax deferral provided.

Similar to deferred comp plans in the U.S., Canada has the RCA, or Retirement Compensation Arrangement. With these plans, the employer typically puts an amount into the employee's RCA. At that time, the contribution (and any future earnings) is subject to a 50% refundable tax that must be remitted to the Canada Revenue Agency. Once the employee has retired from the firm and begins taking withdrawals out of the RCA, the distributions are taxable as ordinary income to the employee. In addition, CRA returns $1 of tax for every $2 withdrawn from the RCA. Although the RCA allows for some tax deferral, 50% of all contributions to the plan (and ensuing income) stays with CRA. When they are returned to the employee, there is no interest paid. In essence, CRA gets an interest-free loan. If you wait until you leave Canada to begin collecting your RCA, Canada-U.S. Tax Treaty rates will apply at a rate of 15% on periodic payments. You could withdraw amounts at a flat 25% withholding rate per the Income Tax Act versus the higher ordinary income tax rates (48% or more) as a resident of Canada. However, in the U.S., all amounts withdrawn are now fully taxable (since October of 2004), but proper tax preparation will ensure offsetting foreign tax credits mitigate your tax liability.

9

Smarten Up!

An investment in knowledge always pays
the best interest. — Benjamin Franklin

In Canada, the primary means of saving for your educational needs is the Registered Education Savings Plan (RESP). You can contribute up to C$4,000 annually to this plan (after tax) and, coupled with the Canada Education Savings Grant of $400 ($500 for those with a household income of less than C$36,378 in 2007), can begin to accumulate funds toward education expenses. In addition, there are the tax credits for the tuition amount, education amount, and student loan interest on your annual Canadian tax return. However, when you move to the U.S., complications can arise. Following are some things to consider in planning for your educational needs when moving to the U.S.

What Happens to My RESP?

Similar to RRSPs, there are varying opinions on the taxation of RESPs in the U.S. We take the position that RESPs do not automatically retain their tax-deferred status with the IRS or your local state. Further, unlike RRSPs, there is no treaty election, IRS form, or revenue procedure to continue the deferral. As a result, you have to declare the income inside the RESPs each year on your U.S. tax return until collapsed along with filing form 3520. Fortunately, CRA will permit non-residents to withdraw funds for "qualified education expenses," including those at a qualified U.S. university. From a Canadian standpoint, funds inside RESPs grow tax deferred until needed for education expenses, and any withdrawals of the gains/income and grant amounts are taxed as ordinary income to the student (who is typically in a lower tax bracket than the contributor). Your original contributions are withdrawn tax free. From a U.S. standpoint, the withdrawal of any amounts should be tax free as well because you have been declaring the income annually on your U.S. tax return. However, this asset will be included in your estate for estate tax purposes and could be subjected to the punishing estate taxes outlined in Chapter 7.

One thorny issue arises if you become a U.S. resident but leave an RESP in Canada and are unable to use it for education expenses. CRA rules state that as a non-resident you cannot withdraw any earnings on your original contributions to an RESP for any purpose other than "qualified education expenses." This means that, even if you are willing to pay the Canadian taxes and penalties, you still can't get the earnings out — only your original principal can be withdrawn (tax free), and you will have to return all of the grant money received back to the Government of Canada. RESPs require some planning to ensure there will be someone in your family (or among relatives) who can benefit from these plans; otherwise, the earnings can be left on "Island Canada" indefinitely. We believe this rule was an oversight by CRA in drafting the laws surrounding RESPs and non-residents of Canada, but we are not sure when, or if, it will be addressed. One final note: there are no provisions to roll your RESP into any education savings account in the U.S. and maintain the tax deferral from a Canadian or U.S. perspective. Further, if you have young children who won't be attending a postsecondary institution any time soon, there are income declaration requirements outlined above but also various reporting requirements in the U.S., such as Form TDF 90.221 — Report of Foreign Accounts, Form 3520: Annual Return to Report Transactions with Foreign Trusts and Receipt of Certain Foreign Gifts and Form 3520A: Annual Information Return of Foreign Trust with a U.S. Owner on your U.S. federal tax return when you leave your RESPs in Canada. Which compliance requirements your state of domicile will have is another matter. Finally, it will be difficult to manage the investments in your RESP because your financial institution will only allow you to sell investments to avoid the ire of the SEC (see Chapter 10 for more details).

Education Saving Opportunities in the U.S.

In the U.S., there are several different ways of saving for your child's education and tax benefits to support those improving themselves through education. An assessment of your tax situation needs to be completed to see which alternatives you are eligible for and fit with your overall financial plan. You then have to decide how much control you want to give your child over these funds. Following is a review of the major plans available in the U.S. to fund your education expenses.

Coverdell Education Savings Account

This plan allows you to put $2,000 after tax away annually per beneficiary. Withdrawals of principal or earnings for qualified education expenses are tax free. These funds can be used for expenses such as tuition, books, computers, Internet connections, and actual living expenses and applies from kindergarten through to university.

UTMA

A Uniform Transfer to Minors Act account can be set up at most brokerage firms in your child's name. You are the custodian on the account. You can then put an unlimited amount of funds in this account, but be aware of the gift tax implications (see Chapter 7). From a tax standpoint, the first $850 in income in 2007 from the account is tax free, with the next $850 taxed at your child's marginal tax rate of 10%. When the income in the account exceeds $1,700, the excess income is taxed at your highest marginal tax rate (as much as 35%) until each child reaches age 18. This is known as the "kiddie tax" and is intended to prevent people from avoiding taxes by simply giving their money to their children to be taxed at their lower tax bracket (similar to the attribution rules on capital gains in Canada). Funds can be taken out for the benefit of the child only and must not be used for "normal" expenses that you as a parent are expected to provide (food or rent in your home). Also be aware that your child gets unrestricted access to the entire UTMA account at the age of majority for the state in which you reside (normally 21), so if he chooses to buy a Corvette, don't blame us!

State College Savings Plans

Known as "Section 529 plans" in the U.S. after their section in the Internal Revenue Code, these state-sponsored programs have become very popular. Every state now has a plan. These plans have a short history and are the result of the 2001 changes to the tax laws, which were made permanent in 2006. What made them suddenly very popular is you make after-tax contributions that can be invested in a wide range of mutual funds. When it comes time for withdrawals for education expenses (room, board, books, tuition), everything (dividends, interest, capital gains) is withdrawn tax free at the federal level and possibly in your state of residence as well. In addition, there are some great estate tax planning advantages that may be applicable in your situation. Most importantly, you retain full control of the funds and can change beneficiaries at any time with no tax or other implications.

Hope Scholarship Credit

In 2007, this tax credit is worth a total of $1,650 for each of your children over a two-year period. In the first year, you are eligible for a $1,100 tax credit if you pay at least $1,100 in college expenses. In the second year, if you pay $1,100 in college expenses, you receive a 50% credit or $550. There are income restrictions to be aware of in qualifying for this credit, and it is available only for the first two years of postsecondary studies.

Lifetime Learning Credit

This tax credit is worth $2,000 annually for each tax-paying family as long as there is a child or parent in school full or part time upgrading his or her skills. There are income restrictions in qualifying for this credit, and you can only select between the Hope Scholarship and the Lifetime Learning Credits in any one year.

Student Loan Interest Deduction

As in Canada, in the U.S. there is an "above the line" deduction (don't have to itemize) on your tax return for any interest paid on student loans. The maximum deduction is $2,500, but there are income restrictions on your eligibility for this deduction.

Tuition and Fees Deduction

Similar to Canada's tuition and education amounts, in the U.S. there is a deduction of up to $4,000 for college tuition and related expenses, but there are income restrictions on whether you qualify or not. Further, you can't take the deduction if you take one of the credits outlined above.

As you can see, there are many alternatives and tax-favorable strategies in the U.S. to save for your education expenses or those of your child. Which options you are eligible for and the pros and cons of each plan depend on your individual financial situation and the level of control you want over the funds. Our firm can provide assistance in determining the best means of achieving your education goals.

Key Differences

There are several key differences in the school systems between Canada and the U.S.

- In Canada, junior high runs from grades 7 to 9. In the U.S., it is just grades 7 and 8 and is called middle school.
- In the U.S., K-12 school generally starts in early-mid-August and runs through May, with longer breaks in between. In Canada, school generally starts in early September and runs through June, with shorter breaks.
- Based on our experience and feedback from others, U.S. undergraduate classes tend to be easier than Canadian undergraduate classes, but U.S. graduate classes tend to be more difficult than Canadian graduate classes.

There are some linguistic differences in education circles you should be aware of as well (see Table 9.1).

Table 9.1

Linguistic Differences in Education

Canada	U.S.
Grade 9 or first year of university	Freshman
Grade 10 or second year of university	Sophomore
Grade 11 or third year of university	Junior
Grade 12 or fourth year of university	Senior
Junior high	Middle school
University	College
Diploma	Associates degree
Marks	Grades

10

Money Doesn't Grow on Trees

Fortunes are made by being highly concentrated,
but fortunes are preserved by being highly diversified.
— Anonymous

Canadians making the transition to the U.S. typically leave some investment accounts or RRSPS/RRIFS in Canada, thinking they will just continue managing their accounts as they always have. The reason most often given for leaving these investments in Canada is they will lose money if loonies are converted to U.S. dollars now (see Chapter 6). What folks don't realize is that it's not "business as usual," and there are complications with the accounts in Canada while they are residing in the U.S. If the decision to move the investment assets to the U.S. is made, there are other complications and unforeseen obstacles to overcome. Following are some of the things you should consider in the area of investment planning.

Keeping Accounts in Canada
Relocating to the U.S. is often followed shortly by a notice from

your brokerage firm saying that it can no longer hold your accounts and that you must move them immediately because you are no longer a resident of Canada. This notice may be due to an overzealous compliance officer who doesn't know what to do with a U.S. address on a Canadian account or a brokerage firm that is not registered in your state of residence. In reality, there is no legal reason for you to move your registered accounts anywhere since Canadian financial institutions can continue to hold accounts for Canadian non-residents. However, Securities and Exchange Commission (SEC) rules cause more complications with regular brokerage accounts (and RESPs), so you may find that you can't place any "buy" trades in the account (only sales are permitted) or be forced to liquidate the entire account and close it.

To get around this issue, some Canadian expatriates attempt to "trick" their financial institutions and the securities regulators by providing a Canadian address of a family member or friend or a post office box number. This tactic can lead to several problems.

- Your financial institution or broker, if proven to be aware of your U.S. residency, could be subject to fines and penalties for putting a Canadian address on your account when you are residing in the U.S.
- For any dividends and interest paid into your brokerage account, no withholding will be taken, as required by the Canada-U.S. Tax Treaty, because your broker believes you are still living in Canada. This creates a compliance issue with the Canada Revenue Agency, and you will have to remit the correct withholding on a tax return to Canada. Further, if you are being issued T3 and T5 slips for this income instead of the required NR4 slips, you could compromise your standing with CRA that you are a non-resident of Canada. You must also declare this income on your U.S. tax return (see Chapter 5).
- Lump-sum RRSP withdrawals or RRIF payments will most

likely have the incorrect withholding taken, as required by the Canada Income Tax Act, and you will be required to remit the correct withholding on a tax return to Canada.

- You will not receive your monthly investment statements or other important information (proxy voting, notification of annual meetings, splits or stock dividends, etc.) in a timely fashion because you will be reliant on your family/friends to send them to you when it is convenient for them.
- Your confidentiality could be compromised if your information ends up at a "trusted" friend's or relative's house.

Also overlooked are the restrictions on trading in your Canadian RRSPs and other registered accounts while you are resident in the U.S. Until recently, the Securities and Exchange Commission prohibited Canadian brokerage firms from making trades in these accounts for U.S. residents because of fears of insider trading and proper accounting of the income in these accounts. The Investment Dealers Association in Canada successfully lobbied the SEC, which agreed in 2000 to allow trading in these accounts (but not RESPs!). However, the states did not readily follow along, and now the Investment Dealers Association is negotiating with all 50 states to allow Canadian financial institutions to continue working with U.S. residents. So far, almost all the states have some form of approval in place, but it depends on the state and on which resolution it has adopted. Before making trades in your account, inquire with your Canadian investment manager to make sure the firm is registered with the SEC and with the state you reside in (your state must have adopted one of the appropriate legislative models to permit that trading).

If you are able to keep your brokerage accounts in Canada (most brokerage firms are no longer permitting U.S. residents to hold brokerage accounts because of SEC rules), be aware of a couple of difficulties. First, as a U.S. resident, you are subject to U.S. taxes on your worldwide income. Your Canadian investment manager/broker likely doesn't know the U.S. tax implications of the transactions he is undertaking and as a result could be conducting investment trades and handing you an unnecessary tax bill on your U.S. return in the process. Research has shown that expenses in the investment and tax efficiency are the two key determinants of investment returns. We recommend that you retain an investment manager well versed in the tax rules in both countries and how the Tax Treaty applies to your situation to ensure your tax liability is mitigated where possible. Another common area overlooked is the difficulty experienced with brokerage accounts in Canada if the account holder dies while resident in the U.S. Typically, the probate process has to be endured twice, once in Canada and once in the U.S., and there is the potential for double taxation (see Chapter 7 for more details).

Setting Up Accounts in the U.S.

When you begin moving your investments to the U.S., you need to select a financial institution. You may approach an institution in your local area that you may never have heard of about setting up an account. Without a doubt, it will be more than happy to get you set up and recommend several "great" investments (review Chapter 12). Following are some things to consider.

Where to Set Up

A common question our firm fields is "Where should I set up an investment account in the U.S.?" We believe the best value for the dollar is at one of the large discount brokerage firms. They offer low commission rates, a wide array of low-cost mutual funds, and exceptional Internet-based services. The custodian of choice for our clients' investments in the U.S. is TD Ameritrade Institutional, the second-largest discount brokerage firm in the world. It offers discounted transaction and trading rates and virtually every institutional mutual fund available as well as having fixed income and stock desks. For our clients in Canada or those with investments remaining there, we use TD Waterhouse Institutional. Again, it offers discounted transaction and trading rates as well as a wide range of institutional mutual funds and an experienced fixed income desk. There are other financial institutions available, but we encourage you to do your research and select a firm that upholds the fiduciary responsibility to you (see Chapter 12).

Temporary Visa

Another issue our firm has been dealing with more often lately is the unwillingness of U.S. financial institutions to open up brokerage accounts to "temporary residents" (e.g., those holding a TN visa). A TN visa is considered a temporary visa renewed annually, so you are not viewed as a permanent resident of the U.S. This means that, for regulatory purposes, many financial institutions are refusing to open up brokerage accounts because of the tragic events of 9/11. Ironically, it's no problem to open up a 401(k) plan with your new employer at the same brokerage firms. This can be a thorny exercise demanding patience.

Social Security Number/ITIN

For those making the transition to the U.S. and wanting to open an account as a U.S. resident, they must have a Social Security Number to put on the account application form (institutions generally won't accept an Individual Taxpayer Identification Number [ITIN] because you are considered a temporary resident). This number ensures any income from the account can be tracked for income tax purposes. For spouses not eligible to work, they need to apply for an ITIN before opening a joint account with the spouse who has a Social Security Number (see Chapter 5 on how to apply). With the tragic events of 9/11, the federal government has determined the best way to fight terrorism is to restrict the access terrorists have to money. As a result, you will find a lot of scrutiny and paperwork to contend with before opening an account. The institution will ask for your employment status, employer's name and address, passport number, and country to determine exactly who is opening the account. In our experience, if you have a non-immigrant visa, you may find it difficult to open an account with most brokerage firms here in the U.S.

Titling Your Account

The other question you will see on the account application form asks how you want the account titled: joint tenancy with rights of survivorship, tenancy in common, tenancy in the entirety, community property, sole and separate property, et cetera. Most Canadians have no idea, so they check any box or don't check one at all, and the brokerage firm uses its default (normally joint tenancy with rights of survivorship). In reality, the option selected can have profound estate planning effects on your family in the event one of you dies or becomes incapacitated. This is not a decision that should be taken lightly, and the answer is probably none of the options provided but an ownership option that never appears on the form. See Chapter 7 for further details on this issue.

Canadian Loonie Accounts

Another big question we get is "Can I set up a Canadian-dollar account in the U.S.?" At the heart of this question is the issue of losing money when exchanging Canadian loonies into U.S. dollars, which we address in Chapter 6. The answer is, essentially, no, you cannot open a Canadian-dollar account in the U.S., whereas in Canada it is common to open a U.S.-dollar account at most Canadian financial institutions. We succeeded once a long time ago in opening a Canadian-dollar account for a persistent client at a U.S. brokerage firm. Some of the many problems we encountered are listed below.

- It was very difficult to even find a brokerage firm in the U.S. to set up a Canadian loonie account.
- There was no end of paperwork to set up the Canadian

loonie account, and once submitted we had to follow up to explain to the firm what the client was doing, and the standard answer was "We can't do that."

- The investment holdings were still reported on the monthly statement in U.S. dollars, so the client still had the "discomfort" of seeing the portfolio in U.S. dollars. It required a monthly call to tell the brokerage firm of the error and have it issue a new statement. By then, next month's statement was already received, and we had to start the process all over again.

- When interest or dividends were paid or a bond matured, the Canadian loonies were automatically converted to U.S. dollars at the prevailing rate plus whatever "shaded" amount the brokerage firm decided on, and everything was swept into a U.S. money market fund. To get this converted back to Canadian loonies required many calls and much paperwork.

The bottom line is that U.S. brokerage firms are just not capable of opening and managing Canadian loonie-denominated accounts effectively because there just isn't sufficient demand for them. With all of the factors listed above, why would you want to try this? It just ends up causing a lot of complexity and frustration in your life.

Moving Investments to the U.S.

Another confusing and potentially frustrating area often encountered is moving your Canadian investments to the U.S. Let's dispel a common myth right off — yes, it's possible to move Canadian investments to the U.S. without having to sell them first. However, as we have personally experienced, the simplest transfers can take months for the unwary. Following is some information to consider when moving your investments to the U.S.

Moving Your RRSP/RRIF

One of the most popular questions our firm fields are "How should I move my RRSP/RRIF to the U.S.? In a lump sum? In stages? Using the annual minimum withdrawal amount? Spouse's first? This year or next?" Unfortunately, the answers to these questions require considerable thought, a current understanding of financial markets, and a thorough understanding of your unique financial situation to determine the Canadian tax implications, U.S. tax implications, and which RRSP(s) to withdraw first. The other thing to consider is, when a prudent withdrawal strategy is developed, what will be done with the money? There simply is no general answer for everyone, but generally it is better to transfer these assets to the U.S. for purposes of estate planning, tax planning, currency exchange, and simplification of life. The answers depend, again, on your individual financial situation and your overall goals and objectives. However, proceed with caution. A c$100,000 lump-sum RRSP withdrawal means at least c$25,000 in Canadian tax — that's a lot of money where we come from. Some proper planning is certainly in order.

Myth: Move Your RRSP to an IRA

One common myth we often have to dispel is moving a Canadian RRSP to a U.S. IRA (Individual Retirement Account). The current rules and regulations simply do not allow a Canadian RRSP to be rolled over to an IRA while maintaining the tax-deferred status in both countries. Your only alternative is to collapse the RRSP and transfer the cash to the U.S. and then make an IRA contribution or leave your RRSP in Canada. Of course, be aware of the tax implications before doing so since you can end up being double-taxed.

Given all these complexities, some people become overwhelmed and simply decide to leave their RRSPs in Canada and forget about them. This is akin to an "ostrich putting its head in the sand." Before doing so, consider the following.

- Under current rules, the maximum tax rate on your RRSPs is only 25%, about half of the tax rate if you had withdrawn it when you lived in Canada. Further, solid foreign tax credit planning can reduce the effective withholding rate on your RRSP withdrawal to less than 25% (see Chapter 5). Even if you are planning on going back to Canada, it can still be a good deal.
- As outlined in Chapter 7, there is the potential for double estate and income taxes between CRA, the IRS and your local state. Further, the overall settlement costs of your estate will be higher as well as create an extra burden for your executor.
- As outlined above, there are U.S. Securities and Exchange Commission and state regulatory requirements restricting Canadian financial institutions from trading in your RRSPs/RRIFs unless registered in your state of residence.
- There are several tax-filing administrative duties you must fulfill every year as long as you keep any RRSP/RRIF accounts in Canada (see Chapter 5). These duties should not be missed under any circumstances since the penalties for doing so can be severe. Further, your state of residence usually has separate rules for dealing with these accounts that you will need to investigate. Overall, this means added complexity and added tax preparation fees . . . every year.
- If you are intent on retiring to the U.S., your future expenses will need to be met with U.S. dollars. If you leave a large part of your investments back in Canada held in Canadian loonies, you could face a decline in your purchasing power in the U.S. due to a declining currency exchange. This is called currency risk, and it introduces unnecessary fluctuations in the future value of your retirement income.
- To cope with the currency exchange issues raised above, your RRSPs should be invested to hedge the U.S. currency and begin generating U.S. income to meet your future expenses in the U.S. The relaxing of the foreign content rules along with the

availability of more U.S.-dollar-based investments in Canada has gone a long way to protect you from the potential currency exchange issues. However, with the limited number of low-cost investment alternatives in Canada versus those in the U.S., it's more difficult to create a low-cost, properly diversified investment portfolio to maintain your desired level of risk and return. If you add up world financial markets, the U.S. is about 48%, while Canada is about 2%. Investing all of your savings in only 50% of the world's markets or investing in mutual funds with huge expenses can directly affect your investment return. It is interesting to note that on May 18, 2006, David Denison, the CEO of CPP was quoted in *The Globe and Mail* stating that "Canada as a single market cannot accommodate the future growth of our organization." As a result, CPP is increasing its current 33% allocation to foreign markets and will begin including emerging markets

• Investment research has shown that there is a direct correlation between the expenses in your portfolio and investment returns. The higher the expenses, the lower your returns. In general, Canadian investment managers, custodians, and mutual funds cost you multiples more than the management and fees of comparable mutual funds in the U.S. Therefore, a substantial annual reduction in your portfolio expenses is generally available for your portfolio on the U.S. side of the border (see "Investing in the U.S." below).

• Another risk you take by leaving your RRSP/RRIF in Canada is that you are at the mercy of the Canadian government's ability to change, for example, the withholding or other rules relating to your registered accounts. A number of years ago, non-residents could have collapsed their RRIFs in a lump sum at a net withholding rate of 15%. Now the withholding rate is 25% on amounts not considered periodic payments. What it will be in the future is uncertain at best, as evidenced by the overnight tax changes on income trusts.

- As you probably have noticed throughout this book, we are big on simplifying your life by consolidating all of your assets in the U.S. at one financial institution. Doing so has benefits most people don't realize at first. A simplified financial situation leads to a better understanding of your overall financial picture, which in turn allows you to have more control, which tends to reduce your stress and bring greater peace of mind. Further, it reduces your complexity at tax time, which can save you a few dollars on tax preparation.

- Finally, you have to deal with it someday. You may be turning 69 and are forced to convert your RRSP to a RRIF to commence the required minimum withdrawals. You may have an unexpected cash need and decide to pull some of it out. Alternatively, your visa came through, and you've decided to stay in the U.S. longer than expected. Or you may just be tired of the complex tax returns and nuisance they cause each year. Whatever the reason, your first withdrawal will cause you to deal with all the issues above. However, the longer the passage of time, the more record keeping required, and the more you have to pay someone to determine the taxable amount of your RRSP/RRIF withdrawal in the U.S.

Despite all of the reasons above, there may be a situation where leaving your RRSPs/RRIFs in Canada is the most prudent thing to do. For example, your RRSP may be in mutual funds with deferred sales charges that will expire soon, or you unexpectedly lose your immigration status and need to return to Canada shortly after moving to the U.S. Or it may make sense to do staged withdrawals of your RRSPs/RRIFs over a longer period of time for foreign tax credit planning purposes or to take advantage of tax-reduced withdrawals using the section 217 filing (see Chapter 5). Our point here is you shouldn't just collapse and move these registered accounts to the U.S. without thinking the process through from beginning to end.

Locked-In Retirement Accounts

Once you decide to move your investments to the U.S., you come across the thorny issue of how to collapse your Locked-In Retirement Account (LIRA). LIRAS are created when you roll your employer pension plan into a self-administered LIRA. LIRAS are exactly that, "locked-in," because the federal or provincial governments don't trust you to roll it into an RRSP and leave it there for your retirement. They feel the need to "help" you leave your retirement funds intact even though they don't provide any restrictions on how you invest them, and if it is a company such as Bre-X you could lose all your funds anyway. We have seen hardship caused by these rules because retirees are restricted in the amounts they can withdraw from their LIFS, particularly for those who don't have other sources of income. For example, someone in her mid-50s who has saved in the company pension all her life and wants to spend more money while she is young and healthy may not be able to support her desired lifestyle because the maximum LIF payment isn't sufficient (and she isn't eligible for CPP or OAS either).

When you tell your broker you want to deregister the funds and withdraw everything to move to the U.S., the standard answer is "You can't." You have to wait until the appropriate retirement age (usually 55), when you can convert your LIRA to a Life Income Fund (LIF) (or a Locked-In Retirement Income Fund or LRIF in certain provinces) and begin taking out the required distributions (there are both minimum and maximum amounts). The problem is that the issues outlined above for keeping RRSPS/RRIFS in Canada apply to LIRAS and LIFS/LRIFS as well. It is possible to get some of them out, but it is not an easy process.

The first item you must contend with is determining whether your employer pension plan falls under federal or provincial rules. If your LIRA falls under provincial rules, you may or may not be able to withdraw it depending on which province governs the employer pension plan from which the LIRA was derived.

Currently, only six provinces allow you to withdraw some of, or your entire, LIRA: British Columbia, Alberta, Saskatchewan (after age 55), Manitoba, New Brunswick, and Quebec. A movement is under way across Canada to change the provincial rules to remove this nuisance. In our opinion, Saskatchewan has one of the more progressive regulations because, once you reach age 55, you can roll your LIRA into a RRIF and make withdrawals as you deem fit. In our conversations with several provincial pension regulators, these rules have been addressed and in some cases included in the next bill to deal with "miscellaneous issues." For example, the Ontario legislature is expected to pass such a bill in the next two or three years for non-residents but for time being, they have instituted some hardship withdrawal rules that may apply to your situation. It is interesting to note that in December of 1999, the Ontario Members of Provincial Parliament passed Bill 27 to amend the Pension Benefits Act that permitted the hardship rules. In the same Bill, they amended the MPPs Pension Act that allowed ex-MPPs to unlock their pensions and move them into an RRSP! We encourage you to get involved in unlocking these Ontario LIRAS for everyone by signing the online petition at www.petitiononline.com/WRC101/ and letting Premier Dalton McGuinty know your thoughts.

If your plan falls under the federal rules (federally regulated industries such as telecommunications, television, airlines, or railroads), you have to be out of the country for at least two calendar years before you can withdraw it. You must file Form NR73 — Determination of Residency Status (Leaving Canada) with CRA, which provides you with a letter in about six weeks confirming you are a non-resident of Canada for the required period. Just present the letter to your financial institution along with your request to collapse and withdraw the funds and you should have your funds in a couple of weeks.

However, you may find the compliance department of your financial institution is unfamiliar with these rules and probably has never received such a request. They will try to hide behind the "letter" of the rules not the "spirit" in which they were intended. They will argue that the rules only apply to the funds if left in the pension plan, not if they are rolled out to a LIRA. Fortunately, in September of 2006, the rules were clarified further for federally regulated pensions rolled to a LIRA and as a result, these financial institutions can no longer hide behind this inconsistency and must unlock your LIRA. Again, we encourage you to get involved in unlocking these Federal LIRAs by signing the online petition at www.petitiononline.com/Unlock06/ and letting the Minister of Finance, James M. Flaherty, know about the issue.

A number of years ago, I had success in moving my own federally regulated LIRA to Alberta and withdrawing it under the provincial rules. The problem is that most financial institutions are getting more diligent in regulating plans from other provinces, and most ask on the LIRA application form which province governs your plan. It is becoming increasingly difficult to achieve, so our hope is that legislative reforms will proceed quickly.

Specific Types of Investments
Following are some of the things you need to consider in moving specific types of investments to the U.S.

- *Stocks:* most individual stocks traded on an exchange in Canada can be moved to a U.S. brokerage firm and sold when requested. It typically means big savings in your pockets because the transaction costs in the U.S. versus those in Canada are typically lower. Stocks listed on both a Canadian and a U.S. stock exchange (e.g., Nortel Networks) will be sold on the U.S. exchange, and the proceeds of the sale will be in U.S. dollars. Likewise, any dividends paid will be issued in U.S. dollars.
- *Bonds:* again, most individual Canadian bonds can be transferred wholesale into a U.S. brokerage account and sold

when requested. However, these bonds will appear on your statement in U.S. dollars. As with stocks, the proceeds of the sale or any interest paid will be in U.S. dollars.

- *Mutual funds:* despite valiant efforts, we have been unable to transfer a single mutual fund from Canada to a U.S. financial institution or mutual fund company. Even U.S.-based mutual fund companies will not permit you to transfer their mutual funds from Canadian subsidiaries to their U.S. head-quarters. I personally tried to move the Templeton International Stock fund and the Templeton International Growth fund (both denominated in U.S. dollars) from Templeton's Canadian subsidiary to the U.S. headquarters to no avail. After countless phone calls and written requests, I gave up, sold the mutual funds, and moved the cash to the U.S. Before selling, analyze and understand the tax implications of doing so as well as the deferred sales charges that may be involved. Without proper planning, moving mutual funds can cost you dearly.

- *Cash:* moving cash is the easiest way to bring your invest-ment portfolio to the U.S. Liquidation of the portfolio avoids a myriad of issues, but you should analyze and understand the tax implications of doing so first. The quickest way to move your cash to the U.S. is to wire it from your bank or brokerage firm to a discount currency exchange broker, who will convert your loonies into U.S. dollars and wire it into your U.S. brokerage or bank account as desired. Whatever you do, don't attempt to take a large amount of cash with you when you leave Canada through a border crossing (see Chapter 4 for more details).

- *Partnerships/unit trusts:* these investments offer you a double whammy because generally you can't move them to the U.S., and they tend to be difficult to sell. You end up stuck with this investment in Canada, which forces you to keep an account open in Canada, any income it produces is subject to

Canadian withholding as well as U.S. taxes, and so on. Over-all, they add a lot of complexity to your life.

Lobbying Your Broker

Occasionally, we have witnessed shameful behavior when your broker/investment manager turns from being "Dr. Jekyll" when your investments are under his management to being "Mr. Hyde" when you tell him that it's in your best interest to move them to the U.S. Typically, these are people with whom you have had a long relationship and have treated you well, but when it no longer suits them they suddenly forget that your interests need to come first (that's the difference between a fiduciary standard versus a suitability standard). We have also seen top-notch investment managers cooperate with their clients to help them meet their needs. You need to be cognizant of any changes in your investment manager and understand what is going on so you can be proactive in expediting the process of moving your assets to the U.S.

First, your investment manager is compensated for the assets housed with his firm. Typically, at the end of the month, a "snapshot" is taken for purposes of compensation, so he will try to delay the transfer of assets at least until then. Second, invest-ment managers typically get compensated more for stock holdings in your portfolio or loaded mutual funds, and they don't want to lose that recurring revenue stream! No doubt you'll see some foot dragging. Third, your investment manager simply will not understand why it's in your best interests to withdraw your RRSPs/RRIFs or move your other investments to the U.S. As Canadians, we are trained from birth to put money into an RRSP and never take it out, so when the request is made it's very "countercultural." To ensure the expeditious movement of your investments, we recommend the following.

1. If possible, initiate the transfer from your U.S. brokerage firm, not your Canadian investment manager. You want to use your U.S.

firm to initiate a "pull" strategy versus relying on your Canadian manager to initiate a "push" strategy.

2. If necessary, have a nice but firm conversation with your investment manager; make it clear that you are doing this and that there's no changing your mind.

3. Follow up, follow up, and follow up. Create a sense of urgency about this move, and keep hounding your investment manager for an update/the status of the transfer so the message is clearly sent.

4. Be sure to obtain the name of your investment manager's supervisor so that, if your investment manager is suddenly "on vacation" or "out of the office," you have a backup person to keep moving the transfer forward.

5. Document, document, and document all phone calls, the subject, the person you talked to, and the outcome.

6. E-mail your broker, and if necessary cc his manager, so that every thing is documented. Investment management firms are required to maintain all e-mail records for regulatory purposes, so a clear history is built and can be referred to in resolving disputes.

Investing in the U.S.

There are several differences between Canada and the U.S. when it comes to investing your money. Unfortunately, for most Canadians making the transition to the U.S., they are unaware of these differences and end up making some costly mistakes or paying too much. This is typically the result of an overzealous broker, a smooth-talking mutual fund salesperson, or an annuity provider. Following are some of the things you need to consider before investing your hard-earned dollars in the U.S.

Investment Expenses

The U.S. is known as one of the most inexpensive places in the world to invest, far below the expenses seen in Canada. This is important because investment research has shown that investment expenses and tax efficiency are two key determinants of portfolio return. Competition in the financial services industry continues to put pressure on brokerage fees, commission rates, and mutual fund expenses. Coupled with the advent of index funds and exchange-traded funds, these factors have reduced investment expenses far more in the U.S. than in Canada (although that is changing . . . but slowly). The most insidious thing about these fees is that most investors don't even know they are paying them unless they look at the prospectuses sent to them (most don't because they trust their advisors, who don't voluntarily disclose them!). Most mutual funds in Canada typically have a 2-3.5% expense ratio compared with an average 0.25%-0.75% in the U.S. For example, $100,000 in Canadian mutual funds can cost you easily 2-3.5% or $2,000 to $3,500 per year (on top of any deferred sales charge), whereas a no-load U.S. mutual fund has expense ratios of approximately 0.25%-0.75% or $250 to $750 per year or less. In addition, there is a much larger selection of low-cost mutual funds in the U.S. that we can use with expense ratios around 0.10% for an S&P 500 Index fund. Canada's high investment costs have made the media as of late, so watch for further news on this issue.

Tax-Preference Investments

There are several tax-preference investment alternatives available in the U.S. not generally available in Canada that may or may not be appropriate for you.

- *Municipal bonds:* if you purchase bonds issued by the municipal governments in your state of residence, the interest is both federal and state tax free (if applicable). As expected, the interest rates on the tax-free bonds are typically lower than those on the fully taxable bonds because of their tax-free status. Interest from municipal bonds purchased from outside your state of residence is tax free federally but taxable on your state return (if applicable).
- *Federal U.S. obligations:* interest from U.S. government

bonds, T-bills, et cetera is tax free at the state level (if applicable) but still taxable at the federal level.

- *Exempt money market:* another alternative is to purchase an exempt money market. These are money market mutual funds that invest only in federal or municipal government bonds that will provide the tax benefits outlined above.

- *Annuities:* you make a contribution to an annuity on a one-time or ongoing basis, and the earnings grow tax deferred. When you are eligible to make withdrawals, your initial contribution is returned tax free, while the earnings are taxed as ordinary income. You should seek competent advice (someone who doesn't sell annuities for a living) before investing in these annuities since they can lock you in for some time and typically have high expenses (hidden) associated with them. Do not move an IRA into an annuity!

- *Life insurance:* there are many insurance policies that allow part of your premium to pay for the life insurance, and the balance goes toward investments. These investments are generally mutual funds that the insurance company offers. The investment income grows tax deferred, and you are able to take out a loan against the cash value that does not have any tax implications. If you withdraw the cash value, any amount above your premium payments made is taxable. Again, you should seek competent advice before investing in these policies, because they typically have high expenses associated with them.

- *Roth IRA:* if you have earned income, you are eligible to make an after-tax contribution to this Individual Retirement Account, invest it, and watch it grow tax free (versus tax deferred). This may be a wonderful alternative for you depending on your unique circumstances (see Chapter 8 for more details).

We have seen many complex schemes, financial products, and complexity added to people's lives in order to reduce their income taxes. We are all for legal tax avoidance techniques used to your benefit. However, sometimes the simplest strategies are the best. For example, if you buy a low-cost, tax-efficient, exchange-traded fund and never sell it, how much tax will you pay? What are the expenses associated with this strategy?

Other Differences

- *Money market "sweep":* dividends or interest payments, maturing bonds, or investment sales result in cash in your account. In Canada, this cash generally sits in an account earning "savings" account interest rates until you choose to invest the cash in a money market mutual fund. These money market funds in Canada may have a deferred sales charge and/or a high management expense ratio, so understand the instrument before investing. In the U.S., any cash in your account is typically "swept" on a daily basis into a money market mutual fund automatically. The nice thing is these are low-cost funds that allow you to take money out at any time penalty free. As a result, you earn the higher money market rate starting the same day your cash hits the account versus a savings account rate, which can be 1-3% less.
- *Mutual funds:* some investors in Canada have researched and become familiar with the different mutual fund families in Canada, such as Altamira, MacKenzie, AIM, Royal Funds, et cetera. In the U.S., however, no such funds exist. The question then becomes "Which mutual fund families should I use in the U.S.?" Vanguard? American? Dimensional Fund Advisors? There are close to 17,000 mutual funds you can select from in the U.S., but it will take you a while to determine which mutual fund is right for your unique circumstances. Our firm can certainly provide assistance in this area.

Foreign Tax Credit Planning

Once you have collapsed your RRSPS/RRIFS/LIRAS, paid the requisite withholding, and moved your cash to the U.S., it is time to invest it again. What many people don't realize is that, by properly structuring your investment portfolio in the U.S. to produce foreign income, you can begin recouping some of the withholding tax you left in Canada on your U.S. income tax return. We have seen folks implement proper foreign tax credit planning strategies withdraw a $1 million RRSP, leave C$250,000 in withholding in Canada, and recoup all of it on their U.S. tax returns before the foreign tax credits expired. This means they withdrew their entire RRSP tax free from Canada. Unfortunately, some firms use this tax-free RRSP withdrawal promise to promote their services, but it is definitely not the norm. We include it as an example to show you the power of proper foreign tax credit planning strategies. Considering your situation, wouldn't you rather pay 5 or 10% withholding on your RRSP rather than 25%? Our firm can analyze your situation and, if applicable, show you how.

The ideal investment to consume your passive foreign tax credits would produce a lot of foreign income annually and not have any foreign taxes withheld. There is a myriad of investments we can use, but which one to use depends on your individual situation and what you are trying to achieve. Don't forget that foreign tax credits have a defined "life" before they expire, so it's important to implement your foreign tax credit planning strategies as soon as your RRSPs are collapsed or at least in a balanced fashion to maximize your benefit (see Chapter 5 for more details).

Our Investment Philosophy

We believe in two simple principles when it comes to investing.

1. Grandma was always right, don't put all of your eggs in one basket. In other words, diversify, diversify, diversify. Why? Because of principle number two.
2. Nobody can predict the future!

Based on these principles, our firm doesn't try to outguess short-term market movements or pick hot managers, stocks, or sectors. We don't try to determine when to be in the market or when to be out because research has shown that accurate predictions can't be made on a consistent, long-term basis (for those who think they can, is it luck, or is it skill?). Instead, our intention is to capture market returns as efficiently and effectively as possible by remaining invested in a broadly diversified portfolio custom-tailored to meet your investment goals and your tolerance for the ups and downs of financial markets. This approach includes an analysis of your long-term projections, current and projected tax situation, current investment portfolio, foreign tax credit inventory, and of course the lifestyle you want now and in the future. In other words, we manage your investment portfolio in an integrated approach to your comprehensive financial plan.

As mentioned earlier, research has shown that the costs of investing along with the tax efficiency of the portfolio are two key determining factors in portfolio returns. As a result, a combination of tax-efficient index funds, exchange-traded funds, and other low-cost vehicles (read no-load) will form the core of your portfolio, with some asset class adjustments as warranted. Our custom-made tools allow us to analyze your Canadian and U.S. investments, consolidate them in one currency for analysis, and determine the right investment strategy to achieve your desired lifestyle. We are approved Dimensional Fund Advisors.

Our firm believes in a broadly diversified investment portfolio that starts with the four basic asset classes: cash, stocks, bonds, and hedging strategies. Stocks are further broken down into domestic (U.S. and Canadian) and foreign (the rest of the world, including Europe, Asia, and emerging markets). This is further broken down into large cap and small cap as well as growth and value. Bonds are also broken down into domestic and foreign. They are broken down further to include short-term, medium-term, and long-term bonds. Hedging strategies consist of asset classes that move out of sync with stocks and bonds. They include real estate, natural resources, energy, precious metals, and other strategies that are not correlated to these other asset classes as they become available.

Finally, our firm believes in a disciplined approach, and this is where we help our clients the most. This means investing when you have the money and selling when you need it again. There is a big difference between speculating and investing, and it is important to note the chasm between them. We find that people invest in one of three ways: by fear, by greed, or by objective. When investing by fear, the slightest drop in financial markets has these speculators selling out everything. Investing by greed leads these speculators to buy when the market is up. Investing by objective looks at your required rate of return on your portfolio to achieve your objectives and structures the portfolio to achieve those objectives over the long term while taking into account your tolerance for market fluctuations.

Our annual retainer service starts by developing an investment policy statement. This document uses your transition plan to outline further details of how your portfolio should be structured. It provides the guidelines on how the portfolio will be governed to meet your objectives. Once the policy is agreed to by all involved, the portfolio is implemented. You should never have anyone invest your money unless you have a written investment policy statement beforehand. Of course, any plan must be monitored closely. As a result, we conduct quarterly reviews of the portfolio, rebalancing it and managing taxes as necessary. The portfolio information is downloaded daily into portfolio accounting software that is used to determine the performance of the portfolio, which in turn enables better decision making. We provide quarterly reporting and rebalancing and are available to answer your questions as the markets move through their natural cycles. If you are interested in having your investments managed in context with your Canada-U.S. transition plan, we'd be happy to assist you. We are able to offer a comprehensive, coordinated solution for your investments in both Canada and the U.S.

11

The Business of Business

Today or tomorrow we will go to this or that city, spend a year there, carry on business and make money. — James 4:13

For business owners, there are more options under their control when moving to the U.S. than for non-business owners. For example, your business can be a ticket to legal U.S. immigration status, health care, or disability coverage. However, business entities also add a lot of complexity to your situation, and there can be many hazards in leaving Canada without getting the requisite planning done. In our experience, business entity planning requires a long lead time (two to three years) and the proper team in place to adequately design and implement the appropriate strategies before entering the U.S. However, if you do this correctly, you can reap huge rewards from both a Canadian and a U.S. perspective.

Emigrate to the U.S.

If you have a "substantive" business in Canada that has been operating for at least two years, you can use it to set up a U.S.

subsidiary. Once the U.S. location is up and running (generating revenues, hired employees, etc.), you as the owner may be able to use that business to obtain an L-1 visa (intracompany transfer) and transfer yourself and your family to the U.S. location. This visa is designed for companies with a presence in both Canada and the U.S. and the need to transfer executives, managers, or others with specialized knowledge between the two locations. The L-1 visa is issued for one year initially for a new U.S. enterprise and can be renewed for a total of seven years. Most importantly, the L-1 visa issued to executives and managers can be a "shortcut" to a green card. With your L-1 visa in hand, you may be able to file for an "adjustment of status," which means you can apply to U.S. CIS to replace your L-1 visa with a permanent resident green card with the intent of operating your business for the foreseeable future in the U.S. Once you obtain a Green Card and hold it for five years, you are eligible to apply for U.S. citizenship if that is your desire. As you can see, you could be discarding a golden opportunity to move to the U.S. if you sell or wind up your business beforehand.

Another alternative is to obtain an E-2 treaty investor visa by investing in the U.S. in a business intent on carrying on substantial trade between the U.S. and Canada or where a substantial investment of capital is made. This visa holder is admitted initially for two years, and then the visa can be renewed indefinitely as long as you are overseeing the investment or carrying on a trade, but it does not lead easily to a green card.

Since 1990, the "gold card" or EB-5 green card has been made available by U.S. CIS for investors who establish a business in the U.S. with an investment of $1 million or $500,000 in a "targeted employment area." The enterprise needs to show how it will benefit the economy and employ at least 10 U.S. workers full time; however, the investor must have some policy-making role in the firm. The "gold card" is issued on a conditional basis for two years. After two years and once the full investment has been completed and the 10 U.S. workers are employed, a petition is filed to remove the conditions and make it a permanent resident green card. Approximately 10,000 of these visas are available annually, but in the past few years only about 1,000 are approved annually because the rules and regulations surrounding them are very specific (see Chapter 3 for more details). The gold card is rarely used, but our firm has direct experience in assisting clients in this area.

Health-Care Coverage

As a business owner in the U.S., you have an opportunity to get health-care coverage for you and your family. One alternative is to install a group health-care plan for yourself, your family, and your employees. Typically, this can be done with as few as two employees, such as a husband-wife team, and any premiums are deductible to the business. If you have more than 50 employees, you can usually avoid underwriting as well. However, the cost of these plans can be prohibitive, and you may be better off to pay for individual plans for you and your employees. A lot depends on which state you will relocate to and which medical plans are available in that state, since each state governs its own health-care insurance industry.

Another important benefit you can get with a business is disability coverage. Statistics show that, if you are under the age of 45, you are more likely to become disabled than you are to die at that age. The problem with disability is your income goes down while your expenses typically go up. To cover this risk exposure as a business owner, you can set up a group disability insurance plan for you and your employees and deduct the premiums through the business. This plan will provide you with some income (usually 60% of your insured salary) in the event you are no longer able to work.

Income Tax Implications

By now, you have an understanding of the personal tax implications when moving to the U.S. However, when you add a business to the mix, the complexity increases dramatically. It has been our experience that your current, trusted team of advisors whom you have worked with for many years are typically incapable of addressing the Canada-U.S. issues adequately when you move to the U.S. In fact, some clients have told us that their advisors said it simply couldn't be done because of the complexity and discouraged them from attempting a move to the U.S. altogether. They were told they should just stay in Canada because the taxes upon their exit would simply consume what has taken them a lifetime to accumulate. It can be done, though, and depending on your individual circumstances the savings in time, effort, and money can be significant. You just have to understand that your current advisors will need to join or be replaced by a new team led by a competent Canada-U.S. transition planner to coordinate all the activities of the team. In addition, the sooner you put this team in place in anticipation of your move, the more fruit the planning process can bear. Following are some of the issues to be aware of when moving to the U.S. when you own a business.

Canadian Tax Implications

When you leave Canada, the shares of your business are subject to the departure tax mentioned earlier in this book. There is typically very little, if any, "cost basis" (original capital contributions) in these shares, which means, in most cases, the fair market value of your business must be declared on your final Canadian exit return. This declaration can cause incredible hardship if the majority of your net worth is tied up in the business and there are no other liquid assets available to pay the tax upon your exit. One option is to file Form T1244 — Election, under Subsection 220(4.5) of the Income Tax Act, to Defer the Payment of Tax on Income Relating to the Deemed Disposition of Property with the Canada Revenue Agency. This option will allow you to defer the tax as long as you can provide acceptable security to the Minister of National Revenue to cover any amounts of federal tax owing in excess of c$14,500. This deferral has the dual effect of "freezing" your departure tax if you expect your business to increase in value and avoid the liquidity issues of the tax owing when you leave Canada.

A unique issue arises with the departure tax if there are assets inside the corporation that have appreciated in value. After you pay the departure tax on the company shares and are comfortably residing in the U.S., if you sell appreciated assets inside the corporation, it needs to declare that income on a T2 tax form and pay Canadian income tax on it again. Another issue is that, if you sell the assets out of the business beforehand instead of the shares, you may be subject to capital cost allowance recapture. The business may face a huge tax bill if the assets inside it have been fully depreciated. The reason is that all of the capital cost allowance you have taken over the years is recaptured in the year of sale, and taxes are owed at that time. You can see that an appreciated or depreciated asset inside a corporation can be subject to double tax . . . once through the departure tax on the company shares and again when the asset is actually sold.

One alternative is to take advantage of the onetime c$500,000 Small Business Capital Gains Exemption on your company shares offered by CRA. If you are able to structure your business and other financial affairs appropriately, you may be able to include your spouse and double the capital gains exemption to offset the first c$1 million in capital gains you face when exiting Canada. Unfortunately, the rules for this exemption are very specific and complex, so competent Canada-U.S. counsel should be retained before such an undertaking.

If you are self-employed and have a sole proprietorship when you leave Canada, it can cause some complications as well. If you directly hold assets that have been depreciated, you could be subject to "depreciation recapture" when you leave Canada. There may be other issues, and they depend on the individual situation, but there is typically very little departure tax to contend with because the primary value of a sole proprietorship is its owner.

As a U.S. resident holding Canadian corporate entities, you quickly face complex tax-filing requirements. First, since the business is located in Canada, you must continue filing Canadian corporate T2 tax returns. Any income withdrawn as wages may have to be declared on a Canadian individual T1 tax return. If the income is paid out as a dividend, you must ensure the appropriate withholding is taken at source, or you will have to file a Part XIII tax letter and Form NR7-R to correct the withholding with CRA.

We have seen people who have neglected to do the requisite planning before leaving Canada with a substantive business entity and, when they realize their situation, start playing tax tie games with CRA. They live in the U.S. but retain tax ties to Canada, so they are not subject to the nasty departure tax on their corporation. In our experience, this is akin to playing "Russian Roulette" with the tax authorities, and it is inevitable that you will commit tax suicide. We don't recommend maintaining tax ties to both countries without seeking the appropriate counsel beforehand to ensure you understand your risks. We have also seen people undertake tremendous planning where most of the taxable portions of the business can be paid out as a dividend subject to a 15% withholding and used as a foreign tax credit on their U.S. returns. The key is having the right team in place and enough lead time to get the planning done.

U.S. Tax Implications

As a U.S. citizen or resident who is a shareholder, officer, or director of a foreign corporation, you must file Form 5471 — Information Return of U.S. Persons with Respect to Certain Foreign Corporations with your U.S. personal income tax filing, which is due April 15th each year. This is simply a reporting requirement (versus a tax return), but if not completed the penalties can be up to US$10,000 for each year the form was not filed. The IRS estimates the average time to prepare the form (exclusive of the requisite bookkeeping) at about 50 hours, but the actual time could be much longer for the uninitiated. Form 5471 appears to be deceptively simple since it is only four pages long, but there are also several worksheets and schedules that must be prepared along with 15 pages of instructions that will test your patience.

Any income taken out of the Canadian corporation as wages or dividends must also be reported on your individual 1040 tax return in the U.S. because you are required to declare your worldwide income on your U.S. tax return. Proper tax preparation should allow you to take offsetting foreign tax credits to avoid double taxation, but you still have to be aware of the other effects the income may have on your itemized deductions, personal exemption, and marginal tax bracket.

Another issue to be aware of is that, once a U.S. person has Sub-Part F income to report from a foreign corporation, the corporation thereafter must switch to a calendar year. This change can cause complications because, if the Canadian corporation has a fiscal year like June 1, you may have to pick up 18 months of income on that return spread out over five years, whereas it is common to operate on a fiscal year end (mid-year) in Canada. This difference causes complications because you have to reconcile your books twice to get the appropriate numbers together for your tax preparer. In addition, reconciling your personal wages, dividends, and varying currency exchange rates from the corporation to align with the mandatory calendar tax year for your individual tax returns in Canada and the U.S. makes things complicated.

When located in Canada, Canadian private corporations get preferred tax rates on the first $300,000 in income (generally less than 20% depending on the province). However, many people move to the U.S. without the requisite planning and as a result, lose the preferential tax rates and are required to pay corporate tax rates at 38% or more. This is particularly true when the date you move to the U.S. is different from the fiscal year end of the corporation. There are some good planning opportunities here that can assist you in retaining the preferential rates.

In Canada, it is common to carry a lot of "retained earnings" inside the corporation. In essence, they provide a form of tax deferral until distributed as wages or dividends. In the U.S., however, accumulated earnings in excess of $250,000 for a C-corporation ($150,000 for certain personal service corporations) require a case to be made with the IRS that the accumulated earnings are required for business purposes (e.g., an investment in capital or having cash available for an expected downturn). Otherwise, the retained earnings could be subject to "accumulated earnings tax" of an additional 15% on top of what is already owing. Table 11.1 is a summary of the corporate tax rates in both Canada and the U.S.

Table 11.1

2007 Federal Corporate Tax Brackets

Canadian taxable income		U.S. taxable income	
0 +	22.1%	0-50,000	15%
Derived as follows:		50,001–75,000	25%
General corporate rate	38.0%	75,001–100,000	34%
Less: federal abatement	(10.0)	100,001–335,000	39%
Equals	28.0	335,001–10,000,000	34%
Add: surtax	1.1	10,000,001–15,000,000	35%
Equals	29.1	15,000,001–18,333,333	38%
Rate reductions	(7.0)	18,333,333+	35%
	22.1%		

U.S. Business Entities

Compared with Canada, there are more business entities in the U.S. that are "flow-through" for tax purposes. This means any income generated by the company flows through to your personal tax return in the U.S. and avoids the higher corporate income tax rates or being taxed twice, as with corporate dividends. Following are some of the most common business entity types in the U.S.

- *C-Corporation:* this is a common corporation that files a corporate Form 1120 tax return, is subject to U.S. corporate income tax rates, and offers liability protection. This is how most large "blue-chip" corporations in the U.S. are structured. These organizations have shareholders (common, preferred, etc.), typically issue bonds, and need to file annual meeting minutes to ensure compliance.
- *S-Corporation:* this is simply a C-Corporation that has taken an "S-Corp" election to pass through all income to the individual shareholders. The company still has shareholders, prepares annual meeting minutes, and offers liability protection, but all income is taxed at the individual's personal income tax rates. The S-Corporation files a Form 1120-S tax return and issues Schedule K-1s to each shareholder to declare on their individual tax returns (similar to the T5013 returns in Canada). Both the "C" and the "S" corporations are more difficult to set up and maintain, but because shares are issued they are easier to transfer.
- *Limited liability company (LLC):* not a corporation per se, this entity has "members" instead of shareholders, and all income is passed through to the members. This is a very popular business entity in the U.S. because it is inexpensive and easy to set up, offers liability protection, and avoids the federal corporate income tax rates. However, you can elect to have an LLC taxed as a C-Corporation in the U.S. if that suits your planning needs.
- *Partnerships:* there are many different kinds of partnerships, and which one to use depends on your needs. For example, there are general partnerships, limited partnerships, limited liability partnerships, limited liability limited partnerships, and so on.

Understanding what you are trying to build helps you to determine which of these tools to use in your situation and depends on your individual financial circumstances, the type of business you want to set up, and what you intend to do with the business over the long term. Needless to say, it is best to do some planning beforehand to select the appropriate entity and get it set up appropriately to avoid complications later.

A Simplified Example

Owning a Canadian corporation when you relocate to the U.S. has its own set of complexities, particularly when entities span the border. We have seen many business entity structures that made sense to the client when presented by a Canadian accountant or attorney but in reality made no sense at all given a full understanding of the rules in both Canada and the U.S. Figure 11.1 is one business structure we worked on, and it provides a vivid illustration of what the wrong structure can do. A husband and wife living in Canada each owned half of the shares of 1234 Canada Inc., a Canadian corporation. Inside this corporation were three investment properties, one located in Canada and two in the U.S. 1234 Canada Inc. owned U.S. Holdings Inc., a U.S. C-Corporation. U.S. Holdings owned two investment properties located in the U.S. This structure was recommended by the clients' Canadian attorney to "protect them from U.S. liability issues" while they lived in Canada, but this "cross-border expert" created a multilayered tax situation for the clients that they weren't aware of until it was explained to them.

Taxation While in Canada

Here is the situation for U.S. Holdings Inc.

- *Tax #1:* all income generated by the two investments inside U.S. Holdings Inc. must be declared on IRS Form 1120 — U.S. Corporation Income Tax Return and taxed at U.S. corporate rates, which can be as low as 15% and as high as 39% (on taxable income over US$100,000) plus state tax (as high as 9.99%, but it depends on which state[s] the corporation operates in or derives income from).

Figure 11.1

Sample Business Structure

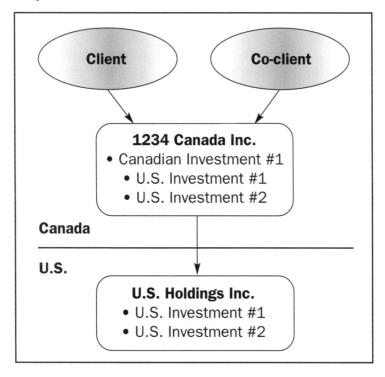

- *Tax #2:* since U.S. Holdings Inc. is owned by 1234 Canada Inc., all dividends moved up to 1234 Canada are subject to a 5% non-resident withholding by the IRS.
- *Tax #3:* all the dividends received from U.S. Holdings Inc. will be declared on a Canadian T2 corporate tax return and taxed at Canadian corporate rates at 22.1%. There will be a foreign tax credit for the 5% withholding but not for the tax paid in the U.S. by U.S. Holdings Inc.
- *Tax #4:* any income from U.S. Holdings Inc. distributed as salary from 1234 Canada Inc. would flow through to the clients' personal tax returns at Canadian rates of 30-45% or more, but 1234 Canada Inc. would get a deduction, so an additional layer of taxes will not occur. However, if distrib-

uted as a dividend, the dividend tax credit applies, but no deduction is available to 1234 Canada, so some double taxation still results.

Note that these taxes are primarily cumulative, with little or no offsetting foreign tax credits for an aggregate tax rate of 60-70% or more! For every dollar in income generated inside U.S. Holdings Inc., only 30-40¢ was actually ending up in the clients' pockets. Even more tragic is the fact that the damage was already done, and little could be done to avoid the steep income tax bill on the income and gains already accrued on the U.S. investments. The clients had no clue this was happening, and with the successful investments they had made they were essentially helping to eliminate the annual deficits in both countries! The primary reason is they had a U.S. accountant preparing their U.S. tax returns and their trusted Canadian accountant preparing their Canadian returns, and the attorney who devised the structure wasn't talking to or coordinating the tax preparation with both sides of the border. The clients were trying to do it themselves, but given the complexity it is no surprise they didn't catch it either. Further, this entity planning did not take into account the clients' desire to move eventually to the U.S. With the requisite planning, the clients would have realized more of the fruit of their investments and had an appropriate structure for an eventual tax-prudent move to the U.S.

We will briefly explain the taxation of the investments inside 1234 Canada Inc., but as you can see double taxation can be avoided for the most part because offsetting foreign tax credits and deductions are available.

- *Tax #1:* the IRS reserves the right to tax any trade or business income connected to the U.S. (except as exempted by the Tax Treaty) plus fixed income such as dividends and interest. Because a Canadian (foreign) corporation held the U.S. investments, any income produced by these two investments must be declared on IRS Form 1120F and taxed at U.S. corporate rates, which can be as low as 15% and as high as 39% (on taxable income over US$100,000) plus state tax (as high as 9.99%).

- *Tax #2:* any income generated by any of the properties held by 1234 Canada Inc. is declared on a Canadian T2 corporate tax return and taxed at Canadian corporate rates at 22.1%. For the two U.S. properties, a foreign tax credit is available for the tax paid on the U.S. corporate tax return.

- *Tax #3:* depending on where the work is performed, any income distributed as salary from 1234 Canada Inc. may be declared as a Canadian source and flows through to the clients' personal tax returns at Canadian rates of 30-45% or more. However, 1234 Canada Inc. would get a deduction for those wages paid, and double taxation is avoided. However, you have to consider any payroll taxes that you may owe in Canada or the U.S. on those wages. However, if distributed as a dividend, the dividend tax credit applies, but no deduction is available to 1234 Canada, so some double taxation still results.

Taxation When Moving to the U.S.

When these folks move to the U.S., their current business structure leaves them in a multilayered tax situation as well. The taxes noted above all remain the same except as outlined below in addition to the departure tax these folks had to face.

- *Departure Tax:* when the owners of the business left Canada, the shares of 1234 Canada Inc. were "deemed" disposed of. Since there were substantive gains in the shares of 1234 Canada Inc. (reflecting the gains in each of the investments inside U.S. Holdings Inc.), the gains are declared on their Canadian "exit" returns, and a large tax liability is created. The problem with the departure tax is that it occurs on the shares of 1234 Canada Inc., not on the gains in the investments inside the company. When these investments are sold and the gains realized, this income will have to be declared and will be taxed again!

- *Distributions:* any income distributed as salary from 1234 Canada Inc. will be declared as a Canadian source, and tax will be paid on T1 personal tax returns at Canadian rates of 30-45% or more, but 1234 Canada Inc. would get a deduction, so an additional layer of taxes will not occur. Because the IRS requires taxpayers to declare their worldwide income, the wages would have to be declared on a U.S. 1040 tax return and U.S. taxes paid with offsetting foreign tax credits for any Canadian taxes paid. If the income is distributed as a dividend from 1234 Canada Inc., no deduction is available to 1234 Canada, and the dividend would be subject to a 15% withholding per the Canada-U.S. Tax Treaty. The dividend would have to be declared on the taxpayers' U.S. 1040 tax returns and U.S. taxes paid with offsetting foreign tax credits for the 15% withholding left in Canada.
- As mentioned earlier, a U.S. resident who is a shareholder, officer, or director of a foreign corporation must file Form 5471-Information Return of U.S. Persons with Respect to Certain Foreign Corporations with your U.S. personal income tax filing, which is due April 15th each year.
- *U.S. estate taxes:* as outlined earlier, when you move to the U.S., you are subject to the U.S. estate tax regime, with punishing tax rates of 45% on amounts over $1.5M million in net worth in 2007. Unfortunately, the value of your worldwide assets, including your Canadian business, is included in this calculation. This means that, if you move to the U.S. without the requisite planning and perish, your heirs may have to conduct a "fire sale" of your business to pay the 45% U.S. estate taxes. The depletion of your estate to your heirs can be significant.

As this simplified example vividly illustrates, the taxation of business entities when leaving Canada can become extremely complex. No wonder so many accountants and tax lawyers simply throw up their hands and declare "It just can't be done." We are thankful for the network of professionals proficient in these transactions who have assisted our clients over the years. They have a thorough knowledge of this area and have a number of strategies and techniques that can be deployed as needed to address most business issues. We have personally witnessed this planning save hundreds of thousands of dollars and countless hours of frustration. The best thing you can do? Hire the appropriate team three to four years in advance of your move to start the planning.

Thanks to Carol Sadler for her contributions to this chapter.

12

Mayday, Mayday

Plans fail for lack of counsel, but with many
advisors they succeed. — Proverbs 15:22

Having read this book, you may feel like crying out "Mayday!"
(*M'aidez!* if you're from Quebec). Indeed, you may be feeling
overwhelmed with all of the things to consider in your move
and the amount of time you have to address them. This feeling
should provide you with the motivation to address them but not
to panic. Although limited, help is available. You have to decide
what you are going to do and where you want help. Some folks
want more help and want to delegate most of the tasks involved,
while others may want to do it on their own just using this book.
We encourage you to determine this upfront since it will help to
guide you in the relationship you are seeking. Your next step is
to go out and find the help you want. This chapter will outline
some of the things you need to consider in your search for a
Canada-U.S. transition planner and be sure to use the checklist
provided in Appendix C.

Selecting a Transition Planner

Today, it seems, everyone is calling himself or herself a "financial planner" or "financial advisor." In our opinion, no industry has so pillaged a term and created such confusion as the financial services industry and the term "financial planner." Any relationship has trust as its underpinning. This trust requires a strict upholding of the fiduciary standard to you (versus a suitability standard). The word *fiduciary* is defined as "of or relating to a holding of something in trust for another." This means your interests are put ahead of the financial planner's, even if you are leaving that firm. With a suitability standard, the product simply needs to be suitable to you (leaving lots of room for the recommender to serve his or her own needs), not necessarily the best thing for you. Essentially, the financial product salesperson does not have to disclose that she is recommending a particular financial product because she has a quota to meet, a bonus for selling it, or a contest to win — it just has to be suitable. Do you see the chasm between these two standards?

An example may help. We fielded a call in 2006 from a sales representative in Denver who found our website and needed some help with a Canadian client. The client had c$1 million in an RRSP in Canada that this salesman had convinced the client to put into a variable annuity. After explaining to the representative that the client would pay c$250,000 in withholding to CRA and that the proceeds should be in a taxable account for foreign tax credit planning purposes, the salesman replied, "This is a $40,000 commission I am not going to forgo." We explained further that there would be tax ramifications on his U.S. federal and Colorado returns that should be quantified beforehand as well, but that didn't matter to him. We finally challenged him to do the right thing for the client because a loss of c$250,000+ could devastate the client's financial projections and because he was not doing the best thing for his client. His response was "I am doing the best thing for the client with the products I am able to sell." After an hour spent trying to save this client money, we hung up the phone in disgust, feeling sorry for this uninformed client. Now let us be clear that caveat emptor applies because the client did not do the requisite research before investing hundreds of thousands of dollars in something. On the other hand, we believe the salesman bears the responsibility to fully disclose the hidden fees, expenses, and, yes, his commission to this client. As long as the product is suitable, he is off the hook. But can he honestly say he put his client's interests ahead of his own? Particularly when we pointed out the issues to him?

Our firm believes the best way to fulfill the fiduciary responsibility to you is to be fee-only (no product sales, no commissions, payment only from you, the client). The planning process should start by having a conversation about you and what you are trying to achieve, not about a particular product, your investments, or a tax-saving strategy that "fits" into your situation. From there, our role is that of a quarterback to coordinate the bevy of attorneys, insurance agents, accountants, investment managers, and other professionals to ensure your best interests are served at all times. The key is to focus everyone on the achievement of your goals and objectives. As a result, your Canadian stockbroker's interests or your U.S. cpa's preferences should come secondary to your needs when moving to the U.S. Here are the things to consider in selecting a Canada-U.S. transition planner.

Competence

The first step in hiring any Canada-U.S. transition planner is to look for the Certified Financial Planner™ designation in both Canada and the U.S. The licence to use the cfp® designation is issued annually by the Certified Financial Planner Board of Standards in the U.S. and the Financial Planners Standards Council in Canada. To hold these designations, one must complete course requirements and a comprehensive exam. In addition, there are work experience requirements (three years) that must be obtained in the financial services industry before use of the designation will be granted. Maintaining these designations requires meeting ongoing continuing education standards to ensure the licensee is current with the changing rules and regulations. Most important, however, is the requirement to abide by a strict code of ethics. An undergraduate and a graduate degree (preferably on both sides of the border) should be considered an asset as well as the RFP designation in Canada and the Tax and Estate Practitioner (TEP) designation given by the Society of Trust and Estate Practitioners.

The next thing to look at is the experience of the transition planner you are considering. You need to ask if he works on a consistent basis in the Canada-U.S. planning arena. Some people call themselves "cross-border" planners, but under further probing it comes to light that they have helped a friend three years ago when he moved to the U.S. or that the bulk of their clients have no international issues at all. Ask about their current clientele and if they themselves have made the move. There is nothing like having someone with the practical experience of having made the move himself to help you with your move. If he hasn't walked in the shoes you are about to put on, run — don't walk — away. We have seen the negative side of so-called experts, and it ends up costing you twice (a good example is tax preparation: you pay once for the initial work and again to adjust or amend your returns to bring you into compliance), plus there is usually little recourse for a job poorly done. When it comes to transition planners, be careful that you are getting what you pay for!

Unfortunately, there is no formal professional training in Canada-U.S. transition planning. It has to come with practical experience, "on-the-job" education, and a comprehensive network of professionals. This means competent Canada-U.S. transition planners are in very short supply, and there are only a handful of people who can competently write a comprehensive financial plan for your transition to the U.S. It often comes down to knowing which questions to ask and how to get effective answers. In addition, there are many potential "gray" areas to consider in any Canada-U.S. move, and often the judgment and experience of a good transition planner are worth more than the fees paid. In the tax preparation arena, there are a greater number of people who can competently deal with Canada-U.S. tax issues and how the treaty between the two countries applies. As always, we recommend you choose your professionals carefully and demand full disclosure of their compensation.

Planning Process

The next thing to focus on is the process the transition planner will follow in developing your financial plan. Lack of a well-defined process is typically indicative of a poor planning approach and, subsequently, poor results. Our years of experience in Canada-U.S. transition planning have led to a very defined process that has proven itself successful many times. As a result, our process is not something we alter or try to find a shortcut around. There are too many small details in any Canada-U.S. move that can create havoc with your unique financial situation. In considering any transition planner, ask if she has a planning process. If so, is it designed for a Canada-to-U.S. transition? Does the process focus on you and what you are trying to achieve, or is it on a particular product, on tax savings, or on an investment system? Any transition plan starts with a thorough exercise setting goals and objectives. This is time consuming but necessary to establish the context in which to place individual Canada-U.S. financial decisions. Ask how much time will be spent understanding your needs and your unique financial situation and how the conversations will be documented. In our experience, this process typically requires two meetings of two to three hours each to fully understand your situation.

Once the process has been completed, you need to ask if a custom-tailored, written report will be issued. Ask to see a sample transition plan. It is important to note the difference between a myriad of colored charts produced by most planning, insurance, or investment software and a financial plan containing detailed analysis of every aspect of your individual financial situation. Be sure that specific recommendations will be given on all aspects outlined above, from cash management and income taxes to Canada-U.S. issues in estate planning.

Client Relationship

Another important attribute in selecting advisors is whether you can work with them or not. Ensure you understand they know whom they are going to serve (you!). Ask if you will be working directly with a principal of the firm or with an associate. If an associate, how does the company assign one to you? Is it random, or is there a personality assessment to find the best fit in the firm? When did that associate make his Canada-U.S. move? When you call in, who will take your call? Is this person technically competent, or does he have to ask someone more senior for every answer? Do you share a common heritage? If not, you will find the "associate" will typically be your "parrot" to someone senior in the firm (who you met in the first meeting and haven't seen since) who really knows the answer, and this can be a frustrating, time-consuming process for you. Is this person fun to work with? Can you work with this person, and is he a "fit" with the way you like to work (in person, via e-mail, etc.)? You should also know, once your plan is complete, who is going to assist you with implementing it and how much that will cost. Be sure you have a detailed understanding of the recommendations being made, the pros and cons of each, and how each will be implemented. Overall, your transition to the U.S. shouldn't be a laborious task, and your consultations should offer healthy interactions that any good relationship is expected to provide.

Nature of the Firm

It is prudent to ask some difficult questions about the firm you are considering. For example, ask about the number of clients lost and gained in the past couple of years. If you get an answer at all, you should ask why people are leaving the firm to glean further insights into your potential relationship with it. If there have been many new clients, you should ask if the firm is on a big marketing push, for you may be lost in the shuffle.

Another difficult question to ask is whether there has been a high rate of employee turnover. If so, it is difficult to retain someone who has an intimate understanding of you and your financial situation, because new "associates" constantly need to be brought up to speed (usually by you because the partners are too busy). A lack of consistency in the relationship can lead to things missed. Also, if there is turnover, you need to ask yourself, "Why isn't this firm able to keep its top employees? Are its hiring practices suspect? Is it just desperate to staff up to handle its marketing growth?"

Find out the strategic direction of the firm and what it is trying to achieve; you will gain insights into the motivation of a relationship with you (are you just a fee, or does the company want to help you build a better life?). If there is no limit to its growth, this may indicate a focus on fees rather than on a relationship with you. Get some details about the principals of the firm, such as their ages and retirement/succession plans, and so on. Look for principals who are committed to their business over the long term and certainly for as long as you intend to have a relationship with them. Ask them if they own the firm outright or if they are part of a larger institution. If so, beware of any new conflicts of interest that could be introduced into your relationship. You should ask for two or three references of clients who have been with the firm (for varying time periods, starting with relatively new to several years) to get a broad perspective on what it is like to work with this firm. How big is the firm, and how many relationships does it currently have? How many relationships does it have per associate? Per principal? The higher the client-associate ratio for relationships, the more difficult it will be to service you. If you visit the firm, is there a sense of organization or chaos? Ask to see the office of the person you will be working with. Are there files stacked all over the floors, desks, and shelves, or is everything relatively clean and in order? A chaotic firm can mean little or no time to service your needs and one focused on fees rather than clients.

Another area to consider is the agreement you will sign with the prospective firm. Ask for a sample agreement, and be sure you understand the details. Is the agreement long and complicated, with the fee buried deep in the agreement or not present at all? Do you understand how the fee is calculated for your situation? Is this an objective or subjective process? Does the fee seem reasonable for services rendered, and how does it compare with other fee quotes? You should also watch for agreements that lock you in for a defined period of time or levy penalties if you want out before the expiration of your agreement. This is all good for the advisor and bad for you. Why would you want to be cemented in a relationship that isn't working? Why can't the advisor earn your business and keep it voluntarily rather than force you into a contractual relationship? Does the financial planner get all or most of your money up front and therefore leave little incentive to continue servicing you afterward? Ask for an estimated completion date for your financial plan. Asking some pointed questions will ensure you have an advisor you can trust to uphold the fiduciary responsibility to you.

Regulatory Compliance

By law, anyone rendering financial advice must be registered with the appropriate government authority. In the U.S., this means your transition planning firm must be registered as a registered investment advisor with the Securities and Exchange Commission or with the appropriate authority in the state where it is located. In Canada, any advisor must be registered with the appropriate provincial authority. In the U.S., you should ask for a Form ADV disclosure statement, which is required by the regulator and should be provided when you inquire about the firm's services. This document must be updated and filed annually, and it contains everything about the financial advisory firm you are considering, including the background of the professionals employed, the services offered, and how they are compensated. You will also be able to check for any disciplinary hearings or other issues that may be important to you. If you are moving to the U.S., it makes the most sense to consider a firm there and vice versa if you are moving to Canada.

You should also check with industry regulators and associations for more information on the firm you are considering. Most of this can be done online with the Securities and Exchange Commission (www.adviserinfo.sec.gov/), the National Association of Securities Dealers (www.nasd.com), and the local state securities regulator. You should also confirm the license to use the CFP® designation at the CFP Board of Standards in the U.S. (www.cfp-board.org) and the Financial Planners Standards Council (www.cfp-ca.org) in Canada or the Institute of Advanced Financial Planners (www.iafp.ca), which governs the Registered Financial Planner designation in Canada. You can also check the background of the licensee, how long she has held the license, and if there have been any disciplinary hearings (and the outcome). Another thing to consider is the advisor's involvement in professional associations. These are a good source of information on the person you are considering to be your trusted financial advisor. In Canada, Advocis (www.advocis.ca) is the largest financial planning organization, and in the U.S. the equivalent is the Financial Planning Association (www.fpanet.org). There is also the National Association of Personal Financial Advisors (www.feeonly.org), where you can check membership, involvement, standing, and so on.

Compensation

Another important thing you should know is how your transition planner is compensated. This is a controversial subject in the industry, so our intent here is to arm you with the information you need so you can make an informed decision and pick the right one for you. Whether they tell you or not, all transition planners get paid . . . nobody works for free. There are basically four methods of compensation.

- *Commission only:* the person gets paid commissions and trailers from financial products sold to you; this is the most common method of compensation in the industry and is evidenced by a focus on your investments and the disclaimer that the person can't offer tax advice.
- *Fee-offset:* advice is rendered for a fee, but if you purchase a financial product afterward the commissions or trailers are reduced by the fee you have paid up front.
- *Fee-based:* this is a combination of a fixed fee for advice rendered and then commissions and trailers for any products sold to you. In our opinion, it's really "double-dipping," and it's telling how the financial plan typically recommends products for which the person will earn a commission on as well.
- *Fee-only:* you pay a fee for advice rendered, and there is no other source of third-party compensation (no commissions, trailers, etc.), similar to how you work today with an accountant or an attorney.

Let us say upfront that our firm is a fee-only financial planning firm, and therefore we are disclosing our bias toward fee-only planning. We believe this method of compensation removes as many conflicts of interest as possible from the relationship with you and puts any firm more firmly on your side in rendering advice in your best interests (upholding the fiduciary responsibility to you). When compensation comes from the sale of financial products to you, it creates an inherent conflict of interest because there is generally a quota to meet or a contest to win. Unfortunately, this is perfectly legal in our society because of two very different standards for financial product salespeople versus true financial advisors. In the case of financial product sales, there is a "suitability" standard, which means the product has to be suitable to your situation in order to avoid the ire of the regulator. With a fiduciary standard, the regulator requires your interests to come ahead of your advisor's, which means the advice rendered should be as conflict-free as possible. We suggest you demand full disclosure and ensure you understand, in dollar terms, how much it will cost to implement any recommendations provided. You should carefully discern between a

- *a financial product salesperson*, who renders advice about a particular product;
- *a financial planner*, who renders advice on specific technical topics such as tax or investments;
- *a financial advisor*, who renders comprehensive financial advice based on an understanding of your entire financial situation and what you are trying to achieve; the focus is on you and your financial goals, not on a particular financial product, technical area, or strategy; and
- *a transition planner*, who is a financial advisor who specializes in your transition from Canada to the U.S.

We have provided a checklist in Appendix C you can use to help you determine exactly what type of advisor you are considering.

It has been our experience that a transition planner well versed personally and professionally in Canadian and U.S. financial matters is typically the best person to assist you with your move to the U.S. It really takes a comprehensive understanding of both sides of the border and continual practice in this area to render the best advice to you.

To save a few dollars, some people believe their Canadian chartered account (CA) and their U.S. certified public accountant (CPA) are all they need to competently cross the border. We have seen Canadian CAs do things for Canadian tax or liability protection purposes with no idea of the consequences in the U.S. As a result, double or even triple taxation has been the result when that person moved to the U.S. (see Chapter 11 for an example). We have seen U.S. CPAs prepare tax returns with no understanding of the IRS or CRA compliance issues. When the first piece of "hate mail" arrives from the IRS or CRA and is presented to the "cross-border tax professional," suddenly calls are no longer returned, or the response "We don't deal with Canadian tax issues" is given. We have seen a Canadian CA complete the Canadian exit return and a U.S. CPA complete the U.S. start-up return with no coordination between the two returns for income and foreign tax credits. As a result, extra taxes are usually paid.

We have seen immigration attorneys simply file a visa application for an unsuspecting client with no explanation of what it means to take up tax residency in the U.S. and no understanding of the Canadian and U.S. tax or estate planning consequences such a visa brings when issued. We have seen estate planning attorneys create estate plans costing thousands of dollars that pay no regard to registered plans or real estate holdings in Canada, the Canadian non-resident trust rules, and the issues non-U.S. citizens bring to the estate planning process. We have seen Canadian "investment managers" trading RRSP, RRIF, and brokerage accounts with no understanding of the U.S. tax consequences they are causing their clients who now reside in the U.S. Come tax time, the unsuspecting client is shell-shocked by the tax bill handed to him by CRA or the IRS. Likewise, we have seen U.S. investment managers managing a portfolio with no understanding of how to use up foreign tax credits, with the excuse that we don't want the "tax tail wagging the investment dog." And, sadly enough, we have often seen people rely on the advice of their current Canadian financial planners to orchestrate their moves to the U.S. with dire tax and estate planning consequences and little regard for the fiduciary responsibility owed to you . . . even putting clients into deferred sales charge mutual funds before they move to the U.S. to lock in the commissions and trailers before they lose the relationship. Unfortunately, these people are rendering advice in an area they are not capable of practicing in . . . a clear violation of principle three of the CFP® Code of Ethics and Professional Responsibility (if they hold the CFP® at all). All of these folks may be welcome on a well-rounded Canada-U.S. transition planning team, but they require a quarterback to coordinate all of the activities together and to ensure that all the right questions are being asked, and answered, along the way. Failure to put in place a well-thought-out plan, unique to your individual situation, and have it coordinated effectively can have many unintended consequences and cause you no end of grief. To assist you in selecting the right transition planner to meet your needs, use the handy checklist we have provided in Appendix C.

Our Firm

Transition Financial Advisors Group uses the tagline "Pathways to the U.S." to clarify that we specialize in helping people make a smooth transition from Canada to the U.S. To that end, our firm operates best as a "financial coordinator," the quarterback of your Canada-U.S. transition planning team. Not only does our firm have the educational background to meet your needs (Terry and I hold both Canadian and U.S. financial planning designations), but we also have the personal experience with our own moves back and forth across the 49th parallel. One of the most important things our firm brings to any relationship is empathy with you in the many joys and frustrations you will experience in moving to the U.S. Why? Because we have walked in the shoes you are about to put on. In addition, we share a common Canadian heritage and can easily talk about hockey, Canadian politics, or fishing in Alberta. Terry and I enjoy many relationships with other professionals across Canada and the U.S. who are competent in Canada-U.S. planning matters and can bring them onto the team as needed. These people include accountants, attorneys, insurance agents, and government contacts. We have chosen this approach over bringing everything in house so we can select the best people to work with you on your Canada-U.S. transition issues. For example, there may be a competent accountant closer to you who will make it more convenient to prepare your taxes. Why should you have to deal with a firm with limited locations?

Our planning fees are typically based on a sliding scale of your net worth. This approach falls in line with our comprehensive financial planning philosophy because our firm looks at everything related to your move. This may include rendering advice on the tax implications of selling your home or converting it to a rental property or providing advice on your homeowner's insurance policy. Our fee is made known up front and put into an agreement that both you and we sign. The fee is then fixed until the engagement is fulfilled, giving you peace of mind that there are no hidden fees or expenses to surprise you later. Obviously, this is how we feed our families, so we don't render advice for free! When we do have time, we are committed to helping our community through pro bono work, so any work we do for free is done in this area only (budget counseling, teaching, etc.).

In our experience, folks who meet the following criteria will benefit the most from our services:

- desire a close, long-term working relationship versus just a transaction;
- willing to delegate financial matters and have done so in the past;
- have a lead time of three to four months before a move to the U.S. is scheduled (longer with business entities);
- believe in our comprehensive transition planning approach and willing to follow our proven process;
- willing and able to expediently implement the plan (with our assistance) once completed;

- make friends easily and willing to share of themselves, expecting the same in return;
- comfortable using the Internet; and
- have a net worth of $2 million or more.

You can contact us for a no-obligation review of your situation and the opportunities and obstacles your unique financial situation presents. Just go to our website under the "Get Started" tab to download our "Introductory FactFinder." Fill it out to the best of your ability and send it to us. We will contact you to set up an appointment, and with your "FactFinder" in hand we can be in a better position to discuss your unique situation.

Head Office

Transition Financial Advisors Group, Inc. — Pathways to the U.S.
Gilbert, AZ
Phone: 480-722-9414
E-mail: book@transitionfinancial.com
Web site: www.transitionfinancial.com/us

Satellite Offices

Calgary, AB
Miami, FL

13

Realizing the Dream

... I still have a dream. It is a dream deeply rooted
in the American dream. — Martin Luther King, Jr.

Now that you have moved, settled in, and begun realizing your lifestyle dream in the U.S., there are some things you will notice. Contrary to popular opinion, there are general cultural differences between Canada and the U.S. that you should be aware of since some of them may be harsh realities. Many of these differences are based on our experiences and the experiences of others we have spoken to who have made the transition to the U.S. For example, Canadians typically tend to be more risk averse, conservative in their relationships, and better savers. Americans tend to be greater risk takers, are more comfortable with debt, are more entrepreneurial in business, and overall tend to be more outgoing. As a result, they tend to save less and carry more consumer debt than Canadians, although in our opinion that appears to be changing based on the number of check-cashing/payday loan stores, stores willing to extend credit, creative financing, and increased comfort with debt we are seeing in Canada. Following is a host of other things you will find interesting in comparing Canada and the U.S.

Military

You will also need to become comfortable with the constant presence of the military (aircraft overhead, equipment on the roads) and military personnel most everywhere you go. In Canada, we rarely saw the military or knew of anyone who had served except maybe an uncle or a great-grandparent in the great wars in Europe. In the U.S., there are numerous military branches and locations throughout the country. Here is a snapshot to give you a working knowledge. All military resides under the Department of Defense and consists of the Army, Navy, Air Force, and Marines (Canada does not have Marines). You also have the National Guard, but it is a state-run (and funded) military organization. You typically see just the Air National Guard and the Army National Guard. They are local to each state, but these branches can be called to active duty by the federal government as needed. The Coast Guard is not part of the military; rather, it is under the Department of Homeland Security along with the Secret Service and Citizenship and Immigration Services. There is also the Reserve Officer Training Corps (more commonly known as the ROTC), while Canada has Cadets. These are high school and university candidates in training for the military. It is strictly voluntary and is intended to prepare them for the military. Each branch of the military has an ROTC, and when you graduate from university you are commissioned as an officer in that branch. Finally, there are the Reserves, who can also be found in Canada. These are people who were in the military, have left it, but can be called back in an emergency.

You will meet people who have served in the military or have children in the military, particularly with the recent Gulf conflict, Afghanistan, and Iraq wars, and military service is done with pride. This relates to another phenomenon with which you will have to become comfortable in the U.S., the profound patriotism here. Canadians could learn a lesson in this area by observing how passionate Americans are about their country. U.S. flags and ribbons are everywhere: hanging from houses, flying on automobiles, hanging in the windows of businesses. Their support for their troops is truly amazing. However, it is interesting to note that Americans do not wear a poppy on Remembrance Day (Veterans Day), and when we have worn ours, many Americans have asked us what it stands for. In our experience, the poem "In Flanders Fields" by Lieutenant Colonel John McCrae is virtually unknown in the U.S., and we haven't heard it recited here.

Government

You will also have to become familiar with the political landscape in the U.S. if you want to engage in an intelligent conversation at parties. There are essentially two political parties at all levels of government in the U.S.: the Republicans (right wing) and the Democrats (left wing) versus four parties in Canada: Conservatives (right wing), Liberals, New Democratic Party (left wing), and Bloc Québécois (separatists). In the U.S. and Canada, it basically comes down to whether you believe in more government, higher taxes, and more social programs (Democratic in your views) or less government, lower taxes, and a more individualistic view of making it in this world (Republican in your political views). In the U.S., you register to vote if you are a citizen, and you get a voter's registration card that declares your party allegiance and in which precinct you vote. If you move, you have to update your registration card; it is a valid form of ID that you can carry with you wherever you go. The mayor of your city in Canada is still the mayor in your city in the U.S., but your premier becomes your governor, and your prime minister becomes your president (see the "Encyclopedia" section below). You can't vote in any elections in the U.S. unless you become a U.S. citizen. However, you can still vote in Canadian elections if you are residing in the U.S. or are a dual citizen, but you have to be careful because, on the Elections Canada voter registration form (Form EC 78600-Application for Registration and Special Ballot for Canadian citizens residing outside Canada), the Section 12 declaration requires you to sign and provide the date you intend to return to Canada. This form may cause problems for you if you are intent on severing your ties with Canada for tax purposes.

It's also interesting to note the differences in law enforcement between the two countries. In Canada, you have your local city police officers or marshals and in their absence the RCMP. Not so in the U.S. Nationally, you have the Secret Service and the Central Intelligence Agency (CIA), which is akin to the Canadian Security Intelligence Service (CSIS), along with the Federal Bureau of Investigation (FBI), the U.S. Marshals Service, the Bureau of Alcohol, Tobacco, Firearms and Explosives (ATF), and the Drug Enforcement Agency (DEA); in Canada, all of these sectors seem to be managed by the RCMP (seems to make sense). You also have the Highway Patrol and State Police, which are run by the state, and the local Sheriff's Department, which is run and funded by the county. You also have local city police forces that overlap with the Sheriff's Department. It gets confusing, but rest assured there are many people available to write you tickets!

Heritage

Most Americans view their heritage as American, while most Canadians know they are of German, Ukrainian, Polish, et cetera descent. Canadians typically know about their family heritage and how their ancestors came to Canada. Ask an American what her heritage is, and she typically won't know or will have to think about it for a while. We attribute this difference to the fact that America is a much older nation and has been settled longer. It is not uncommon to find fifth- and sixth-generation Americans, while it is not uncommon to find first- and second-generation Canadians. I am a second-generation Canadian born to first-generation Canadian parents who in turn were born to my grandparents, who were from Germany. As Canada wanted to settle its land, it opened the doors to many immigrants, who came to homestead in Canada and escape the unrest in Europe. As Canada continues its program of diversity through immigration policies, there is a whole new group of first-generation Canadians emerging particularly from Asia and India.

Sports

Another cultural phenomenon is the much different sports scene in the U.S. We grew up when Saturday night was spent watching Hockey Night in Canada on CBC with Don Cherry and Ron MacLean bantering back and forth. Hockey was everywhere in the news, on the radio, and on the TV, and it was easy to keep informed. In Arizona, hockey news is relegated to the back page or simply not reported at all despite Wayne Gretzky leading the Phoenix Coyotes in the local market. Instead, you have to get used to "football Sunday" from September to January. The NFL rules on Sunday, and it is common for people to wake up at 9 a.m. on Sunday and watch NFL football until 10 p.m. If it's not football (or the culmination of the Super Bowl in January), it will be the NBA (basketball) from January on till the summer, when MLB (baseball) takes over until the fall, when the NFL starts again. Then you have to add in college (university) sports, which are huge in the U.S. compared with Canada. The support Americans provide to their college athletes is incredible, and it is typical to have 50,000 people attend a college football game. Again, we think Canadians could learn from Americans in supporting their local university athletes. Saturdays in the U.S. are reserved for college football until "March Madness" hits and the National Collegiate Athletic Association (NCAA) basketball championships are played. We must admit that, during the hockey lockout, we acquired a taste for college basketball and the NFL. And what about you avid curlers? Forget it. You won't even hear about curling until the Winter Olympics coverage starts again.

Food

One of the biggest adjustments we had to make in moving to the U.S. was the difference in food between the two countries. Yes, we said food. What do we mean? Here are some of our favorites that we have had to learn to do without because these items are hard to find in the U.S.

- Perogies, although we have found them occasionally at Trader Joe's
- Butter tarts and crumpets
- Ginger beef — thin strips, coated with a sweet sauce
- Pancake mix — Mrs. Nunweiler's or Coyote brand (nice and hearty!)
- Snacks — all Old Dutch potato chips, Popcorn Twists, Hostess Hickory Sticks and Shoestrings, Hawkins Cheezies
- Chocolate bars — Jersey Milk, Eat-More, Caramilk, Coffee Crisp, Aero, Smarties, Mirage, Wunderbar, Cadbury Bars, Oh Henry!, Glosettes, Maltesers, Crispy Crunch, Crunchie, Big Turk, Mr. Big, Mack Toffee, Malted Milk, Neilson (Coconut Fingers, Golden Buds, Macaroons, Slowpokes, Willocrisp), Bridge Mixture, Cherry Blossoms
- Cookies — Dare (Wagon Wheels, Chocolate Fudge, Coffee Break), Christie (Fudgeo's, Maple Leaf), Dad's (Oatmeal, Oatmeal Chocolate Chip, Oatmeal Raisin)
- Candy/gum — Thrills, Maynard's Wine Gums
- Sauces/syrups/spreads — Roger's Golden syrup, Summerland Sweets syrups, HP Sauce, E.D. Smith Lemon Spread, Shirriff Caramel Spread, Imperial Cinnamon Spread
- Cereals — Post Shreddies, Muesli, Red River, Sunny Boy, Quaker Harvest Crunch
- Beverages — Tim Hortons coffee, Red Rose tea, Mott's Clamato juice, Sun-Rype juice, and of course almost all Canadian beers!
- 222's pain reliever
  Other Canadians in the U.S. have noticed they can't find

these items, so they have set up websites from which you can order such items. Check our website at: www.transitionfinancial.com/us for links to some of these companies.

Here are some other differences we have found or been told about.

- Fruitcake is considered a delicacy in Canada and is found in most wedding cakes and during the Christmas season. In the U.S., it is considered a social faux pas to give or receive fruitcake.
- You can't find Nanaimo bars anywhere!
- Dairy Queen Brazier in Canada is far better than in the U.S.
- Dairy Queen ice milk soft serve is creamier tasting in Canada than in the U.S.
- McDonald's offers muffins in Canada, while breakfast burritos are available in the U.S.
- KFC is crispier and better tasting in Canada than in the U.S.
- KFC gravy is much more flavorful in Canada than in the U.S. (fries and gravy are uncommon).
- Tim Hortons coffee is available primarily in the border states in the U.S.
- Earls is starting to open some restaurants in the U.S. (Scottsdale, AZ, and Lone Tree, CO).
- Boston Pizza has many restaurants in the U.S. now.
- The Keg is starting to open some restaurants in the U.S. (AZ, CO, TX, WA).

Here is a list of items we can't find in Canada when we visit there.

- Poore Brothers potato chips
- Chocolate bars — Hershey's milk chocolate, Almond Joy, Mounds, Baby Ruth, Three Musketeers, Payday, 100 Grand, Milk Duds, Mr. Goodbar

- Malt-O-Meal cereal
- Krispy Kreme doughnuts are much harder to find.
- Aleve pain reliever

However, here are some things we and others have noted when back in Canada.

- P.F. Chang's Chinese Bistro (Pei Wei is the takeout) is nowhere to be found.
- Ruth's Chris Steakhouse is absent except at one location in Toronto.
- Good Mexican food and good barbeque food are hard to find.
- Portions are generally bigger in the U.S., and eating out is cheaper (before the exchange rate).
- The number of restaurants that offer buffet service all day is much greater in the U.S. than we have found in Canada.
- The selection in most grocery and retail stores is far greater in the U.S. than in Canada.
- Most "sin" taxes are higher in Canada than in the U.S. (liquor, wine, beer, cigarettes, cigars, chewing tobacco, gasoline).

If you have something to add to this list, please e-mail us at book@transitionfinancial.com and tell us about it.

The Postal System

- It is a postal code in Canada and a zip code in the U.S.
- A first-class stamp costs 42¢ in the U.S. versus 52¢ in Canada in 2007.
- Mailing a postcard costs 27¢ in the U.S. versus 52¢ in Canada.
- First-class postage for a regular #10 envelope from the U.S. to Canada costs 66¢ (est.) versus 93¢ from Canada to the U.S.
- It takes approximately 7-10 calendar days for first-class mail

to reach Canada from the U.S., but it takes approximately 10-14 days for mail in Canada to reach the U.S.

- In the U.S., a letter mailed for delivery in the same city will typically be delivered the next day, whereas in Canada it can be two to three business days.
- In the U.S., mail is delivered on Saturdays. Not so in Canada.
- If you have friends or relatives in Canada who are mailing out wedding invitations to you in the U.S., tell them a U.S. stamp is required for the return postage. Putting a Canadian stamp on a return envelope that originates in the U.S. is not recognized by the U.S. postal system (however, such letters have been known to slip by).

The English Language

The American version of English is different from the British version used in Canada, so words such as cheque, labour, harbour, centre, and litre become check, labor, harbor, center, and liter. That is why your computer's spell checker may highlight these words as misspelled. Table 13.1 shows other differences in the way Canadians use the English language versus Americans.

Table 13.1

Canadian versus American English

Canada	U.S.
Pop	Soda or Cokes
Caesar	Bloody Mary
Barbecue	Cookout
Housecoat	Robe
Chesterfield	Sofa/couch
Car accident	Car wreck
Holidays	Vacation
Ensuite	Master bath
Dinner	Lunch
Icing Sugar	Powdered Sugar

Canada	U.S. cont'd
Cubby Hole	Glove Box
Penitentiary	Prison
Donair	Gyro
Supper	Dinner
Felts	Markers
Chocolate bar	Candy bar
Garbage	Trash
Buns	Rolls
Thongs	Flip flops
Slacks	Pants
Runners	Tennis shoes/Sneakers
Golf shirt	Polo shirt
Squares	Dessert
Garburator	Garbage disposal
Washroom	Restroom
Marks	Grades
Junior high	Middle school
University	College
Floating rate	Adjustable rate
Cutlery	Silverware
Pot holders	Hot pads
Tea towels	Wash towels
Porridge	Oatmeal
Toque	Toboggan hat
Brown bread	Wheat bread
Sucker	Lollipop
Soother	Pacifier
Licken	Spanking
Standard	Stick shift
Needle	Shot
Slippers	House shoes
Guaranteed investment certificate (GIC)	Certificate of deposit (CD)

The Metric System

After you have moved to the U.S. and are settled in, you will start talking in terms of gallons, Fahrenheit, et cetera. However, when you are talking with your friends and family back home in Canada, they will be talking in terms of liters, celsius, et cetera. The following should help you in these conversations.

- Celsius can be converted to Fahrenheit quickly by doubling the Celsius number and adding 30 (e.g., 30°C x 2 = 60 + 30 = approximately 90°F). For negative numbers, the calculation works like this: –30°C x 2 = –60 + 30 = approximately –30°F.
- If you want an exact conversion, use (°F – 32) x 5/9 = °C.
- The boiling point is 212°F versus 100°C.
- Freezing occurs at –32°F versus 0°C.
- Room temperature is 70°F versus 20°C.
- Body temperature is 98.6°F versus 37°C.
- Mr. Fahrenheit was the only glass blower in his day who could blow a symmetrical, thin cylinder (thermometer) to record temperatures. He set –32°F as his starting point because it was the lowest temperature he could record with his device.
- 100 km/hr = approximately 60 mph.
- 1 mile = 1.61 km or 1 km = 0.62 mile.
- 1 inch = 2.54 centimeters.
- 1 meter = 3.28 feet.
- The U.S. adheres to the metric system for track and field, while Canada uses yards for football.
- 1 liter = 1.06 quarts.
- 1 ton = 1.1 tonnes (pronounced "tawns").
- 1 imperial gallon = 4.5 liters.
- 1 U.S. gallon = 3.8 liters.
- 1 imperial gallon = 0.84 U.S. gallon.
- 1 kilogram = 2.2 pounds.
- 500 grams = 1.1 pounds.

Encyclopedia

Geography

- The Russian Federation is the largest country in the world, Canada is second, China is third, the U.S. is fourth, and Brazil is fifth.
- Canada covers 3,849,674 square miles (9,970,610 square km), of which 291,576 square miles (755,180 square km) are inland water (7.6%), while the U.S. covers 3,717,811 square miles (9,629,091 square km), of which 181,519 square miles (470,131 square km) are inland water (4.9%).
- Quebec is the largest province, and Ontario is second, while Alaska is the largest state, and Texas is second (note: the Yukon, Northwest Territories, and Nunavut are territories, not provinces).
- Texas is 13,314 square miles larger than Alberta.
- The population of Canada is about the same as the population of California (about 32.6 million). The population of the U.S. crossed 300 million in October of 2006 (approximately 10 times that of Canada).
- The largest metropolitan populations in the U.S. are New York with approximately 20 million and Los Angeles at approximately 15 million. In Canada, Toronto has approximately 4.3 million, and Montreal has approximately 3.3 million.
- Canada shares a 5,527 mile (8,895 km) border with the U.S. spanning 12 states and is the largest unprotected border in the world.
- The lowest temperature ever recorded in Canada was $-81°F$ ($-63°C$) in Snag, Yukon, while the highest was $115°F$ ($46°C$) at Gleichen, Alberta.
- The lowest temperature every recorded in the U.S. was $-79.8°F$ ($-62.1°C$) at Prospect Creek Camp along the Alaska pipeline 20 miles north of the Arctic Circle
- In the contiguous 48 states, the lowest temperature was $-69.7°F$ ($-56.5°C$) in Rogers Pass just west of Helena, Montana, while the highest temperature was $134°F$ ($56.7°C$) in

Death Valley, California
- It is interesting to note that the record low ever recorded in Hawaii was 12°F (-11.1°C)

Government
- In the U.S., Congress creates the laws governing the land (legislative branch) and is made up of the Senate and the House of Representatives. In Canada, the Parliament is made up of the Senate (upper house), the House of Commons (lower house), and the Sovereign (represented by the governor general).
- Canada is a constitutional monarchy under the queen, while the U.S. is an independent republic.
- Canada has a parliamentary-cabinet government versus a presidential-congressional government in the U.S. This means that in the U.S. the president is both the head of state and the head of government. In Canada, the queen (represented by the governor general) is the head of state, while the prime minister is the head of government.
- The Republicans (the GOP, for Grand Old Party — the elephant) are most akin to the Conservatives in Canada (the Tories).
- The Democrats (whose symbol is the donkey) are akin to the Liberals (Grits) in Canada.
- It is a governor who heads the state government in the U.S., while in Canada it is a premier who heads the provincial government.
- The Canadian equivalent to the CIA (Central Intelligence Agency) in the U.S. is CSIS (Canadian Security Intelligence Service).
- The Canada Pension Plan can be collected as early as age 60, whereas U.S. Social Security can be collected as early as age 62.
- Canada is part of the British Commonwealth (along with Australia, New Zealand, and India, among other countries),

while the U.S. is not.

- Unlike in Canada, U.S. health-care coverage (Medicare) does not start until age 65; for those under this age, it is available for the indigent through Medicaid. Many people receive health insurance as a benefit from their employers, but if you are self-employed or a part-time worker you have to "go bare" or obtain coverage on your own.

- There are 11 statutory holidays in both Canada and the U.S. In the U.S., Thanksgiving is on the last Thursday in November versus the second Monday in October in Canada; Memorial Day in the U.S. is the fourth Monday of May versus Remembrance Day in Canada on November 11th; Victoria Day in Canada is the third Monday of May; while Independence Day in the U.S. is July 4 versus Canada Day on July 1. There is no holiday for Good Friday or Boxing Day in the U.S.

Miscellaneous Trivia

- Both Saskatchewan and Arizona do not change their clocks for daylight savings time.
- U.S. banks typically do not offer currency exchange services, Canadian banks do.
- Canadian banks charge a fee for each check, while most U.S. banks offer free checking.
- Americans refer to grades 7 and 8 as middle school, while in Canada grades 7, 8, and 9 are known as junior high.
- American high school is grades 9, 10, 11, and 12; the grades are referred to in collegiate fashion as freshman, sophomore, junior, and senior.
- In NFL football, the field is 100 yards long, and the game has four downs, while the CFL field is 120 yards long, and the game has three downs.
- Winnie the Pooh and the telephone were both created in Canada.
- Basketball and hockey were both created in Canada

- In the U.S., the big shopping day is the day after Thanksgiving, while in Canada it is Boxing Day
- In the U.S., the biggest newspaper is typically Sunday versus Saturday in Canada

The Tax System

- Tax-filing deadlines are April 15th in the U.S. and April 30th in Canada for personal taxes.
- In Canada, you get a Social Insurance Number (SIN), while in the U.S. you get a Social Security Number (SSN).
- One return is filed per married couple in the U.S. versus one return per person in Canada.
- A W-2 slip in the U.S. is equivalent to a T4 slip in Canada.
- A 1099-INT or 1099-DIV slip is generally equivalent to a T3 or T5 slip in Canada.
- In Canada, only Quebec has a separate return and collects its own taxes. In the U.S., 43 states have separate returns and collect their own taxes (the other seven do not have state income taxes).
- Both Canada and the U.S. allow a tax deduction for medical expenses but limit it by 3% of net income and 7.5% of adjusted gross income respectively.
- The closest thing to an RRSP in the U.S. is an Individual Retirement Account (IRA); unlike the IRA, RRSP contributions are always deductible.
- In Canada, lottery winnings are not taxable and are paid out in a lump sum. In the U.S., lottery winnings are taxable and are paid out over a 20-year period unless the cash option is requested in advance.
- Both tax systems have an alternative minimum tax.

Appendices

Appendix A

Glossary

AHCCCS — Arizona Health Care Cost Containment System

AMT — Alternative Minimum Tax

ATF — Bureau of Alcohol, Tobacco, Firearms and Explosives (U.S.)

ATM — Automatic Teller Machine

CA — Chartered Accountant (Canada)

CBC — Canadian Broadcasting Corporation

CCA — Capital Cost Allowance (Canada)

CFP — Certified Financial Planner

CIA — Central Intelligence Agency (U.S.)

CMHC — Canada Mortgage and Housing Corporation

COBRA — Consolidated Omnibus Budget Reconciliation Act (U.S.)

CPA — Certified Public Accountant (U.S.)

CPI — Consumer Price Index

CPP — Canada Pension Plan

CRA — Canada Revenue Agency

CSIS — Canadian Security Intelligence Service

DEA — Drug Enforcement Agency

DPSP — Deferred Profit Sharing Plan

EA — Enrolled Agent

EIN — Employer Identification Number

ERISA — Employee Retirement Income Security Act (U.S.)

FBI — Federal Bureau of Investigation

FHA — Federal Housing Authority

FPA — Financial Planning Association (U.S.)

GST — Goods and Services Tax (Canada)

GSTT — Generation Skipping Transfer Tax (U.S.)

IRA — Individual Retirement Account (U.S.)

IRS — Internal Revenue Service

ISO — Incentive Stock Option (U.S.)

ITIN — Individual Taxpayer Identification Number (U.S.)

LIF — Life Income Fund

LIRA — Locked-In Retirement Account

LLC — Limited Liability Company

LRIF — Locked-In Retirement Income Fund

NAFTA — North American Free Trade Agreement

NAPFA — National Association of Personal Financial Advisors

NQ — Non-Qualified Employee Stock Option (U.S.)

OAS — Old Age Security (Canada)

PBGC — Pension Benefit Guaranty Corporation (U.S.)

POA — Power of Attorney

QDOT — Qualified Domestic Trust (U.S.)

QPP — Quebec Pension Plan

RCA — Retirement Compensation Arrangement (Canada)

RCMP — Royal Canadian Mounted Police

RESP — Registered Education Savings Plan (Canada)

ROTC — Reserve Officer Training Corps

RFP — Registered Financial Planner

RPP — Registered Pension Plan (Canada)

RRIF — Registered Retirement Income Fund (Canada)

RRSP — Registered Retirement Savings Plan (Canada)

S&P — Standard and Poors (U.S.)

SEC — Securities and Exchange Commission (U.S.)

SEP — Simplified Employee Pension

SIN — Social Insurance Number (Canada)

SS — Social Security

SSA — Social Security Administration

SSN — Social Security Number (U.S.)

STEP — Society of Trust and Estate Practitioners

TEP — Trust and Estate Practitioner

TN — Trade NAFTA (visa)

U.S. — United States of America

U.S. CIS — U.S. Citizenship and Immigration Services

U.S.-VISIT — United States Visitor and Immigrant Status Indicator Technology

UTMA — Uniform Transfer to Minors Act Account (U.S.)

VA — Veterans Administration (U.S.)

VWP — Visa Waiver Permanent Program Act

WEP — Windfall Elimination Provision (U.S.)

Appendix B

Resources You Can Use

In our digital age, there is a multitude of information that can be obtained with the simple click of a button. Following are a host of websites, publications, and firms of relevance to each chapter in this book. If the link is out of date, feel free to check our website for updated resources at: www.transitionfinancial.com/us

Chapter 1: American Aspirations

Financial Planners Standards Council — www.cfp-ca.org
CFP Board of Standards — www.cfp.net
Advocis — www.advocis.ca
Financial Planning Association — www.fpanet.org
Institute of Advanced Financial Planners — www.iafp.ca
National Association of Personal Financial Advisors — www.feeonly.org
Society of Trust and Estate Practitioners — www.step.org
Transition Financial Advisors — www.transitionfinancial.com/us

Chapter 2: Cover Your Assets

For a list of health-care consultants we recommend, see the risk management section of our website at: www.transitionfinancial.com/us.

U.S. Medicare — www.medicare.gov
Life Insurance Quotes — www.accuquote.com
Auto Insurance Quotes — www.insweb.com
Homeowners Insurance Quotes — www.accucoverage.com
Health Insurance Quotes — www.ehealthinsurance.com
All Types of Insurance Quotes — www.insure.com

Alberta Health and Wellness — www.health.gov.ab.ca
BC Ministry of Health — www.health.gov.bc.ca
Manitoba Health — www.gov.mb.ca/health/

New Brunswick — www.gnb.ca
Newfoundland and Labrador — www.health.gov.nl.ca/health
Nunavat — www.gov.nu.ca/hsssite/hssmain.shtml
NWT — www.hlthss.gov.nt.ca
Ontario — www.health.gov.on.ca
PEI — www.gov.pe.ca/health/index.php3
Quebec — www.msss.gouv.qc.ca
Saskatchewan Health — www.health.gov.sk.ca
Yukon — www.hss.gov.yk.ca

Chapter 3: A Pledge of Allegiance
For a list of immigration attorneys we recommend, see the immigration section of our website at:
www.transitionfinancial.com/us

U.S. Citizenship and Immigration Services — www.uscis.gov
U.S. Department of State — http://travel.state.gov/

Citizenship and Immigration Canada — www.cic.gc.ca
Foreign Affairs and International Trade Canada — www.dfait-maeci.gc.ca

Immigration Attorneys
American Immigration Lawyers Association — www.aila.org

Chapter 4: Moving Your Stuff
U.S. Customs and Border Protection — www.cbp.gov
Bureau of Alcohol, Tobacco, Firearms and Explosives — www.atf.gov
U.S. Department of Transportation — www.dot.gov
U.S. Environmental Protection Agency — www.epa.gov
Car History — www.carfax.com
House Valuations — www.zillow.com
American Moving and Storage Association — www.moving.org

Canada Border Services Agency — www.cbsa-asfc.gc.ca
Canadian Import Restrictions — www.beaware.gc.ca
GST Refund for Visitors to Canada —
www.cra-arc.gc.ca/tax/nonresidents/visitors/

Chapter 5: Double Taxes, Double Trouble

For a list of Canada-U.S. tax preparers we recommend, see the
income tax section of our website at:
www.transitionfinancial.com/us

IRS — www.irs.gov
> **Publication 54** — *Tax Guide for U.S. Citizens and Resident Aliens*
> **Publication 213** — *Check Your Withholding*
> **Publication 501** — *Exemptions, Standard Deductions, and Filing Information*
> **Publication 514** — *Foreign Tax Credits*
> **Publication 519** — *U.S. Tax Guide for Aliens*
> **Publication 521** — *Moving Expenses*
> **Publication 527** — *Residential Rental Property*
> **Publication 597** — *Information on the United States-Canada Income Tax Treaty*
> **Publication 733** — *Rewards for Information Given to the IRS*
> **Publication 901** — *U.S. Tax Treaties*
> **Publication 1915** — *Understanding Your Individual Taxpayer Identification Number*
> **Publication 2193** — *Too Good to Be True Trusts*
> **Publication 4261** — *Do You Have a Foreign Bank Account?*
> **Publication 4446** — *IRS Best Websites, Phone Numbers, and Other Useful Info*

U.S. Department of Treasury — www.treas.gov
State Income Tax Links — www.taxsites.com/state.html
State Sales Tax Links — www.retirementliving.com/RLtaxes.html

CRA — www.cra-arc.gc.ca

Interpretation Bulletins

> **IT161R3** — *Non-Residents: Exemption from Tax Deductions at Source on Employment Income*
>
> **IT171R2** — *Non-Resident Individuals: Computation of Taxable Income Earned in Canada and Non-Refundable Tax Credits*
>
> **IT221R3** — *Determination of Canadian Residency Status*
>
> **IT262R2** — *Losses of Non-Residents and Part-Year Residents*
>
> **IT298** — *Canada-U.S. Tax Convention: Number of Days "Present"*
>
> **IT420R2** — *Non-Residents: Income Earned in Canada*

Provincial Income Tax Links — www.ctf.ca/links.asp

Provincial Sales Tax Links —
www.taxtips.ca/provincial_sales_tax.htm

Chapter 6: Show Me the Money

International Salary Calculator —
www.homefair.com/homefair/servlet/ActionServlet?pid=500&
homefair&to=ActionServlet%3Fpid%3D244%26cid%3Dhome
fair&pagename=199&internal=T

U.S. Salary Calculators — www.homefair.com/homefair/calc/sal-
calc.html?NETSCAPE_LIVEWIRE.src=homefair
www.salary.com

Currency Exchange Rates —
www.bankofcanada.ca/en/rates/exchform.html

Custom House Currency — www.customhouse.ca

Free Credit Report —
www.annualcreditreport.com

FICO Scores — www.myfico.com/

Chapter 7: Till Death Do Us Part

For a list of competent estate planning attorneys we recommend, see the estate planning section of our website at: www.transitionfinancial.com/us.

IRS — www.irs.gov
>   **Publication 555** — *Community Property*
>   **Publication 559** — *Guide for Survivors, Executors, and Administrators*
>   **Publication 950** — *Introduction to Estate and Gift Taxes*

Estate Planning Information — www.estateplanninglinks.com

Estate Planning Attorneys

Wealth Counsel — www.wealthcounsel.com

National Network of Estate Planning Attorneys — www.nnepa.com

American College of Trust and Estate Counsel — www.actec.org

Chapter 8: Financial Freedom

CPP/OAS — www.sdc.gc.ca/en/gateways/nav/top_nav/program/isp.shtml

U.S. Social Security — www.ssa.gov

IRS — www.irs.gov
>   **Publication 560** — *Retirement Plans for Small Business*
>   **Publication 575** — *Pension and Annuity Income*
>   **Publication 590** — *Individual Retirement Accounts*
>   **Publication 915** — *Social Security*
>   **Publication 939** — *General Rules for Pensions and Annuities*
>   **Publication 4333** — *SEP Retirement Plans for Small Business*
>   **Publication 4334** — *SIMPLE IRA Plans for Small Business*

Retirement Living — www.retirementliving.com

Sperling's Best Places to Live — www.bestplaces.net

Moving.com — www.moving.com/find_a_place/relosmart

Chapter 9: Smarten Up!

U.S. Department of Education — www.ed.gov
Federal Student Aid Website — www.studentaid.ed.gov
College Savings Plans Network — www.collegesavings.org
IRS — (Publication 970 — *Tax Benefits for Education*)

Chapter 10: Money Doesn't Grow on Trees

Investment Dealers Association — www.ida.ca
Toronto Stock Exchange — www.tsx.ca
Montreal Stock Exchange — www.msx.ca
NASDAQ Canada — www.nasdaq-canada.com
Morningstar Canada — www.morningstar.ca
Dimensional Fund Advisors Canada — www.dfacanada.com
Barclay's Global Investors iShares — www.ishares.ca/

Securities and Exchange Commission — www.sec.gov
National Association of Securities Dealers — www.nasd.com
American Stock Exchange — www.amex.com
New York Stock Exchange — www.nyse.com
NASDAQ — www.nasdaq.com
Chicago Board of Trade — www.cbot.com
Chicago Board Options Exchange — www.cboe.com
Index Funds — www.indexfunds.com
Morningstar U.S. — www.morningstar.com
Dimensional Fund Advisors — www.dfaus.com
Barclay's Global Investors iShares — www.ishares.com
IRS — www.irs.gov
   Publication 550 — *Investment Income and Expenses*
   Publication 551 — *Basis of Assets*
   Publication 564 — *Mutual Fund Distributions*

Chapter 11: The Business of Business

IRS — www.irs.gov
   Publication 541 — *Partnerships*
   Publication 542 — *Corporations*

Publication 583 — *Starting a Business and Keeping Records*
Publication 587 — *Business Use of Your Home*
Publication 1635 — *Understanding Your EIN*
Publication 3402 — *Tax Issues for Limited Liability Companies*

Chapter 12: Mayday, Mayday

Transition Financial Advisors — www.transitionfinancial.com/us, or call us at 480-722-9414

Financial Planners Standards Council — www.cfp-ca.org/plannersearch/plannersearch.asp, or call 1-800-305-9886

Institute of Advanced Financial Planners —www.iafp.ca, or call 1-888-298-3292

Advocis — www.advocis.ca/content/find-ad-form.aspx, or call 1-800-563-5822

CFP Board of Standards — www.cfp.net/search/, or call 1-888-237-6275

U.S. Securities and Exchange Commission — www.adviserinfo.sec.gov/

National Association of Personal Financial Advisors — www.fee-only.org, , or call 1-800-366-2732

Financial Planning Association —www.plannersearch.org, , or call 1-800-647-6340

Society of Trust and Estate Practitioners — www.step.org/searchuser.pl?n=1000

Chapter 13: Realizing the Dream

For a list of other resources you may find useful, see the trivia section of our website at www.transitionfinancial.com/us

Government of Canada — www.gc.ca
Canadian Embassy Initiative — www.connect2Canada.com

Elections Canada — www.elections.ca

Royal Canadian Mounted Police — www.rcmp-grc.gc.ca

Canadian Security Intelligence Service — www.csis-scrs.gc.ca

Canada Post — www.canadapost.ca

U.S. Government — www.firstgov.gov

Federal Bureau of Investigation — www.fbi.gov

Bureau of Alcohol, Tobacco, Firearms and Explosives — www.atf.treas.gov

Drug Enforcement Agency — www.dea.gov

U.S. Military

    Army — www.army.mil

    Navy — www.navy.mil

    Airforce — www.airforce.com

    Marines — www.marines.com

United States Postal Service — www.usps.com

Appendix C

Transition Planner Interview Checklist

Competence

1. Do you hold both the Canadian and the U.S. CFP® designations?
2. What other designations, degrees, or training do you have in transition planning?
3. How long have you been practicing specifically in the area of Canada-U.S. transition planning?
4. How long have you been working at the firm? What is your next career step in the firm?
5. What percentage of your clients are Canada-U.S. clients versus others?
6. Tell me about your own personal experiences in transitioning between Canada and the U.S.

Planning Process

1. Describe in detail the planning process you have to address the needs of my Canada-U.S. transition.
2. How do you determine my goals and objectives for my transition?
3. How do you integrate my goals and objectives into my transition plan?
4. Do you have a written sample plan I can review?

Client Relationship

1. Tell me about your firm. How long have you been in business? Please provide me with your Form ADV or other regulatory disclosures.
2. How many employees do you have? How many clients per employee? Per principal?
3. What are your assets or net worth under management?
4. Will I be working directly with a principal or an associate? Why?
5. How do you determine the person I will be working with in the firm?

6. How much employee turnover have you had in the past two years? Why?

7. What is your typical client? What is his or her net worth?

8. What are the principals' goals and objectives for the firm in the next five to 10 years?

9. How old are the principals? What are their plans for retirement and succession? When will that take place?

10. What personalities work best with you? Your firm? Why?

11. How many clients have left the firm over the past two years? Why?

12. How many clients have you gained in the past two years? Why?

13. Where do you custody investment accounts? Why? Are there any conflicts of interest I need to be aware of?

14. What are your personal interests?

Compensation

1. How are you paid? When are you paid?

2. How do you calculate your fees? What is my fee in dollars? Specifically, show me the calculations for my fee.

3. How do you ensure that your fiduciary responsibility to me is given the highest priority?

4. Can I see a sample agreement? How long does my agreement last? How can I terminate it?

Professional Affiliations and Associations

You can consult with the following professional organizations to confirm any credentials or affiliations for the transition planner you have interviewed.

1. *Financial Planners Standards Council:* the organization that licenses and governs the Canadian CFP designation (www.cfp-ca.org/plannersearch/plannersearch.asp, or you can call 1-800-305-9886).

2. *CFP Board of Standards:* the organization that licenses and governs the CFP® designation in the U.S. (www.cfp.net/search/, or call 1-888-237-6275).

3. *Institute of Advanced Financial Planners:* the organization that licenses and governs the use of the RFP designation in Canada (www.iafp.ca/, or you can call 1-888-298-3292).

4. *U.S. Securities and Exchange Commission:* this is the regulatory body in the U.S. that governs financial advisors (www.adviserinfo.sec.gov/).

5. *National Association of Personal Financial Advisors:* the only organization in the U.S. and Canada comprised of fee-only financial advisors (www.fee-only.org, or call 1-800-366-2732).

6. *Financial Planning Association:* the largest association of financial planners in the U.S. (www.plannersearch.org, or call 1-800-647-6340).

7. *Advocis:* the largest association of financial planners in Canada (www.advocis.ca/content/find-adform.aspx, or call 1-800-563-5822).

8. *Society of Trust and Estate Practitioners:* the global organization for those practicing advanced trust and estate matters (http://www.step.org/searchuser.pl?n=1000).

Appendix D
100 Questions Typically Asked by the U.S. CIS Examiner

1. What are the colors of our flag?
2. How many stars are there in our flag?
3. What color are the stars on our flag?
4. What do the stars on the flag mean?
5. How many stripes are there in the flag?
6. What color are the stripes?
7. What do the stripes on the flag mean?
8. How many states are there in the union?
9. What is the 4th of July?
10. What is the date of Independence Day?
11. Independence from whom?
12. What country did we fight during the revolutionary war?
13. Who was the first president of the United States?
14. Who is the president of the United States today?
15. Who is the vice-president of the United States today?
16. Who elects the president of the United States?
17. Who becomes president of the United States if the president should die?
18. For how long do we elect the president?
19. What is the Constitution?
20. Can the Constitution be changed?
21. What do we call change to the Constitution?
22. How many changes or amendments are there to the Constitution?
23. How many branches are there in our government?
24. What are the three branches of our government?
25. What is the legislative branch of our government?
26. Who makes the laws in the United States?
27. What is Congress?
28. What are the duties of Congress?
29. Who elects Congress?
30. How many senators are there in Congress?

31. Can you name the two senators from your state?
32. For how long do we elect each senator?
33. How many representatives are there in Congress?
34. For how long do we elect the representatives?
35. What is the executive branch of our government?
36. What is the judiciary branch of our government?
37. What are the duties of the Supreme Court?
38. What is the supreme law of the United States?
39. What is the Bill of Rights?
40. What is the capital of your state?
41. Who is the current governor of your state?
42. Who becomes president of the United States of America if the president and the vice-president should die?
43. Who is the chief justice of the Supreme Court?
44. Can you name the 13 original states?
45. Who said "Give Me Liberty, or Give Me Death"?
46. Which countries were our enemies during World War II?
47. What are the 49th and 50th states of the union?
48. How many terms can a president serve?
49. Who was Martin Luther King, Jr.?
50. Who is the head of our local government?
51. According to the Constitution, a person must meet certain requirements in order to be eligible to become president. Name one of the requirements.
52. What are the 100 senators in the Senate?
53. Who selects the Supreme Court justices?
54. How many Supreme Court justices are there?
55. Why did the pilgrims come to America?
56. What is the head executive of state government called?
57. What is the head executive of city government called?
58. What holiday was celebrated for the first time by the American colonists?
59. Who was the main writer of the Declaration of Independence?
60. When was the Declaration of Independence adopted?
61. What is the basic belief of the Declaration of Independence?

62. What is the national anthem of the United States?
63. Who wrote "The Star-Spangled Banner"?
64. Where does freedom of speech come from?
65. What is the minimum voting age in the United States?
66. Who signs bills into law?
67. What is the highest court in the United States?
68. Who was the president during the Civil War?
69. What did the Emancipation Proclamation do?
70. What special group advises the president?
71. Which president is called the "Father of Our Country"?
72. What Immigration and Naturalization Service form is used to apply to become a naturalized citizen?
73. Who helped the pilgrims in America?
74. What is the name of the ship that brought the pilgrims to America?
75. What were the 13 original states of the United States called?
76. Name three rights of freedoms guaranteed by the Bill of Rights.
77. Who has the power to declare war?
78. Name one amendment that guarantees or addresses voting rights.
79. Which president freed the slaves?
80. In what year was the Constitution written?
81. What are the first 10 amendments to the Constitution called?
82. Name one purpose of the United Nations.
83. Where does Congress meet?
84. Whose rights are guaranteed by the Constitution and the Bill of Rights?
85. What is the introduction to the Constitution called?
86. Name one benefit of being a citizen of the United States.
87. What is the most important right granted to U.S. citizens?
88. What is the United States capital?
89. What is the White House?
90. Where is the White House located?
91. What is the name of the president's official home?
92. Name one right guaranteed by the first amendment.

93. Who is the commander in chief of the U.S. military?

94. Which president was the first commander in chief of the U.S. military?

95. In what month do we vote for the president?

96. What month is the new president inaugurated?

97. How many times may a senator be reelected?

98. How many times may a congressman be reelected?

99. What are the two major political parties in the United States today?

100. How many states are there in the United States?

Pilot Exam Questions

1. Name one important idea found in the Declaration of Independence.

2. What is the supreme law of the land?

3. What does the Constitution do?

4. What does "We the People" mean in the Constitution?

5. What do we call changes to the Constitution?

6. What is an amendment?

7. What do we call the first ten amendments to the Constitution?

8. Name one right or freedom from the First Amendment.

9. How many amendments does the Constitution have?

10. What did the Declaration of Independence do?

11. What does freedom of religion mean?

12. What type of economic system does the U.S. have?

13. What are the three branches or parts of the government?

14. Name one branch or part of the government.

15. Who is in charge of the executive branch?

16. Who makes federal laws?

17. What are the two parts of the United States Congress?

18. How many United States Senators are there?

19. We elect a U.S. Senator for how many years?

20. Name your state's two U.S.Senators.

21. How many U.S.Senators does each state have?

22. The House of Representatives has how many voting members?

23. We elect a U.S. Representative for how many years?

24. Name your U.S. Representative.

25. Who does a U.S. Senator represent?

26. Who does a U.S. Representative represent?

27. What decides each state's number of U.S. Representatives?

28. How is each state's number of Representatives decided?

29. Why do we have three branches of government?

30. Name one example of checks and balances.

31. We elect a President for how many years?

32. How old must a President be?

33. The President must be born in what country?

34. Who is the President now?

35. What is the name of the President of the United States?

36. Who is the Vice President now?

37. What is the name of the Vice President of the United States?

38. If the President can no longer serve, who becomes President?

39. Who becomes President if both the President and the Vice President can no longer serve?

40. Who is the Commander-in-Chief of the military?

41. How many full terms can a President serve?

42. Who signs bills to become laws?

43. Who vetoes bills?

44. What is a veto?

45. What does the President's Cabinet do?

46. Name two Cabinet-level positions.

47. What Cabinet-level agency advises the President on foreign policy?

48. What does the judicial branch do?

49. Who confirms Supreme Court justices?

50. Who is the Chief Justice of the United States?

51. How many justices are on the Supreme Court?

52. Who nominates justices to the Supreme Court?

53. Name one thing only the federal government can do.

54. What is one thing only a state government can do?
55. What does it mean that the U.S. Constitution is a constitution of limited powers?
56. Who is the governor of your state?
57. What is the capital (or capital city) of your state?
58. What are the two major political parties in the U.S. today?
59. What is the highest court in the U.S.?
60. What is the majority political party in the House of Representatives now?
61. What is the political party of the majority in the Senate now?
62. What is the political party of the President now?
63. Who is the Speaker of the House of Representatives now?
64. Who is the Senate Majority Leader now?
65. In what month are elections held in the United States?
66. What is the current minimum wage in the U.S.?
67. When must all males register for the Selective Service?
68. Who is the Secretary of State now?
69. Who is the Attorney General now?
70. Is the current President in his first or second term?
71. What is self-government?
72. Who governs the people in a self-governed country?
73. What is the "rule of law"?
74. What are "inalienable rights"?
75. There are four amendments to the Constitution about who can vote. Describe one of them.
76. Name one responsibility that is only for United States citizens.
77. Name two rights that are only for United States citizens.
78. Name two rights of everyone living in the U.S.
79. What is the Pledge of Allegiance?
80. Name one promise you make when you say the Oath of Allegiance.
81. Who can vote in the U.S.?
82. Name two ways that Americans can participate in their democracy.
83. When is the last day you can send in federal income tax forms?

84. Name two of the natural, or inalienable, rights in the Declaration of Independence.
85. Who wrote the Declaration of Independence?
86. When was the Declaration of Independence adopted?
87. Name one reason why the colonists came to America?
88. What happened at the Constitutional Convention?
89. Why did the colonists fight the British?
90. When was the Constitution drafted?
91. There are 13 original states. Name three.
92. What group of people was taken to America and sold as slaves?
93. Who lived in America before the Europeans arrived?
94. Where did most of America's colonists come from before the Revolution?
95. Why were the colonists upset with the British government?
96. Name one thing Benjamin Franklin is famous for.
97. Name one famous battle from the Revolutionary War.
98. Who is called the "Father of Our Country"?
99. Who was the first President?
100. Name one of the writers of the Federalist Papers?
101. What group of essays supported passage of the U.S. Constitution?
102. Name one of the major American Indian tribes in the United States.
103. Name one war fought by the United States in the 1800s.
104. What territory did the United States buy from France in 1803?
105. What country sold the Louisiana Territory to the United States?
106. In 1803, the United States bought a large amount of land from France. Where was that land?
107. Name one of the things that Abraham Lincoln did.
108. Name the U.S. war between the North and the South.
109. Name one problem that led to the Civil War.
110. What did the Emancipation Proclamation do?
111. What did the abolitionists try to end before the Civil War?

112. What did Susan B. Anthony do?

113. Name one war fought in the United States in the 1900s.

114. Who was President during World War I?

115. The United States fought Japan, Germany, and Italy during which war?

116. What was the main concern of the United States during the Cold War?

117. What major event happened on September 11, 2001, in the United States?

118. What international organization was established after World War II (WWII) to keep the world at peace?

119. What alliance of North America and European countries was created during the Cold War?

120. Who was President during the Great Depression and World War II?

121. Which U.S. World War II general later became President?

122. What did Martin Luther King, Jr. do?

123. Martin Luther King, Jr. had a dream for America. What was his dream?

124. What movement tried to end racial discrimination?

125. What is the longest river in the United States?

126. What ocean is on the West Coast of the United States?

127. What country is on the northern border of the United States?

128. Where is the Grand Canyon?

129. Where is the Statue of Liberty?

130. What country is on the southern border of the United States?

131. Name one large mountain range in the United States.

132. What is the tallest mountain in the United States?

133. Name one U.S. territory.

134. Name the state that is in the middle of the Pacific Ocean.

135. Name one state that borders Canada.

136. Name one state that borders on Mexico.

137. What is the capital of the U.S.?

138. Why does the flag have 13 stripes?

139. Why do we have 13 stripes on the flag?

140. Why does the flag have 50 stars?

141. What is the name of the National Anthem?

142. On the Fourth of July we celebrate independence from what country?

143. When do we celebrate Independence Day?

144. Name two national U.S. holidays.

Appendix E

Comprehensive Case Study: Working Couple

John and Jenny Movers hired Transition Financial Advisors to assist them in making a smooth transition to the U.S. (although based on a real-life fact pattern, all names and numbers have been changed). Following are the financial planning issues, obstacles, and opportunities our proven planning process revealed for the Movers. This is intended not to be blanket advice applicable to all situations but to increase your understanding of the many things that must be taken into account when considering a move to the U.S. Each person's situation is unique and requires a custom analysis to determine the best course of action. As any good transition planner should, we review the following eight areas of planning: customs, immigration, cash management, income tax, financial independence, risk management, estates, and investments; each is part of a comprehensive transition plan.

Background

On April 30th, 2001, John and Jenny received good news. John's U.S.-based employer accepted his transfer request to move him down to Arizona from Ontario. Better yet, his employer agreed to pay his current salary of c$100,000 (bonus averaging c$40,000) in U.S. dollars (us$100,000 + us$40,000 bonus). Aged 53 and 52 respectively, married, with no children, both John and Jenny are Canadian citizens only. Jenny will resign from her current position as a marketing manager to pursue employment in the U.S. The Movers have a net worth of c$2,650,000 comprised as follows.

Table E.1

The Movers' Net Worth

Asset	Fair market value ($)	Cost basis ($)	Titling
Canadian brokerage account	750,000	500,000	Joint
RRSP	450,000	-	John
RRSP	300,000	-	Jenny
LIRA	100,000	-	Jenny
Checking/savings accounts	50,000	50,000	Joint
Vested stock options exercise	450,000	-200,000	John
Employee stock purchase plan	100,000	30,000	John
Principal residence	600,000	375,000	John
mortgage	-100,000		
Autos (x 2)	50,000	75,000	One Each
Personal/household /jewelry	100,000	200,000	Joint
Total	C$2,650,000		
		C$1,325,000	John
		C$425,000	Jenny
		C$900,000	Joint

Life Planning

Like any good financial plan, we start by determining where John and Jenny are "going," where they "are" now (net worth, financial circumstances), and how they are going to get "there." The "plan" allows individual financial decisions to be placed in context and ensure limited resources are channeled toward achieving their plan. Following is a summary of their intentions.

- John and Jenny would like to remain in the U.S. for five to seven years and then return to Canada.
- They would like to take advantage of John's employment opportunities and the lower tax rates in the U.S. to build their net worth and then move back to Canada.
- The Movers would like to be financially independent by John's age 60 through a combination of work in Canada and the U.S.
- When they are independent, they would like to purchase a five-acre piece of land in Ontario near family with a modest home and a guest retreat.
- When independent of work, the Movers would like to be involved in full-time charitable work and offer their home and retreat at no charge to charity workers.
- They might "snowbird" two to three months per year in the U.S. after becoming financially independent and moving back to Canada.
- They would simplify their lives wherever possible and lead a relatively simple life.
- The bulk of their estate would go to their respective parents who survive them, some to siblings, and the balance to charitable organizations.

Customs Planning

The Movers wanted to take their 1999 Lexus with them to the U.S. to replace it there later. They were going to sell their 2001 Mercedes. We pointed out that their Lexus might not pass the strict emissions standards in Arizona. Further, the odometer and speedometer are denominated in kilometers, and the car has been exposed to salt on Canada's roads, potentially reducing its value in the U.S. Given their lifestyle choices, we advised them to sell their car before moving and lease new vehicles during their temporary stay in the U.S., which made it easier to register with the State of Arizona. They completed a full inventory of their personal goods when packing and donated a host of items to charity. Because they decided to sell their home, most of their sweaters, winter clothing, and sporting goods were stored with family until their return at Christmas. We informed them that they had to pass the written portion of the Arizona driving exam along with a valid Canadian driver's license in order to get an Arizona driver's license.

Immigration Planning

John's company sponsored him for an L-1 visa (intra-company transfer), while Jenny would enter on an L-2 visa (dependent of an L-1). However, at the time of their transition, we pointed out that Jenny's visa did not offer work authorization, and the loss of her salary would seriously retard achievement of their independence goals. The Movers began negotiations with John's employer in an attempt to get some sponsorship for Jenny that would permit her to work, but the negotiation process had gone too far to include that. The Movers made the transition to the U.S., and Jenny remained dormant for 18 months before she got a break. In 2002, the U.S. Immigration and Naturalization Service changed the rules for L-2 visa holders, enabling her to work and resolving a key issue for the Movers' financial situation.

We assured Jenny in particular that in moving to the U.S. she would not lose her Canadian citizenship and that dual Canada-U.S. citizenship was a possibility if they wanted it. The L-1 visa when issued to executives or managers is a "short cut" to a green card, and once a green card is held for five years they would be eligible to become naturalized citizens of the U.S. However, in looking at the Movers' intention to reside back in Canada permanently, we pointed out that U.S. citizens must file a U.S. tax return no matter where they live in the world. To avoid this nuisance, we recommended that John and Jenny retain their current L-1 and L-2 visas (can be renewed for a maximum of seven years). If they proceeded to obtain a green card and stayed longer than expected, we cautioned them, they could be subject to the new expatriation rules for green card holders. Based on their current plan, if they move back to Canada in five to seven years, they simply hand in their visas or green cards at the border, and typically their tax-filing obligation ceases.

Cash Management Planning

In moving to the U.S., the Movers had concerns about how to move the proceeds of the sale of their Canadian house to the U.S. (see "Income Tax Planning" below). They were concerned about the "loss" when exchanging Canadian loonies for U.S. dollars. We empathized but educated them on currency exchange and emphasized that their retirement investments should remain in Canadian dollars where appropriate investment vehicles existed. Since they intended to move back to Canada for their financial independence, their future needs will be in Canadian dollars, so converting everything into U.S. dollars and subjecting it to currency exchange fluctuations needed to be considered carefully. We also analyzed the cost-of-living differences between Canada and the U.S. for the Movers' desired lifestyle. They tracked their expenses for six months in the U.S. and found that they weren't significantly different. We recommended a discount currency exchange firm that allowed them to conveniently move their cash to the U.S., saving currency exchange costs in the process.

Another issue the Movers had to face is qualifying for a mortgage in the U.S. since they have no U.S. credit rating. We worked with their lending institution to educate it on how to "pull" a Canadian credit report and ensure it was valued in the loan application process. With the support of John's employer and the "can do" attitude of their lender, the Movers succeeded in getting a mortgage to buy a house (using the house proceeds from Canada as a down payment). Through the credit union John's employer has in the U.S., the Movers were able to get a credit card issued in their names as well. We also advised John to pay off the Home Buyer's Plan on his RRSP before exiting Canada; otherwise, it would be considered a distribution and fully taxable in Canada.

Income Tax Planning
Key Assumptions

- John's salary: $140,000
- Capital gains joint: $35,000 ($10,000 short term)
- Interest: $7,500
- Dividends: $12,500 ($10,000 qualified dividends)
- Standard deduction used for U.S. scenario
- No exchange rates used (to show the net tax effect of the move)
- No tax planning included

Table E.2

2006 Tax Comparison

Canada	John	Jenny	C$	U.S.	US$
Federal	$34,786	$708	$35,494	Federal	$34,722
Ontario	20,507	555	21,062	Arizona	6,920
Subtotal	$55,293	$1,263	$56,556		$41,642
Payroll taxes	2,640	0	2,640		7,206
Total	$57,933	$1,263	$59,196		$48,848
% of income			30.4%		25.1%
Health insurance			$1,000		$4,500
Grand total			$60,196		$53,348
			30.9%		27.4%
		U.S. tax	C$54,275	Cdn tax	US$53,276
		Difference	C$4,921		<US$4,428>

In the Movers' situation, the move resulted in a tax savings of C$4,921 (US$4,428) in 2006 (using an exchange rate of C$1=US90¢). Factoring in health insurance premiums (pretax) levels the playing field more, but if the Movers have a mortgage and property taxes, move to a state with no income tax, and take into account the exchange rates and Canada's sales taxes versus those in the U.S. the table tilts further toward the U.S. However, if the Movers decided to move to California, their tax situation would be as follows.

Table E.3

2006 Move to California

Canada	John	Jenny	C$	U.S.	US$
Federal	$34,786	$708	$35,494	Federal	$34,722
Ontario	20,507	555	21,062	California	13,243
Subtotal	$55,293	$1,263	$56,556		$47,965
Payroll taxes	2,640	0	2,640		7,206
Total	$57,933	$1,263	$59,196		$55,171
% of income			30.4%		28.3%
Health insurance			1,000		4,500
Grand total			$60,196		$59,671
			30.9%		30.6%
		U.S. tax	C$61,301	Cdn tax	US$53,276
		Difference	<C$2,105>		US$1,895

Since California state tax would be approximately US$13,243, it tilts the table back in favor of Canada to the tune of C$2,105 once assumed exchange rates are taken into account. Other factors that may have to be considered in this analysis include all RRSP income needs to be declared in California, mortgage interest, property tax payments, et cetera. As this analysis clearly reveals, it is not a black-and-white decision to move to the U.S. for strictly tax reasons.

Canadian Filing Requirements

John and Jenny each need to file a Canadian "exit" return by April 30th following the year they left Canada. On this return, they are subject to the "departure tax" that CRA imposes on expatriates on "taxable Canadian property." Since the stock options and RRSPS are not considered taxable Canadian property by CRA (attachable in some way to ensure payment of any tax), the only items subject to the departure tax are the employee stock purchase plan and their brokerage account. Our analysis indicated there are embedded gains of c$70,000 in the employer's stock and c$250,000 in the brokerage account, leading to a departure tax of c$31,193 for John and c$16,635 for Jenny. To mitigate this departure tax, we were able to equip John with this information to negotiate higher moving expenses and signing bonus from his employer, delay his employment start date in the U.S. (and ensuing exit date from Canada), net some gains and losses together, and make RRSP contributions to offset some of the income. Despite the departure tax, the Movers decided to move to the U.S. because of the opportunity to reduce their income tax through planning, an increased signing bonus, the payment of moving expenses, better career opportunities, and a desired lifestyle.

To clearly demonstrate that they were severing their ties with Canada, the Movers canceled their Ontario driver's licenses, canceled OHIP, consolidated their banking to one account for convenience, sold their home, sold their vehicles, and moved the bulk of their goods to Arizona. In addition, Jenny turned down an offer to remain an additional three months with her employer after John's departure because of the complications of remaining a tax resident of Canada while John took up tax residency in the U.S. At our prompting, the Movers also notified all Canadian financial institutions (brokerage firms, banks, life insurance companies, mutual fund firms, etc.) that they were now non-residents of Canada and residents of the U.S. As a result, they were now subject to the appropriate withholding on any Canadian source income, as outlined in the Canada-U.S. Tax Treaty. Failure by a couple of financial institutions to withhold the appropriate amount (and in one case overwithholding) required a Part XIII tax return to be filed in Canada to correct the withholding, further complicating the Movers' situation.

U.S. Filing Requirements

The Movers were required to file a U.S. "start-up" return by

April 15th following the year they took up tax residency. To do so, they took our advice: John applied for a Social Security Number and Jenny applied for an ITIN upon entering the U.S. Our analysis revealed there was US$240,000 of embedded gains in the RRSPs (using the appropriate exchange rates). We "stepped-up" the cost basis for U.S. purposes in the Movers' RRSPs prior to departure because the IRS considers them fully taxable and doesn't recognize the tax deferral that CRA does. In addition to filing the appropriate tax forms for the RRSPs and the LIRA, we also took a Canada-U.S. Tax Treaty election on the U.S. return to step-up the gains in the employer's stock and brokerage account for U.S. purposes. Our analysis also revealed that it was in the Movers' best interest to take a specific U.S. income tax election and be declared U.S. residents for the entire year and file jointly. Our analysis further revealed that, after they became residents of the U.S., it was worthwhile to collapse some of their RRSPs in Canada and transfer them to the U.S. in a staged fashion (they can't be transferred to an Individual Retirement Account, or IRA, in the U.S.). John created foreign tax credits with the 25% withholding rate, and Jenny was able to get some of her RRSPs out tax free while ineligible to work in the U.S. Through our structuring of their investment portfolio in both Canada and the U.S., we were able to use up some of these foreign tax credits on their U.S. tax returns (see "Investment Planning" below). We also ran a tax projection in the U.S. to give insights about John's W-4 form, instructing his employer how much income tax to withhold from his pay to ensure he wasn't over- or underwithheld. Finally, we informed John that, if he took up tax residency in the U.S. and exercised his stock options, he would have to file a Canadian T1 tax return to declare the income as well as declare that income on his U.S. return with offsetting foreign tax credits. As a result, he decided to exercise some stock options prior to taking up tax residency in the U.S.

Independence Planning

In reviewing the Movers' financial projections, we determined that a move to the U.S. would enable them to achieve independence from work at John's age 59. If they were to remain in Canada the entire time, John would have to work until age 63 because of the higher income taxes, the fewer career advancement opportunities, and the lost tax benefits when reentering Canada. It appeared they would need a net worth of approximately c$3 million to live their desired lifestyle for the balance of their lives, so a disciplined savings plan was put in place but balanced with their desired lifestyle in Arizona to accumulate another $500,000 before moving back.

In reviewing the different alternatives available for retirement savings, John began contributing to his employer's 401(k) plan only (no IRAS), with any surpluses going into their joint taxable portfolio. This approach set them up well for their pending move back to Canada.

Because both John and Jenny will contribute to the U.S. Social Security system while in the U.S., they will qualify for a Social Security retirement benefit at age 62 even if they have moved back to Canada. This is due to the Canada-U.S. Totalization Agreement, which allows both John and Jenny to use their working years in Canada to qualify for a retirement benefit in the U.S. as well. Further, since Jenny's working visa was delayed, she will pay less into the system and therefore can collect the greater of her benefit or half of John's at her age 62.

Both John and Jenny qualified for a Canada Pension Plan benefit before moving to the U.S. Although they will lose some contribution years during their absence from Canada, their current benefit will not diminish, and if they elect to stay after John's age 60 in the U.S. he could begin collecting his CPP benefit early if doing so fits into their overall financial plan. The Movers will both qualify for Old Age Security when they return to Canada because they will have fulfilled the 40-year residency requirement after age 18.

Risk Management Planning

Besides a valid visa, the other item that is a "must have" before considering a move to the U.S. is some form of health insurance. The Movers' OHIP coverage ceased when they left Canada, but John is eligible for U.S. health benefits through his employer, and Jenny is included without any waiting period. This includes vision and dental care. Since John is the primary breadwinner, he has a C$500,000 term life insurance policy. The problem is that, if he dies in the U.S., the death benefit is only US$450,000 (assuming a 90¢ exchange rate). Based on our analysis and the Movers' new financial situation in the U.S., the death benefit is not sufficient for Jenny, so John is underwritten for a new 10-year term insurance policy in the amount of US$750,000 to replace his old policy.

We pointed out to the Movers that, with each year they work in the U.S., they accumulate credits toward Medicare. If they returned to Canada after just five years, they would have accumulated only 20 quarters of eligibility, so they would have to pay the full amount for Medicare Part A if they ever wanted to retire back in the U.S. However, if they stayed the full seven years as they desired and delayed resigning from John's employer until the start of the next year, they could accumulate 32 quarters of eligibility, enabling them to qualify for a discount of approximately 45% on Medicare Part A premiums should they return to the U.S. in the future. If they elected to remain in the U.S. for 10 years, they would be eligible for free Medicare Part A.

Estate Planning

In preparation for moving to the U.S., John and Jenny went to their local estate planning attorney in Ontario and had their wills updated. However, we pointed out the flaws of their current estate plan and the fact that their Canadian wills would not avoid the probate process in both Arizona and Ontario. To gain the greatest control in the event of death while in the U.S., John and Jenny elected to get a full trust-centered estate plan prepared in the U.S. We cautioned them on naming Canadian beneficiaries and being caught in the Canadian non-resident trust rules. They elected to change their estate plan to accommodate that, and we encouraged them to contact us before moving back to Canada so the requisite preentry planning could be done with their living trust in place. After implementing their estate plan, they took more comfort with John's travels through work because, in the event of death, incapacity, or disability, their wishes would be implemented.

Using the information and titling provided in table E-1, the Movers' U.S. estate tax situation without a U.S. estate plan in place is estimated at US$384,100 at the second spouse's passing (13.5% depletion). However, because John put their home and his life insurance in his name only, he and Jenny were shocked to find out that she would have to write a check for US$21,850 in estate taxes if John predeceased her. By adding a QDOT as part of their U.S. estate plan and gifting some assets from John to Jenny, the Movers reduced their current estate tax liability to zero.

If the Movers had stayed in Canada, the deemed disposition at death tax is estimated at C$391,481, including the RRSPS, LIRA, and brokerage account at the second spouse's death. Once they moved to the U.S., their Canadian deemed disposition at death was reduced to C$212,500 on the RRSPS and LIRA because of the 25% withholding (they took our advice and moved their brokerage account to the U.S. as well).

Investment Planning

As the collapsed RRSPS and brokerage accounts were transferred to the U.S., they were invested in a low-cost, tax-efficient, well-diversified investment portfolio with ample foreign exposure (outside the U.S. and Canada). The foreign exposure creates the right type of income to begin using up the foreign tax credits on the U.S. tax returns through the collapse of John's RRSPS as well as hedges the Canadian loonie for their future retirement expenses in Canada. Further, the asset allocation we developed took advantage of the limited investment choices in John's 401(k) plan while maximizing the consumption of the foreign tax credits, all the while preparing the Movers for a potential move back to Canada.

Appendix F

Comprehensive Case Study: Retired Couple

Ed and Nettie Canuck hired Transition Financial Advisors to assist them in making a smooth transition to the U.S. (although based on a real-life fact pattern, all names and numbers have been changed). Following are the financial planning issues, obstacles, and opportunities our planning process revealed for the Canucks. This is intended not to be blanket advice applicable to all situations but to increase your understanding of the many things that must be taken into account when considering a move to the U.S. Each person's situation is unique and requires a custom analysis to determine the best course of action. As any good transition planner should, we review the following eight areas of planning: customs, immigration, cash management, income tax, financial independence, risk management, estates, and investments; each is part of a comprehensive transition plan.

Background

After many years of "wintering" in the U.S., Ed and Nettie decided they wanted to stop "snowbirding" and move permanently from Alberta to Florida to spend the rest of their lives. They were tired of watching the calendar, counting the days and filing IRS form 8840 to show their closer tax connection to Canada (see our companion book "The Canadian Snowbird in America.") They had some reservations about leaving their children, grandchildren, and friends but decided that visiting Canada rather than living there year round was more appealing. They recently wound up and sold their business for C$3.5 million and thought it was time to seize the opportunity to move to the U.S. Aged 65 and 62 respectively, married with three grown children and four grandchildren, both Ed and Nettie are Canadian citizens, with Nettie being an American citizen as well. The Canucks have a net worth of approximately C$7,833,333, comprised as follows.

Table F.1

Canucks' Net Worth

Asset	Fair market value ($)	Cost basis ($)	Titling
Canadian brokerage account	4,000,000	3,750,000	Joint
RRSP	600,000	-	Ed
RRSP (spousal)	900,000	-	Nettie
IRA – U.S. (US$100,000)	111,111	-	Nettie
Checking/savings accounts	150,000	150,000	Joint
Principal residence (Alberta)	1,000,000	775,000	Joint
Florida home (US$650,000)	722,222	450,000	Joint
Autos (x 2)	100,000	100,000	Joint
Personal/household/jewelry	250,000	500,000	Joint
Total	**C$7,833,333**		
		C$600,000	**Ed**
		C$1,011,111	**Nettie**
		C$6,222,222	**Joint**

Life Planning

We started by determining where Ed and Nettie are "going," where they "are" now, and how they are going to get "there." The "plan" allowed individual financial decisions to be placed in context and ensure that limited resources were channeled toward achieving their plan. Following is a summary of their intentions.

- Ed and Nettie want to move permanently to Florida, severing their tax ties with Canada but spending summer months in Alberta close to their family.
- Now independent of work, they want to remain financially independent in the U.S.
- The Canucks want to pass their estate on prudently to their heirs in both Canada and the U.S., with a portion going to their church in Canada.

Customs Planning

The Canucks wanted to keep their home in Canada, along with

a vehicle, for their visits in the summer months. We encouraged them to sell their home and take all of their personal goods with them to Florida, including their art collection, family heirlooms, and antiques, to ensure they properly severed their tax ties to Canada. Ed and Nettie elected to hire a reputable moving company to take care of all the details of moving their personal goods to the U.S., including development of a full inventory of goods to present to the U.S. Customs and Border Protection agent. To establish a defensible value for tax purposes, we advised them to get appraisals on their Florida home near the time they left Canada. We informed the Canucks that the vehicle they leave at their Florida residence would not be subject to the departure tax for CRA purposes.

Although "empty nesters," Ed and Nettie still had two babies: Dollar the collie and Loonie the yellow Lab. In preparation for their move, we suggested Ed and Nettie have both of their dogs examined by a vet and get a health certificate to assure their good health. At the same time, the veterinarian gave each dog a rabies shot and provided a letter confirming this treatment. When it came time to move to the U.S., the Canucks had no problems taking their dogs through U.S. Customs when they drove to Florida.

Immigration Planning

Since Nettie is an American citizen, she sponsored Ed for a green card. They had no set schedule for when they wanted to move, so their plans accommodated the lengthy time it took to apply for his green card. We told Ed he should refrain from entering the U.S. while his green card application was being processed since he could jeopardize the entire filing. As a result, their immigration attorney applied for "advanced parole" at the same time the green card application went in so Ed and Nettie could come back to Canada in the summer after settling in Florida. Once he received his green card package from U.S. CIS, we instructed him not to open it or he would delay his entry into the U.S. because he would have to wait for another one. The green card package must be opened by the U.S. cis agent at the border when he crosses into the U.S. to take up residency there. In addition, Ed and Nettie were able to complete all of the preentry planning to mitigate their tax liability before Ed executed his green card package and took up tax residency in the U.S. After holding his green card for three years, Ed reviewed the pros and cons of U.S. citizenship with us and based on our conversation with him, he decided to become a U.S. citizen. They also used their citizenship to sponsor one of their grown children for a green card so she could realize her dream of moving to the U.S. as well.

Cash Management Planning

To expediently move their financial assets to the U.S., the Canucks selected a discount currency exchange firm to exchange all of their available Canadian loonies into U.S. dollars. These funds were wired into the Canucks' investment account in the U.S., so we were able to begin investing them the next day. This approach also avoided the required government paperwork surrounding the transfer of large amounts of cash to the U.S.

Ed and Nettie wondered about getting a U.S.-based credit card since they believed their Canadian U.S.-dollar credit card might be considered a tie to Canada. We advised them that a bank such as rbc Centura Bank in Florida was comfortable with obtaining their Canadian credit report and based on it would issue them a U.S.-based credit card. To ease their move, the Canucks closed all of their checking and savings accounts except the one they would use for convenience when back in Canada during the summers. They also filed the necessary paperwork to have their cpp and oas checks deposited directly into their checking account so their automated bill payments would be covered for their Canadian home.

Income Tax Planning

Key Assumptions

- CPP: Ed $10,135, Nettie $4,300
- OAS: Ed $5,816 (clawed back)
- Capital gains joint: $75,000 ($25,000 short term)
- Interest: $42,000
- Dividends joint: $83,000 ($70,000 qualified dividends)
- Standard deduction used for U.S. scenario
- No exchange rates used (to show the net tax effect of the move)
- No tax planning included

Table F.2

2006 Tax Comparison

Canada	Ed	Nettie	C$	U.S.	US$
Federal	$12,828	$10,193	$23,021	Federal	$20,445
Alberta	5,366	4,353	9,719	Florida	0
Subtotal	$18,194	$14,546	$32,740		$20,445
OAS clawback	5,816	0	5,816	AMT	2,050
Total	$24,010	$14,546	**$38,556**		**$22,495**
% of income			**17.5%**		**10.2%**
Health insurance			1,000		4,524
Grand total			39,556		$27,019
			18.0%		**12.3%**
		U.S. tax	C$24,994	Cdn tax	US$34,700
		Difference	C$13,562		<US$12,205>

In the Canucks' situation, the move resulted in annual tax savings of C$13,562 (US$12,205) in 2006 (using an exchange rate of C$1=US90¢). Both Ed and Nettie were thrilled to find out that Ed would no longer be subject to the OAS clawback (nor would Nettie in the future), increasing their income every year in the U.S. by an inflation-adjusted C$11,631! Further, since OAS and CPP are taxed a maximum of 85% in the U.S., the Canucks had an even larger windfall. We were able to increase this differential by structuring their portfolio to integrate with their overall tax and financial plan. Through proper foreign tax credit planning and the use of other tax preference items, we were able to mitigate their U.S. tax liability even further and still meet their U.S. income requirements while maintaining their investment risk tolerance objectives.

Canadian Filing Requirements

Ed and Nettie each needed to file a Canadian "exit" return by April 30th following the year they left Canada. On this return, the Canucks were subject to the "departure tax" that CRA imposes on expatriates. Included in this calculation, to the Canucks' surprise, were their Canadian brokerage account and their Florida residence. Our analysis indicated there were embedded gains of C$250,000 in the brokerage account and C$272,222 in their Florida home, leading to a departure tax of C$41,981 for Ed and C$41,981 for Nettie. To mitigate their departure tax, we accelerated the Canucks' exit date from Canada, netted some gains and losses together, and made RRSP contributions to offset some of the departure income. We also coordinated Ed and Nettie's charitable intentions with their tax situation so that a large charitable contribution could be made to their church before leaving Canada that we could use for tax purposes in both countries. These strategies, coupled with the reduced taxes outlined above, were more than satisfactory for the Canucks to realize their desired lifestyle and offset the departure tax they faced upon exit.

To clearly demonstrate that they were severing their ties with Canada, the Canucks canceled their Alberta driver's licenses, canceled their Alberta health care, consolidated their banking to one account for convenience, and moved the bulk of their personal goods to Florida. They also canceled all but one of their Canadian credit cards and established a credit card in the U.S. Further, they discontinued all of their subscriptions and memberships in Canada and reestablished them in Florida, including buying a membership at their local golf club.

U.S. Filing Requirements

Since Nettie is a U.S. citizen, both she and Ed were shocked to find out that she was required to file U.S. federal tax returns (married filing separately) since moving to Canada in 1972 and declare the income that had been accruing in her RRSPs on her U.S. return. We filed the past tax returns required along with a notice of the situation to bring Nettie into compliance with the IRS. Further, these tax returns were needed as part of her sponsorship of Ed's green card. Based on our analysis, we pointed out that Ed was required to file IRS Form 8840 — A Closer Connection Exception Statement with the IRS because he had exceeded 121 days in the U.S. for the previous three years. We filed this form to bring Ed into compliance with the IRS as well. Both he and Nettie were pleased to learn that Florida repealed its Intangibles Tax, so they would have no filing obligation with the state to contend with when they moved there.

When the Canucks moved to the U.S., Ed would simply be added to Nettie's tax return (married filing jointly) filed by April 15th. Our analysis revealed filing jointly with the specific income tax election to declare Ed a resident for the entire year was in their best interest to mitigate their U.S. tax obligation. Nettie had an existing Social Security Number, but Ed had only an ITIN because of the previous sale of a U.S. property. We advised him that upon executing his green card package at the border, he would apply for a Social Security Number that would replace his ITIN at that time.

Our analysis revealed there was US$75,000 of embedded gains inside Ed's RRSP (using the appropriate exchange rates), which we "stepped-up" for U.S. tax purposes prior to executing his green card package. However, for Nettie, the embedded gains were more difficult to determine in her RRSP because she is a U.S. citizen. She began working with her brokerage firm while in Canada to establish a history in the account so we could determine the tax implications upon withdrawal.

Independence Planning

In reviewing the Canucks' projections, we determined that a move to the U.S. would not hamper them from maintaining their desired lifestyle for the balance of their lives (even with the departure tax they faced). Further analysis revealed they have a high probability of success in their projections and in fact have surplus funds that would allow for some lifetime gifting to heirs, philanthropy to their church, or enhancing their lifestyle. Further, their projections revealed that Ed and Nettie don't need to take much risk in their investment portfolio to achieve their financial objectives.

They were thrilled to find out they would retain their current CPP benefits if they moved to the U.S. in addition to both of them being able to collect OAS. An even greater surprise came when Nettie found out she could double-dip into both Canadian and U.S. government pensions because she is eligible to collect her Social Security benefits at age 62 (US$6,000 annually after the windfall elimination provision is applied). Of even greater surprise was that Ed would automatically get half of her benefits or US$3,000 annually without having contributed a nickel to the system. We advised Nettie to contact the Social Security Administration to arrange for her and Ed's benefits to commence.

Nettie had concerns about her IRA in the U.S. From a tax standpoint, we advised her that it retained its tax-deferred status in the U.S. and in Canada. She would have to commence the required minimum distributions when she turned 70 1/2, and they would be fully taxable to her. We encouraged her to change the beneficiary on the IRA from her estate to Ed so he could maintain the tax-deferred status of the account in the event she predeceased him.

Risk Management Planning

One of the primary reservations Ed and Nettie had in moving to the U.S. was leaving the socialized medical system in Canada.

We alleviated their concerns by showing them they could self-insure a larger amount of their medical expenses and get underwritten for a catastrophic coverage health insurance policy at a cost of approximately US$2,500 per year for both of them. We further assured them that if something went very bad they could relocate back to Alberta for medical care because there is no waiting period there to obtain health care. Finally, because Nettie was a U.S. citizen and had established 40 quarters of coverage before getting married and moving to Canada, she would qualify for free Medicare Part A when she turns 65. At that time, Ed would automatically qualify as well for free Medicare Part A, saving them US$9,432 in premiums in 2006. Part B would still cost them US$2,124 annually, and they would get on a basic Part D prescription plan for $144 annually.

The Canucks didn't have any life insurance, but we suggested they consider life insurance in the amount of $1.5 million for estate liquidity purposes (see estate planning section below). However, to keep the value of their life insurance out of the value of their estate for estate tax purposes, we needed a more sophisticated estate plan. Given the complication this would add to their lives, Ed and Nettie decided not to proceed with this alternative.

Estate Planning

Given the size of Ed and Nettie's estate and because Ed — at the time of our initial planning — was not a U.S. citizen, comprehensive estate planning integrated with their financial plan was critical. Using the information and titling provided above, the Canucks' U.S. estate tax, without a new estate plan, was estimated at US$2,323,000 at the second death if Ed predeceased Nettie. If Nettie predeceased Ed, he was shocked to find out, he would have to write a check for US$701,500 to the tax authorities for estate taxes due at her death! At his death, another check for US$2,000,310 would have to be written before the balance of their estate could pass to their heirs (depletion of 38.3%). This amount did not include any probate, attorney, or court costs in both Canada and the U.S. After their estate plan was put in place, the U.S. estate tax liability was still us$1,403,000 at the second spouse's death (depletion of 19.9%).

An additional complication was the fact that Ed and Nettie had heirs remaining in Canada who would receive a substantial inheritance at their passing. In most cases, a U.S. trust-centered estate plan is appropriate for a couple like Ed and Nettie. However, given that they have heirs in Canada, the establishment of a U.S. trust could be caught under Canada's non-resident trust rules. In this case, we looked at the role of wills (as opposed to living trusts) with specific U.S. tax language to include a QDOT so no estate tax would be owing at Nettie's death if she predeceased Ed. We also looked at increased lifetime gifting and a greater charitable gift at the second death that would be sufficient to reduce the U.S. estate tax to zero. Since the Canucks wanted their gift to go to their church in Canada, we informed them that their gift would remain estate tax deductible in the U.S. under the Canada-U.S. Tax Treaty. We looked at the role of insurance as a means to replace the charitable gift or estate tax at the second death to go to their Canadian heir(s), but because of the complications it caused they elected not to go this route. Depending on how the U.S. estate tax rules change over the next few years, and if any of their Canadian heirs move to the U.S., a complete review of their estate plan is needed.

If the Canucks had stayed in Canada, the deemed disposition at death tax is estimated at c$721,231, including the RRSPs, brokerage account, and Florida home at the second spouse's death. Once they moved to the U.S., their Canadian deemed disposition at death was reduced to c$375,000 on the RRSPs because of the 25% withholding (they took our advice and moved their brokerage account to the U.S. as well).

Investment Planning

As the collapsed RRSPs and brokerage accounts were transferred to the U.S., they were invested in a low-cost, tax-efficient, well-diversified investment portfolio with ample foreign exposure (outside the U.S. and Canada). The foreign exposure created the right type of income to begin using up the foreign tax credits in the U.S. generated with the collapse of their RRSPs (they have a "shelf life" of the current year plus 10 years in the U.S.). Further, the asset allocation we developed generated U.S.-dollar income to meet the Canucks' new living expenses in the U.S. while further reducing their income tax liability (see "Income Tax Planning" above). We left a portion in Canadian dollars in Canada to meet their Canadian-dollar obligations for their home in Canada, et cetera. Their Canadian investment manager, unfamiliar with the Canada-U.S. transition planning issues, was eager to get the proceeds from the sale of their business working for them. She wanted to invest in a number of Canadian mutual funds. After consulting with us, the Canucks decided to leave their current investment manager, and some investments were made in Canada but in investment assets that were easily transferable to their U.S. brokerage account. The rest was left in cash and wired through a discount currency exchange firm where we were able to implement investment strategy shortly thereafter.

Index

DISCLAIMER

This book presents general information including the author's investment philosophy. This information is not intended as personalized investment advice and should not be relied upon by any individual as the basis for investment decision-making. Readers are encouraged to discuss their specific investment needs, goals, and objectives with a qualified investment professional.

Additionally, this book contains legal and tax information related to relocating from Canada to the United States. While the information contained in the books is deemed to be reliable, the author does not intend to provide comprehensive legal or tax advice. As the issues are quite complex and each individual situation requires specific advice, readers are encouraged to seek the assistance of qualified legal and tax professionals regarding their specific legal and tax needs.